First World War
and Army of Occupation
War Diary
France, Belgium and Germany

16 DIVISION
Divisional Troops
180 Brigade Royal Field Artillery
16 February 1916 - 28 June 1919

WO95/1963/1

The Naval & Military Press Ltd
www.nmarchive.com
Published in association with The National Archives

Published by

The Naval & Military Press Ltd

Unit 10 Ridgewood Industrial Park,
Uckfield, East Sussex,
TN22 5QE England
Tel: +44 (0) 1825 749494

www.naval-military-press.com
www.nmarchive.com

This diary has been reprinted in facsimile from the original. Any imperfections are inevitably reproduced and the quality may fall short of modern type and cartographic standards.

Contents

Document type	Place/Title	Date From	Date To
Heading	WO95/1963/1		
Heading	16th Division 180th Brigade R.F.A. Feb 1916-Jun 1919		
War Diary	Bordon	16/02/1916	18/02/1916
War Diary	Hause	17/02/1916	17/02/1916
War Diary	Berguette	18/02/1916	18/02/1916
War Diary	Blessy	18/02/1916	18/02/1916
Heading	180 Bde R.F.A. 16th DW Vol. 2		
War Diary	Berguette	26/02/1916	07/03/1916
War Diary	Ames	08/03/1916	06/04/1916
War Diary	Ames La Trimmans	07/04/1916	07/04/1916
War Diary	La Trimmans	08/04/1916	09/04/1916
War Diary	Ames	10/04/1916	15/04/1916
War Diary	Maguirgabe	16/04/1916	30/06/1916
Heading	War Diary 180th Brigade Royal Field Artillery 1st. July to 31st. July 1916. Volume No. 6		
War Diary	Maguirgabe	01/07/1916	27/07/1916
Heading	War Diary 180th Brigade RFA. Month Of August 1916. Volume		
War Diary	Hulluch Sector	01/08/1916	08/08/1916
War Diary	Loos Sector	08/08/1916	26/08/1916
War Diary	Ames	27/08/1916	30/08/1916
War Diary	Doeur	31/08/1916	31/08/1916
Miscellaneous	New Formation 180 Brigade R.F.A.		
Heading	War Diary 180th Brigade Royal Field Artillery For Month Of September 1916 Volume 8		
War Diary	Daours	01/09/1916	01/09/1916
War Diary	L.9 Central	02/09/1916	14/09/1916
War Diary	T.25d. 1/10000 Loneveval	14/09/1916	15/09/1916
War Diary	T 25d. 1/10000	16/09/1916	18/09/1916
War Diary	T25d	18/09/1916	27/09/1916
War Diary	T16.a.	27/09/1916	30/09/1916
Operation(al) Order(s)	Right-Centre Artillery Operation Order No. 1.	23/09/1916	23/09/1916
Operation(al) Order(s)	Issued with Operation Order No. 1. Right Centre Artillery.	25/09/1916	25/09/1916
Operation(al) Order(s)	Addendum to Right Centre Artillery Operation Order No. 1	23/09/1916	23/09/1916
Miscellaneous	Reference par. 6, Right Centro Artillery Operation Order No. 1,	24/09/1916	24/09/1916
Operation(al) Order(s)	Amendments to Right-Centre Artillery Operation Order No. 1	24/09/1916	24/09/1916
Operation(al) Order(s)	Memorandum. Right Centre Artillery. 4.5th Howitzer Programme from Zero, 25th September, 1916	25/09/1916	25/09/1916
Map	Identification Trace for use with Artillery Maps.		
Heading	War Diary Month Of October, 1916. Volume 9 180th Brigade R.F.A.		
War Diary	Ocarnoy	01/10/1916	01/10/1916
War Diary	Athuiele	02/10/1916	02/10/1916
War Diary	Boubers	03/10/1916	03/10/1916
War Diary	Ecques	05/10/1916	05/10/1916
War Diary	Coq-de-Paille	06/10/1916	08/10/1916

War Diary	Hallebast	09/10/1916	17/10/1916
War Diary	Wippenhoek	18/10/1916	19/10/1916
War Diary	Ypres.	20/10/1916	31/10/1916
Heading	War Diary. For Month Of November, 1916. Volume 10 180th Brigade R.F.A. Vol 10		
War Diary	Ypres	01/11/1916	29/11/1916
Heading	War Diary For Month Of December, 1916. Volume 11 180 Brigade R.F.A. Vol XI		
War Diary	Ypres	01/12/1916	27/12/1916
War Diary	Dranoutre	28/12/1916	31/12/1916
Heading	War Diary for month of January, 1917. Volume 12 180th Brigade R.F.A. Vol 12		
War Diary	Dranoutre	01/01/1917	29/01/1917
War Diary	Little Kemmel.	30/01/1917	31/01/1917
Operation(al) Order(s)	Operation Order No. 2. by Lieut. Col. L.R.S. Ward. D.S.O. R.F.A. Commanding Spanbroek Group. R.F.A.	27/01/1917	27/01/1917
War Diary	Battery Yasks.		
Operation(al) Order(s)	Spanbroek Operation Order No. 4. by Lieut. Col. L.M.S. Ward. D.S.O. R.F.A. Commanding Spanbroek Group R.F.A.	30/01/1917	30/01/1917
Heading	War Diary. For Month Of February, 1917. Volume 13 Unit 180th Brigade R.F.A. Vol 13		
War Diary	Little Kemmel.	01/02/1917	28/02/1917
Miscellaneous	M.S. 39. Headquarters 16th D.A.		
Miscellaneous	Headquarters. 16th Divl. Arty. Headquarters 47th Inf. Bde. (For Information) File.	01/02/1917	01/02/1917
Miscellaneous	180th Brigade. R.F.A. No. S. 118/1.	03/02/1917	03/02/1917
Operation(al) Order(s)	Spanbroek Operation Order No. 5. by Lieut-Col. L.N.S. Ward D.S.O., R.F.A., Commanding Spanbroek Group. R.F.A.	09/02/1917	09/02/1917
Operation(al) Order(s)	Spanbroek Operation Order No. 6. by Lieut. Col. L.E.S. Ward. D.S.O., R.F.A. Commanding Spanbroek Group. R.F.A.	10/02/1917	10/02/1917
Miscellaneous	Table Of Battery Tasks.		
Operation(al) Order(s)	Spanbroek Operation Order No. 7. by Lieut-Col. L.E.S. Ward D.S.O. R.F.A. Commanding Spanbroek Group R.F.A.	12/02/1917	12/02/1917
Operation(al) Order(s)	Ammendment to Spanbroek Operation Order No. 7.	12/02/1917	12/02/1917
Map	Secret		
Operation(al) Order(s)	Spanbroek Operation Order No. 8 by Major N.A. Stebbing., D.S.O. R.F.A. Commanding Spanbroek Group. R.F.A.	14/02/1917	14/02/1917
Miscellaneous	Table Of Battery Tasks.		
Miscellaneous	Rates Of Fire.		
Operation(al) Order(s)	180th Brigade R.F.A. No. S.F./26 Reference Spanbroek Operation Order No. 8., dated 14-2-17	14/02/1917	14/02/1917
Operation(al) Order(s)	Spanbroek Operation Order No. 9 by Major N.A. Stebbing, D.S.O., R.F.A.,	22/02/1917	22/02/1917
Operation(al) Order(s)	Spanbroek Operation Order No. 10. by Major N.A. Stebbing. D.S.O., R.F.A.	23/02/1917	23/02/1917
War Diary	War Diary For Month of March, 1917. Volume 14 180th Brigade R.F.A.		
War Diary	Little Kemmel	01/03/1917	17/03/1917
War Diary	Westoutre	18/03/1917	22/03/1917
War Diary	Laclytte	23/03/1917	30/03/1917

Operation(al) Order(s)	Spanbroek Operation Order No. 12. by Lieut-Colonel L.E.S. Ward. D.S.O., R.F.A.	01/03/1917	01/03/1917
Miscellaneous	Table of Tasks		
Miscellaneous	Table of Tasks.		
Operation(al) Order(s)	16th Divisional Artillery Operation Order No. 47. 25th Feb. 1917	25/02/1917	25/02/1917
Miscellaneous	Bombardment Table February 27th. 1917	27/02/1917	27/02/1917
Miscellaneous	Table Of Tasks.		
Miscellaneous	180th. Bde. R.F.A. No. S.F/33/3	28/02/1917	28/02/1917
Operation(al) Order(s)	16th Divisional Artillery Operation Order No. 51. 3rd March 1917.	03/02/1917	03/02/1917
Miscellaneous	Tasks For Night 4th/5th March.		
Miscellaneous	16th D.A. No. R. 2708/38. 3rd Mar. 1917	03/03/1917	03/03/1917
Operation(al) Order(s)	16th Divisional Artillery Operation Order No. 50. 3rd March 1917	03/03/1917	03/03/1917
Miscellaneous	Bombardment Table "B" Day.		
Miscellaneous	Spanbroek Group Date 8th March 1917	08/03/1917	08/03/1917
Miscellaneous	Spanbroek Group Date 9 March 1917	09/03/1917	09/03/1917
Miscellaneous	Spanbroek Group. Date 9th March 1917	09/03/1917	09/03/1917
Miscellaneous	Vierstraat Group. Spanbroek Group. D.T.M.O.	09/03/1917	09/03/1917
Miscellaneous	Report On Hostile Raid On Night 8/9th. March.	09/03/1917	09/03/1917
Miscellaneous	Report On Hostile Attacks In The Spanbroek Section On Afternoon March 8th. 1917	08/03/1917	08/03/1917
Miscellaneous	Precis of Orders etc. emanating from Spanbroek Group Hdqrs. in connection with a hostile raid on 8.3.17	08/03/1917	08/03/1917
Miscellaneous	Report by Major A.K. Digby. D.S.O. Observing Officer at K. 18.		
Miscellaneous	47th Inf. Bde. No. G. 1609.	09/03/1917	09/03/1917
Operation(al) Order(s)	Spanbroek Operation Order No. 13. by Lieut-Colonel L.E.S. Ward D.S.O., R.F.A. Commanding.	13/03/1917	13/03/1917
Operation(al) Order(s)	Reference Spanbroek O.O. No. 13.	13/03/1917	13/03/1917
Operation(al) Order(s)	180th. Brigade R.F.A. Operation Order No. 14. Lieut-Colonel L.E.S. Ward., D.S.O., R.F.A. Commanding.	20/03/1917	20/03/1917
Miscellaneous	Relief Table.		
Miscellaneous	Relief Table		
Operation(al) Order(s)	180th. Bde. Operation Order No. 15. by Lieut-Colonel L.E.S. Ward. D.S.O., R.F.A., Commanding.	27/03/1917	27/03/1917
Miscellaneous	Relief Table		
Heading	War Diary For Month Of April, 1917 Volume 15 Unit. 180th Brigade R.F.A.		
War Diary	Westoutre	01/04/1917	08/04/1917
War Diary	Nielles-Lez-Blequin	09/04/1917	22/04/1917
War Diary	Godwaers-Velde	23/04/1917	23/04/1917
War Diary	Locre	24/04/1917	30/04/1917
Operation(al) Order(s)	180th. Brigade Operation Order No. A.1. by Major N.A. Stebbing, D.S.O., R.F.A., Comdg.		
Operation(al) Order(s)	180th. Brigade Operation Order No. 19.	29/04/1917	29/04/1917
Miscellaneous	Relief Table.		
Operation(al) Order(s)	180th. Brigade, Operation Order No. 16 by Lieut-Colonel L.E.S. Ward. D.S.O., R.F.A., Commanding.	31/03/1917	31/03/1917
Miscellaneous	Barrage Table		
Operation(al) Order(s)	180th. Bde. R.F.A. No. S.F. 64. Reference 180th. Bde. O.O. dated 31.3.17	31/03/1917	31/03/1917
Map	18 Pdr. Barrages		
Miscellaneous	General March Orders by Lieut-Colonel L.E.S. Ward, D.S.O., R.F.A., Comdg.	04/04/1917	04/04/1917

Operation(al) Order(s)	180th. Brigade Operation Order No. 17. by Lieut-Colonel L.E.S. Ward, D.S.O., R.F.A., Commanding.	05/04/1917	05/04/1917
Operation(al) Order(s)	16th Divisional Artillery Operation Order No. 62. 3rd April, 1917	03/04/1917	03/04/1917
Operation(al) Order(s)	180th. Brigade R.F.A. Order No. 180	06/04/1917	06/04/1917
Operation(al) Order(s)	180th. Brigade Order No. 185. by Lt-Colonel L.E.S. Ward, D.S.O., R.F.A., Commanding.	07/04/1917	07/04/1917
Miscellaneous	Programme Of Training.		
Operation(al) Order(s)	180th. Brigade Order No. 260. by Lieut-Colonel L.E.S. Ward, D.S.O., R.F.A., Commanding.	20/04/1917	20/04/1917
Operation(al) Order(s)	180th. Brigade Order No. 268 by Lieut-Colonel L.E.S. Ward, D.S.O., R.F.A., Commanding.	21/04/1917	21/04/1917
Heading	War Diary Volume 16 For Month Of May, 1917 Unit 180th Brigade R.F.A.		
War Diary	Locre	30/04/1917	01/05/1917
War Diary	La Clytte	02/05/1917	07/05/1917
War Diary	Scherpenberg	09/05/1917	09/05/1917
War Diary	La Clytte	10/05/1917	12/05/1917
War Diary	Locrestraat Farm	13/05/1917	27/05/1917
War Diary	Rossignol Wood	28/05/1917	31/05/1917
Miscellaneous	180th. Bde. R.F.A. No. S.F.114	08/05/1917	08/05/1917
Operation(al) Order(s)	180th. Brigade Operation Order No. 21. by Lieut-Colonel L.E.S. Ward. D.S.O., R.F.A., Commanding.	10/05/1917	10/05/1917
Operation(al) Order(s)	180th. Brigade Operation Order No. 22 by Lieut-Colonel L.E.S. Ward. D.S.O., R.F.A., Commanding.	18/05/1917	18/05/1917
Operation(al) Order(s)	Ross Group Operation Order No. 1. by Lieut-Colonel L.E.S. Ward. D.S.O., R.F.A., Commdg.	27/05/1917	27/05/1917
Operation(al) Order(s)	Ross Group Operation Order No. 2 by Lieut-Colonel L.E.S. Ward. D.S.O. R.F.A., Commdg.	31/05/1917	31/05/1917
Heading	War Diary. For Month Of June, 1917 Volume Unit 180th Brigade R.F.A.		
War Diary	Rossignol Wood	01/06/1917	07/06/1917
War Diary	Irish House N 23 c 95	07/06/1917	07/06/1917
War Diary	Irish House	07/06/1917	09/06/1917
War Diary	S.P. 13	10/06/1917	10/06/1917
War Diary	Byron Farm	11/06/1917	28/06/1917
War Diary	M8c 04.	30/06/1917	30/06/1917
Operation(al) Order(s)	Right Group Operation Order No. 3. by Lieut-Colonel L.E.S. Ward. D.S.O., R.F.A., Comdg.	01/06/1917	01/06/1917
Miscellaneous	Creeping: Practice Barrage Table.		
Operation(al) Order(s)	16th Divisional Artillery Operation Order No. 79. 2nd June, 1917.	02/06/1917	02/06/1917
Miscellaneous	Gas Shell Bombardment Table 2nd/3rd June.		
Miscellaneous	Gas Shell Bombardment Table For 3rd/4th June.		
Operation(al) Order(s)	Right Group Operation Order No. 5. by Lieut-Colonel L.E.S. Ward. D.S.O., R.F.A., Comdg.	02/06/1917	02/06/1917
Miscellaneous	Table of Tasks.		
Operation(al) Order(s)	Right Group Operation Order No. 6. by Lieut-Colonel L.E.S. Ward. D.S.O., R.F.A., Comdg. June 3rd, 1917	03/06/1917	03/06/1917
Miscellaneous	Table of Tasks		
Operation(al) Order(s)	Right Group Operation Order No. 7 by Lieut-Colonel L.E.S. Ward, D.S.O., R.F.A., Commdg.	03/06/1917	03/06/1917
Miscellaneous	Creeping Barrage		
Miscellaneous	Standing Barrage		
Operation(al) Order(s)	Reference Right Group Operation Order No. 7	04/06/1917	04/06/1917
Map	Second Army Barrage Map. June, 1917		

Operation(al) Order(s)	Right Group Operation Order No. 9. by Lieut-Colonel, L.E.S. Ward, D.S.O., R.F.A., Comdg.	05/06/1917	05/06/1917
Miscellaneous	47th Inf. Bde. No. G. 3221	03/06/1917	03/06/1917
Miscellaneous	Barrage Table to accompany 47th Infantry Brigade No. G. 3221		
Operation(al) Order(s)	Left Artillery Group 19th Division Operation Order No. A.1 12th June 1917	12/06/1917	12/06/1917
Miscellaneous	180. Bde. RFA. No. SF. 186	14/06/1917	14/06/1917
Operation(al) Order(s)	19th Divisional Artillery Operation Order No 125 14th June 1917	14/06/1917	14/06/1917
Operation(al) Order(s)	Left Artillery Group 19th Division Operation Order No. A.2.	14/06/1917	14/06/1917
Miscellaneous	Relief Table 27th/28th. June. O.O.A.2.		
Miscellaneous	180. Bde. RFA. No. SF. 186	14/06/1917	14/06/1917
Operation(al) Order(s)	16th. Divisional Artillery Operation Order No. 88. 16th. June. 1917	16/06/1917	16/06/1917
Operation(al) Order(s)	180th. Brigade Operation Order No.A.2. by Major N.A. Stebbing, D.S.O., R.F.A., Commanding. 26th. June, 1917	26/06/1917	26/06/1917
Heading	War Diary For Month of October, 1917. Unit 180 Brigade R.F.A. Volume Number 21		
War Diary	Near St Leger. G 22 a 28	05/10/1917	20/10/1917
War Diary	Near St Leger.	21/10/1917	30/10/1917
Heading	War Diary For Month Of November, 1917. Volume:- 22 Unit:- 180th Bde R.F.A.		
War Diary	T.28 a 28 Near Leger	01/11/1917	30/11/1917
Heading	War Diary For Month Of December, 1917 Volume:- 23 Unit 180th Brigade R.F.A. Original		
War Diary		29/12/1917	30/12/1917
War Diary	St Leger	01/12/1917	20/12/1917
War Diary	Near Ervillers	20/12/1917	21/12/1917
War Diary	Near Beaulencourt	22/12/1917	22/12/1917
War Diary	Haut Allaines	23/12/1917	23/12/1917
War Diary	Near Roisel	24/12/1917	25/12/1917
War Diary	Seemilie	26/12/1917	29/12/1917
Heading	War Diary, For Month Of January, 1918. Volume:- 24 Unit:- 180th Brigade R.F.A.		
War Diary	Ste Emilie	01/01/1918	31/01/1918
Heading	War Diary. For Month Of February, 1918. Volume:- 25 Unit:- 180th Brigade R.F.A.		
War Diary	Marquaix	01/02/1918	18/02/1918
War Diary	Tincourt	19/02/1918	27/02/1918
War Diary	Quarry Near Ste Emilie	28/02/1918	28/02/1918
Heading	16th Divisional Artillery. 180th Brigade R.F.A. March 1918 Appendix attached:- Battle Casualties.		
War Diary	Quarry Near Ste Emilie	01/03/1918	31/03/1918
Miscellaneous	Battle Casualties.		
War Diary	Near Of Bois De Waire Nr. Hamel	01/04/1918	01/04/1918
War Diary	Fouilloy	03/04/1918	18/04/1918
War Diary	Homes Billes	20/04/1918	30/04/1918
Miscellaneous	Battle Casualties		
War Diary	Hamet Billet (near St. Venant)	01/05/1918	07/05/1918
War Diary	Hamet Billet	08/05/1918	29/05/1918
War Diary	Hamet Billet Near St Venand	01/06/1918	15/06/1918
War Diary	Hamet Billet	15/06/1918	22/06/1918
War Diary	Enquin-le-23 Mines	23/06/1918	23/06/1918

War Diary	Bois Du Hazois	24/06/1918	30/06/1918
War Diary	Bois du Hazois	01/07/1918	01/07/1918
War Diary	ACQ	17/07/1918	17/07/1918
War Diary	Avias	18/07/1918	31/07/1918
War Diary	Arras	01/08/1918	16/08/1918
War Diary	East of Arras	16/08/1918	31/08/1918
Miscellaneous	East of Fampoux	01/09/1918	04/09/1918
War Diary	Fampoux Anzin	05/09/1918	05/09/1918
War Diary	Vielfort	06/09/1918	07/09/1918
War Diary	Annequin	08/09/1918	13/09/1918
War Diary	H.Q. Annequin	14/09/1918	30/09/1918
War Diary	Annequin	01/10/1918	03/10/1918
War Diary	Auchy	04/10/1918	10/10/1918
War Diary	Billy	15/10/1918	15/10/1918
War Diary	Annoelin	16/10/1918	16/10/1918
War Diary	Camphin	17/10/1918	17/10/1918
War Diary	Powtamma	18/10/1918	18/10/1918
War Diary	Templeuve	19/10/1918	19/10/1918
War Diary	Sentier	20/10/1918	20/10/1918
War Diary	Taintignies	21/10/1918	01/11/1918
War Diary	Rumes	05/11/1918	13/11/1918
War Diary	Enevelin	15/11/1918	15/11/1918
War Diary	Wahagnies	16/11/1918	18/11/1918
War Diary	Mons En Pevele	20/11/1918	28/12/1918
War Diary	Mons-En-Pevele	01/01/1919	26/02/1919
War Diary	Cappelle (Chateau du Bron.)	01/05/1919	10/05/1919
War Diary	Wattines	12/05/1919	07/06/1919
War Diary	Cappelle	08/06/1919	21/06/1919
War Diary	Dunkerque	28/06/1919	28/06/1919

16TH DIVISION

180TH BRIGADE R.F.A.

FEB 1916-JUN 1919

Instructions regarding War Diaries and Intelligence Summaries are contained in F. S. Regs., Part II. and the Staff Manual respectively. Title Pages will be prepared in manuscript.

WAR DIARY
or
~~INTELLIGENCE SUMMARY~~
(Erase heading not required.)

Army Form C. 2118

180th Brigade R.F.A. No 1.

Place	Date	Hour	Summary of Events and Information	Remarks and references to Appendices
Bordon	Feb 1916 16th 17th 18th		The Brigade left Bordon by rail and embarked at Southampton as follows:— On S.S. Southwest Miller, Headquarters and "A" Battery, on S.S. Bellerophon "B" and "C" Batteries, on S.S. Archimedes "D" and B.A.C.	
Havre	Feb 17th		"A" "B" "C" and Headquarters disembarked at Havre on the morning of the 17th, "D" + the B.A.C. in the Evening of the same day. The Brigade, with the exception of the B.A.C. entrained on the Evening of the 17th and proceeded by rail to Berguette where it arrived at 10.30 P.M on the 18th Feby, disentrained	
Berguette	Feb 18th		and marched 14 Km. to Blessy. The B.A.C. entrained at Havre on the Evening of the 18th and arrived at Blessy on the morning of the 20th Feby.	
Blessy	Feb.		The Brigade remained in billets at Blessy till the 26th Feby on which date it marched to a new billeting area	

1875 Wt. W593/826 1,000,000 ... R. C. & A. A.D.S.S./Forms/C. 2118.

180 Bde
R.F.A
16th Div
Vol 2

Army Form C. 2118

Instructions regarding War Diaries and Intelligence Summaries are contained in F. S. Regs., Part II. and the Staff Manual respectively. Title Pages will be prepared in manuscript.

WAR DIARY
or
~~INTELLIGENCE SUMMARY~~
(Erase heading not required.)

180th Brigade R.F.A. No. 2

Place	Date	Hour	Summary of Events and Information	Remarks and references to Appendices
Berguette	1916 Feb 26 to Feb 29th		at Berguette a distance of 12 km. The Brigade remained in billets at Berguette till the end of the month.	
"				

J. Cochrane
Lt. Col. R.F.A.
Comm'g 180th Bde R.F.A.

1875 Wt. W593/826 1,000,000 ... L.B.C. & A. A.D.S.S./Forms/C. 2118.

Instructions regarding War Diaries and Intelligence Summaries are contained in F. S. Regs., Part II. and the Staff Manual respectively. Title Pages will be prepared in manuscript.

WAR DIARY
or
INTELLIGENCE SUMMARY
(Erase heading not required.)

180th Bde RFA Army Form C. 2118

No 2.

Place	Date 1916	Hour	Summary of Events and Information	Remarks and references to Appendices
Berguette.	Mar 1st		The Brigade still in back billets at Berguette.	
			Two officers from H. Q. and two officers and twelve men per Battery joined the 12 D.A. in the Vermelles sector for a three days' course.	
~~Berguette~~.	~~Mar 2nd~~		The following officers went:- Lt-Col. J. E. C. J. Cochrane D.S.O. Major N. Stebbing. Capt C. D. Hope. Lieut. G. C. J. Wood. 2 Lt. Ivan Firth. 2 Lt. O. Steven. 2 Lt. J. R. Kent. 2 Lt. B. K. Mumbey. 2 Lt. J. R. D. Martin, and 2 Lt. D. Mackay.	
			2 Lt. H. B. Harwood joined the Brigade, and was posted to 'A' Battery.	
Berguette.	Mar 3rd		The course returned from the 12th D.A, and joined their own units.	
Berguette.	Mar 4th		Major N. Stebbing joined 8th Artillery Course at Aires.	
Berguette	Mar 5th		The following officers and another 12 men per Battery joined 12th D.A for a three days course:- Capt. E. B. Maxwell. Capt. A. K. Digby. D.S.O. 2 Lt. A. R. Lister. Lt. T. R. J. Lynch. 2 Lt. A. E. Edwards: 2 Lt. H. W. Lilley Lt. S. D. J. Saunders. Lt. H. C. Richardson.	
			Lt. P. A. Brooke joined the Brigade, & was posted to 'B' Battery.	
Berguette.	Mar 6th		2 Lt. F. F. Newman joined the Brigade, and was posted to 'C' Battery.	
Berguette.	Mar 7th		2 Lt. A. A. Tindall joined the Brigade, and was posted to 'D' Battery.	
			The Brigade marched from Berguette to another billeting area at Ames.	
Ames.	Mar 8th		The course returned from 12th D.A.	
Ames.	Mar 9th		The following officers, and one section per Battery went for course to 1st D.A.	

Instructions regarding War Diaries and Intelligence Summaries are contained in F. S. Regs., Part II. and the Staff Manual respectively. Title Pages will be prepared in manuscript.

WAR DIARY
or
INTELLIGENCE SUMMARY
(Erase heading not required.)

180th Bde RFA. Army Form C. 2118

No 2.

Place	Date	Hour	Summary of Events and Information	Remarks and references to Appendices
Ames.	Mar 9th (cont.)		Lt. and Adjt. P.W. Woods. 2Lt. B.K. Mambey. 2Lt. D. Steven. Lt. J.T.R.G. Lynch. 2Lt. J.A.D. Martin. Lt. G.S.J. Wood. 2Lt. J.R. Kent. 2Lt. D. Mackay. 2Lt. A.A. Tindall. Lt. W.P. Balls. 2Lt. T.G. Key.	
Ames.	Mar 10th		Major N. Stebbing rejoined his unit.	
Ames.	Mar 12th		The course returned from 1st D.A.	
Ames.	Mar 13th		The following officers and another section per Battery joined 1st D.A. for another course:– 2Lt. A.R. Lister. 2Lt. H.B. Harwood. Lt. P.A. Brooke. 2Lt. J.E. Edwards. 2Lt. H.W. Tilley. 2Lt. F.F. Newman. Lt. S.D.J. Saunders. 2Lt. D. Mackay, and 2Lt. D. Schofield.	
Ames.	Mar 19th		On the return of this course the following officers went with section for a week course in the firing line in 1st Corps area. Capt. A.K. Digby. D.S.O. Capt. Maxwell. 2Lt. Ivan Firth. Lt. L.T.R.G. Lynch. 2Lt. H.D.R. Martin. 2Lt. A.R. Lister, and 2Lt. D. Mackay.	
Ames.	Mar 26th		This course returned, and the following officers with sections joined 15th D.A. for a weeks course:– Lt.-Col. J.E.C.J. Cochrane. D.S.O. Major N. Stebbing. Capt. Hope, and eight subalterns.	
Ames.	Mar 29th		Capt. A.K. Digby D.S.O joined C/71 15th D.A. for three days. The Brigade remained in billets in Ames till end of month.	

P.W. Woods Lt RFA
Adjt 180th Bde RFA

1875 Wt. W593/826 1,000,000 4/15 J.B.C. & A. A.D.S.S./Forms/C. 2118.

180th Brigade R.F.A.

Army Form C. 2118

Vol 3

XVI

Instructions regarding War Diaries and Intelligence Summaries are contained in F. S. Regs., Part II. and the Staff Manual respectively. Title Pages will be prepared in manuscript.

WAR DIARY
or
~~INTELLIGENCE SUMMARY~~

(Erase heading not required.)

Place	Date	Hour	Summary of Events and Information	Remarks and references to Appendices
Annes	April 1		The Bde back in billets at Annes. 2Lt R.A. Smith joined the Bde on 30/3/16 & was posted to "B" Battery.	
	2		Col. J.C. Cochrane D.S.O. returned from 71st Bde. R.F.A. L 36179 Sgt Harris R D/180 was wounded while on duty at B. HQ. at Loos & was evacuated	
	3		The sections at the front of B and D Batteries returned to their units. Single sections from "A" and "C" went into the line to relieve 116 & 117 Batteries respectively. Lt H.C. Richardson R.F.A. was evacuated to England sick and struck off the strength of the Brigade. 116 & 117 Batteries took over the billets horse lines &c of "A" & "C" Batteries. Major H.C.V. Harrison 18th D.A.C. was buried at Lillers	
	4		The remaining sections of A and C Batteries left for the Front and corresponding sections of 116 & 117 came into reserve attached to the Bde for discipline only.	
	5		2Lt F.F. Newman returned from 1st Army Trench Mortar School at St Venant.	
	6		Lt. P.A. Brooks with NCO & 6 men joined the Trench Mortar School at St Venant on a course.	

1875 Wt. W593/826 1,000,000 4/15 J.B.C. & A. A.D.S.S./Forms/C. 2118.

Army Form C. 2118

Instructions regarding War Diaries and Intelligence Summaries are contained in F. S. Regs., Part II. and the Staff Manual respectively. Title Pages will be prepared in manuscript.

WAR DIARY
or
~~INTELLIGENCE SUMMARY~~
(Erase heading not required.)

Place	Date	Hour	Summary of Events and Information	Remarks and references to Appendices
Arnes / La Tirmand	7		The Brigade less A & C Batteries was attached to 15th (Scottish) Division and marched under 44th Infantry Bde into billets at La Tirmand. These billets were unsuitable for Artillery owing to lack of watering facilities. The Divisional Commander inspected the Division en route. 2Lt F.F. Newman remained at Arnes in charge of details	
La Tirmand	8.		Under orders from 44th I.B the Bde marched into special Artillery Manoeuvre Area through Bonny and took up a position, returning to billets about 6pm.	
	9		Brigade returned to Arnes, inspected en route by Divisional Commander.	
Arnes	10.		L37702 Gnr. W.J. Ferguson was wounded while on Trench Mortar digging fatigue.	
Arnes	11		One section B & D Batteries left for the front attached to 12 D.A.	
Arnes	12		Remainder of B & D left to relieve D/62 12 D.A. One section of A & C took over their billet line	
Arnes	13		Lt P.A. Brooke RFA returned from Trench Mortar Course. Remainder of A & C Batteries returned to reserve	

1875 Wt. W593/826 1,000,000 4/15 J.B.C. & A. A.D.S.S./Forms/C. 2118.

Instructions regarding War Diaries and Intelligence Summaries are contained in F. S. Regs., Part II. and the Staff Manual respectively. Title Pages will be prepared in manuscript.

WAR DIARY
or
~~INTELLIGENCE SUMMARY~~
(Erase heading not required.)

Army Form C. 2118

Place	Date	Hour	Summary of Events and Information	Remarks and references to Appendices
Annes	15.		The 180 Bde RFA commence taking over from 71st Bde RFA H.Q. at Mazingarbe: Battery positions near Fosse 7 Battery positions A: G26d77. B: G26.d.42. C: G27c1.2 D: G33a8.5.	
Mazingarbe	16.		Taking over Completed. Fosse 7 positions heavily shelled in the morning with 4.2 + 5.9 Howitzers. At 3.30 pm the last of the Loos Pylons was shelled to the ground.	
	17		L 37710 Bdr L. Key was wounded mending telephone line Fosse 3 and Quality St shelled with 4.2s in the afternoon. Otherwise all quiet	
	18		Light was bad, Weather unfavourable for artillery observation Enemy quiet	
	19.		Enemy quiet. Registration carried on	
	20.		Wind still high. Enemy quiet. 101947 Gnr Skinner Ch. A/180 was wounded by 5.9 while on duty as linesman	

1875 Wt. W593/826 1,000,000 4/15 J.B.C. & A. A.D.S.S./Forms/C. 2118.

Army Form C. 2118

Instructions regarding War Diaries and Intelligence Summaries are contained in F. S. Regs., Part II. and the Staff Manual respectively. Title Pages will be prepared in manuscript.

WAR DIARY
or
~~INTELLIGENCE SUMMARY~~
(Erase heading not required.)

Place	Date	Hour	Summary of Events and Information	Remarks and references to Appendices
Mazingarbe	21		No 101947 Gnr Skinner C. dies during the night at 33 C.C.S. Weather fine. Congratulatory letter from the General of the Div complimenting Col Cochrane D.S.O. Capt A Maxwell A/180 on the splendid shooting of his Battery when relieving 117 Battery. Much aerial activity. The enemy shelled Philosophe, Fosse 8 & Quality St with 4.2 5.9 from 7.30 am to 11 am. with little effect. Experiment in wire cutting tried with Medium Trench Mortars 10 Rds fired Judged not a success by our observing officers	
	22		Weather very wet Enemy quiet. 2/Lt Ias Millar joined the Bde & was posted to BAC/180.	
	23		Weather cleared. Barometer rose from 29.2" to 30" in about 12 hrs. Enemy shelled Fosse 8 & Mazingarbe 4 Balloons up	
	24		Weather very fine Enemy shelled Fosse 3 and B/180 Battery positions with 5.9. Second experiment with Medium Trench Mortars was judged a success by our officers who observed. 2/Lt E.D. Masson joined the Bdge & was posted to B Battery.	

1875 Wt. W593/826 1,000,000 4/15 J.B.C. & A. A.D.S.S./Forms/C. 2118.

Instructions regarding War Diaries and Intelligence Summaries are contained in F. S. Regs., Part II. and the Staff Manual respectively. Title Pages will be prepared in manuscript.

WAR DIARY
or
~~INTELLIGENCE SUMMARY~~

(Erase heading not required.)

Army Form C. 2118

Place	Date	Hour	Summary of Events and Information	Remarks and references to Appendices
Mazingarbe	25		Weather fine Barometer 30.2 Wind S.E. Gas alert was ordered. Major Stebbing observes the fire of his Battery from Kite Balloon. Much rifle fire was heard from 8pm to 9pm on 1st Div Zone near the Double Crassier. Later there was much firing near the Hohenzollern.	
	26.		Weather still fine. Four Sections from the 71st Bde joined the Bde to occupy the reinforcing positions. The Heavies near Mazingarbe fired for 2½ hrs in the afternoon. Officer of D Battery reports the presence of suspected Gas Cylinders near Sap 43. Battery ~~[illegible]~~ got 2 direct hits & smashed the cylinder. No gas emitted.	
	27		About 5 am heavy bombardment by enemy was proceeding along our front. About 5.45 am all Bde lines were cut by shell fire. At 5.10 am enemy released gas from his trenches S of Hulluch supporting it with an artillery Barrage along our sector (Puits 14 Bis). Second cloud was released at 7.30 am. There was specially heavy bombardment of Chalk Pit salient. Infantry attack was then launched which succeeded in getting a footing in our trenches over 300 yds. Enemy were driven out again at 8 am leaving many dead in trenches & No Man's Land	

1875 Wt. W593/826 1,000,000 4/15 J.B.C. & A. A.D.S.S./Forms/C. 2118.

Army Form C. 2118

Instructions regarding War Diaries and Intelligence Summaries are contained in F. S. Regs., Part II. and the Staff Manual respectively. Title Pages will be prepared in manuscript.

WAR DIARY
or
~~INTELLIGENCE SUMMARY~~
(Erase heading not required.)

Place	Date	Hour	Summary of Events and Information	Remarks and references to Appendices
27th			We took several prisoners. Our Batteries were heavily shelled by 4.2 and 5.9s till Mid-day. Gas Attack was signalled at 6 pm from Hillock Sector but no attack followed. Casualties as follows. L 36045. A/Bdr. Cattel A A/180 killed. L 40058 Bdr Hunter T D/180 wounded & sent to Hospital	
28th			Hostile Gas Attack reported at 5.30 am from Hillock Sector. Much rifle fire on our left. Our Batteries fired on their zones. The Gas attack alarm was a false one. "A" & "B" Batteries were heavily shelled with 4.2" & 5.9" Hows. L36262 Bdr Hendry L B/180 was killed at Battery position. L39228 Gnr Jones G. A/180 was wounded and L39229 Gnr Maunders JH A/180 B.S.M. at duty. 16n. H.B. Little 2Lt R.F.A. joined the Brigade & was posted to A Battery	
29th			Heavy firing heard at 4.30 pm. Gas Attack from S of Hillock took place. Our Batteries shelled with 4.2" and 5.9" from the direction of Auchy till after 6 am. The gas attack is reported to have caused many casualties in our trenches. Remainder of the day was very quiet. Letters of congratulation from 48th & 49th Infantry Brigades were received by the O.C. R.A. on the excellent shooting of his Batteries. Several linesmen &c were brought to notice during the recent operations	

1875 Wt. W593/826 1,000,000 4/15 J.B.C. & A. A.D.S.S./Forms/C. 2118.

Instructions regarding War Diaries and Intelligence Summaries are contained in F. S. Regs., Part II. and the Staff Manual respectively. Title Pages will be prepared in manuscript.

WAR DIARY
or
~~INTELLIGENCE~~ SUMMARY

(Erase heading not required.)

Army Form C. 2118

Place	Date	Hour	Summary of Events and Information	Remarks and references to Appendices
Mazingarbe	30.		Very quiet day. but some large shells were sent near the Battery positions	

[signature]
LIEUT. COL. R.F.A.
COMMANDING 180th BRIGADE, R.F.A.

1875 Wt. W593/826 1,000,000 4/15 J.B.C. & A. A.D.S.S./Forms/C. 2118.

Instructions regarding War Diaries and Intelligence Summaries are contained in F. S. Regs., Part II. and the Staff Manual respectively. Title Pages will be prepared in manuscript.

WAR DIARY
or
~~INTELLIGENCE SUMMARY~~
(Erase heading not required.)

XVI

180th Bde. R.F.A.

No 4.

Army Form C. 2118

Vol 4

Place	Date	Hour	Summary of Events and Information	Remarks and references to Appendices
Mazingarbe	May 2		Lieut. S. Antliff of 1 East Lancs. Bde. R.F.A. was attached from England for 14 days' instruction. C/180 was shelled heavily this morning with 8" + D/180 with 4.2" Hows. L 36135 Gnr. Abbott B. and 120494 Gnr Gubbins W. both of C/180 were killed in a dugout by a shell.	
	3.		Two false gas alarms today one at 2 a.m. and another at 9 p.m.	
	5		Lt S. D. J. Saunders went to St Venant on a course of Trench Mortars.	
	6		16th Divisional Artillery School opened today in the Chateau next Mazingarbe church - Lt. Col. J. E. C. J. Cochrane D.S.O., 180th Bde. Commanding - Five Officers joined.	
	11		Battery positions at Fosse 7 heavily shelled from 4 pm till 7 pm. during an enemy attack on the South of the Hohenzollern Redoubt.	

1875 Wt. W593/826 1,000,000 R. C. & A. A.D.S.S./Forms/C. 2118.

Instructions regarding War Diaries and Intelligence Summaries are contained in F. S. Regs., Part II. and the Staff Manual respectively. Title Pages will be prepared in manuscript.

WAR DIARY
or
~~INTELLIGENCE SUMMARY~~
(Erase heading not required.)

Army Form C. 2118

180th Bde. R.F.A.
No. 4.

Place	Date	Hour	Summary of Events and Information	Remarks and references to Appendices
Mazingarbe	12.		No L36257 Dvr. Hasemore J. W. A/180 was tried by FGCM on the 30th April and sentenced to suffer death by being shot for wilful defiance of authority. The Sentence was duly carried out 4.25 am. this morning.	
	15		Much rifle and artillery fire just south of the Hohenzollern. Fosse 7 and Mazingarbe Church shelled with 5.9" Hows.	
	17.		Lt. S.D.J. Saunders and 2/Lt. D. Schofield returned to duty from Hospital.	
	18		Lt. S.D.J. Saunders returned to Hospital 33 C.C.S.	
	19.		Lt. G.S.J. Wood C/180 went to Hospital and was evacuated to West Riding Clearing station.	
			41154 Sgt. Murphy E. A/180 and L37717 Br. Breedon J.C. A/180 were wounded by shell fire but remained at duty.	
	21		Artillery School first course closed. From mid day till nearly 9 pm Fosse 7 and Mazingarbe Batteries were heavily shelled with lachrymatory and other heavy shell during a German attack on the Vimy Ridge.	

Instructions regarding War Diaries and Intelligence Summaries are contained in F. S. Regs., Part II. and the Staff Manual respectively. Title Pages will be prepared in manuscript.

WAR DIARY
or
~~INTELLIGENCE SUMMARY~~
(Erase heading not required.)

180th Bde. R.F.A. Army Form C. 2118

No. 4.

Place	Date	Hour	Summary of Events and Information	Remarks and references to Appendices
Mazingarbe	22		The Brigade Ammunition Column was absorbed into the 16th D.A.C. The following Officers were transferred: Capt. The Hon. G. C. Nugent, Lt. S. D. J. Saunders, Lt. W. P. Balls, 2Lt. B. Harwood.	
	28		L37776. Gnr. Kimbley W. D/180, wounded but remained at duty.	
	30.		These telephonists belonging to A/180 + H.Q./180 have received parchment certificates from the G.O.C. 16th Division awarded for devotion to duty on the 27th and 28th April. L39228 Gr. Jones G. A/180 R.F.A. L36223 Gr. Coombs H.D. H.Q/180 R.F.A. L36336 Dr. Pettitt W.J. do " 97080 Gr. Turnbull G. do L36211 Gr. Binks S.J. do.	

P. M. [signature]
Lieut. R.F.A.
Adjutant 180th (West Ham) Brigade R.F.A.

1875 Wt. W593/826 1,000,000 [illegible] L.B.C. & A. A.D.S.S./Forms/C. 2118.

Instructions regarding War Diaries and Intelligence Summaries are contained in F. S. Regs., Part II. and the Staff Manual respectively. Title Pages will be prepared in manuscript.

WAR DIARY
or
INTELLIGENCE SUMMARY
(Erase heading not required.)

Army Form C. 2118

XVI 180th Bde R.F.A.
WO 5. Vol 5

Place	Date	Hour	Summary of Events and Information	Remarks and references to Appendices
Mazingarbe	June 1		Batteries of the Brigade are still in action round Fosse VII where they have greatly strengthened their positions during the previous months	
	2		Under the reorganisation of the Divisional Artillery D/180 Bde was transferred to the 77th Bde R.F.A. and became B/77th R.F.A. The following officers left the Brigade with the Battery: Major Sir Charles D Hope-Dunbar Bart. Lt ~~J.S. Firth~~ Lt ~~F.E. Edwards~~ Lt A.A. Tindall Lt ~~E.D. Masson~~ A/77th Bde R.F.A. took the place of D/180, joined the Brigade & became D/180. The following officers joined with their Battery: Capt R.A. Spencer Lt R.A. Allhusen Lt H.O. Hughes Lt T.G. Hipwell 2nd Lieut C.F. Lewis (at present attending 16th R.A. School)	
	3	z	~~Capt~~ W.P. Reid A.V.C. rejoined H.Q. 180th Bde from the old B.A.C. of the Brigade, to which he had been attached	
	4-12		Weather alternately dull & fine. Very little activity	
	13-17th		Lt Col J.E.C.A. Cochrane D.S.O. took over Command of the Left Group 16th Div Artillery during the absence of Lt Col Thomas on leave to England	

1875 Wt. W593/826 1,000,000 4/15 J.B.C. & A. A.D.S.S./Forms/C. 2118.

Instructions regarding War Diaries and Intelligence Summaries are contained in F. S. Regs., Part II. and the Staff Manual respectively. Title Pages will be prepared in manuscript.

WAR DIARY
or
INTELLIGENCE SUMMARY
(Erase heading not required.)

Army Form C. 2118

180th Bde R.F.A.
No 5.

Place	Date	Hour	Summary of Events and Information	Remarks and references to Appendices
Maqnipabe	18.		Lt H.B. Little A/180 R.F.A. was posted to X 16th T.M. Battery while attending the Divisional Artillery School	
	"		Lt D.A. Brooke went to 33rd C.C.S. suffering from an old wound in the leg.	
	19.		Lt C.F. Lewis R.F.A. was posted from D/180 to A/180 in place of Lt H.B. Little evacuated as above	
			Lt J Miller was posted from HQ 180th Bde to D/180 in room of Lt C.F. Lewis	
	22		No 115383 Gnr Wallwin R. C/180 was wounded in action	
	23		"A"/180 had five direct hits with 5.9" shell on their Gun pits without any material damage being done	
	24-29		Our artillery has been very active. Several successful raids have been carried out on our front.	

1875 Wt. W593/826 1,000,000 4/15 J.B.C. & A. A.D.S.S./Forms/C. 2118.

Instructions regarding War Diaries and Intelligence Summaries are contained in F. S. Regs., Part II. and the Staff Manual respectively. Title Pages will be prepared in manuscript.

WAR DIARY
or
INTELLIGENCE SUMMARY
(Erase heading not required.)

Army Form C. 2118

180th Bde R.F.A.
No 5.

Place	Date	Hour	Summary of Events and Information	Remarks and references to Appendices
Mazingarbe	29		Mazingarbe was shelled four times with 4.2" Gun shell at 9.45 am (24 rounds); at 3pm (20 rounds) when three R.E.'s horses were killed; at 10.15 pm near the Brigade H.Qrs and 1 am near the Church. This time 4 men were killed + 14 wounded. There was much firing on our right during the night 29/30th.	
	30		Three mines were blown up by the Division on our right at 9.15 after 5 minutes intense artillery preparation.	

P M Woods Lieut. R.F.A.
Adjutant 180th (West Ham) Brigade R.F.A.

1875 Wt. W593/826 1,000,000 4/15 J.B.C. & A. A.D.S.S./Forms/C. 2118.

W A R D I A R Y

180th Brigade

Royal Field Artillery.

1st. July to 31st. July 1916.

VOLUME No. 6

16 — July

180 RFA

Vol 6

Instructions regarding War Diaries and Intelligence Summaries are contained in F. S. Regs., Part II. and the Staff Manual respectively. Title Pages will be prepared in manuscript.

WAR DIARY
or
~~INTELLIGENCE SUMMARY~~
(Erase heading not required.)

~~Army Form~~ C. 2118

180th Bde. R.F.A.

No. 6

Place	Date	Hour	Summary of Events and Information	Remarks and references to Appendices
Mazingarbe	July 1.		Intimated that ~~Lt~~ S. O. J. Wood R.F.A. C/180 was evacuated to England 1.6.16. Enemy shelled Mazingarbe twice with 4 inch gun. Several fell near the Artillery School. Over 200 shells ~~were~~ fired at Water Tower Maroc near our B/180 O.P. without doing any damage.	
	2.		Sergt Catheral C/180 was slightly wounded but remained at duty.	
	3-5.		Quiet on our Front, during the days. Raids nightly.	
	6.		About 8.45 pm our Batteries at Fosse 7 were shelled by Lachrymatory Shell. Nearly 1000 are reported to have fallen near the Fosse.	
	7		Mazingarbe has been shelled for the last three days with 4" gun several times ~~per~~ day. The area near the Church has become distinctly unhealthy, although the weather has not been good for artillery Observation	

Instructions regarding War Diaries and Intelligence Summaries are contained in F. S. Regs., Part II. and the Staff Manual respectively. Title Pages will be prepared in manuscript.

WAR DIARY
or
~~INTELLIGENCE SUMMARY~~
(Erase heading not required.)

Army Form C. 2118

180th BDE R.F.A.
No 6

Place	Date	Hour	Summary of Events and Information	Remarks and references to Appendices
Mazingarbe	8		Weather has cleared. Mazingarbe has not been ~~shelled~~.	
	10		2Lt C.F. Lewis R.F.A. A/180 was admitted to No 3 C.C.S.	
			Intimated that Lt P. Brooke evacuated to England on 23/6/16.	
	12.		2Lt J.W. Dean R.F.A. from England posted to Brigade, and posted to A/180. 2Lt A.B. Lythgoe R.F.A. posted to B/180	
	13.		2Lt C.F. Lewis R.F.A. A/180 to England per hospital Ship	
	17		Our Batteries at Fosse 7 were shelled during the forenoon.	
	18		No 28418 Gnr Sparkes. H. A/77th Bde R.F.A. attached to 16th Div Artillery School was wounded in the School and admitted to Hospital. Mazingarbe billets were shelled by 4.2" How - universal shell at 4pm Several soldiers were killed & wounded.	
	21		2Lt J.W. Dean A/180 proceeded on Course at 16th Div. Arty School.	

1875 Wt. W593/826 1,000,000 ... J.B.C. & A. A.D.S.S./Forms/C. 2118.

Army Form C. 2118

180TH BDE R.F.A.
No 6

Instructions regarding War Diaries and Intelligence Summaries are contained in F. S. Regs., Part II. and the Staff Manual respectively. Title Pages will be prepared in manuscript.

WAR DIARY
or
~~INTELLIGENCE SUMMARY~~
(Erase heading not required.)

Place	Date	Hour	Summary of Events and Information	Remarks and references to Appendices
Mazingarbe	23		"A" and "B" Batteries of this Brigade moved from Battery positions at Fosse 7 to positions to left of and nearly adjoining the Cemetery of Vermelles. "D" Battery (How.) is transferred to the Right Group.	
	24.		Brigade Headquarters move to House lately occupied by 182nd Bde. R.F.A.	
	25		The 16th D.A. School in charge of 180th Bde H.Q. moved to rooms at Head Quarters. Officers are now billeted in former Headquarters of 180th Bde.	
	27		Officers from the 32nd Divisional Artillery are being attached to the various Batteries.	

R.W.Woods
Lieut. R.F.A.
Adjutant 180th (West Ham)
Brigade R.F.A.

1875 Wt. W593/826 1,000,000 ... J.B.C. & A. A.D.S.S./Forms/C. 2118.

Vol 7

W A R D I A R Y .

180th Brigade RFA

MONTH OF AUGUST, 1916.

VOLUME:- 7

Instructions regarding War Diaries and Intelligence Summaries are contained in F. S. Regs., Part II. and the Staff Manual respectively. Title Pages will be prepared in manuscript.

Army Form C. 2118

WAR DIARY
or
INTELLIGENCE SUMMARY
(Erase heading not required.)

Place	Date	Hour	Summary of Events and Information	Remarks and references to Appendices
HULLUCK SECTOR.	1/8/16	—	Very quiet day, our trenches lightly shelled during the morning to which we retaliated. Details of proposed raid by 48th Inf Bde received. Details of pending move received from 16th D.A.	[illegible]
"	2/8/16	—	Enemy artillery slightly more active today, our support and front line trenches were shelled at intervals during the day. We retaliated effectively, and also fired on enemy front line for machine gun fire on our aeroplanes. Our T.M's engaged enemy wire at various points	[illegible]
"	3/8/16	—	Enemy activity normal, retaliation was given for hostile fire on our front and support line, during the day. Enemy retaliated rather heavily on account of our T.M fire	[illegible]
"	4/8/16	—	Fairly Quiet day. Enemy T.M's were active during the morning and evening. Registrations carried out. Wagon lines moved back to NOEUX-LES-MINE, in view of forthcoming move.	
"	5/8/16	12.30 AM	Zero time for raid by 48th Inf. Bde. The raid took place over the whole Bde front, the infantry intending to enter at 16 different points. The following Btys were engaged. A/182. B/182. C/182. D/182 C/77. A/180 B/180. D/77. These Btys belong to Lt Group. Assistance of A/77 and 32nd Bty of the 8th D.A. also obtained. The 60 pdrs and 6" Hows were granted. Col Askwith CMG R.A. was at Inf Bde H.Q. directing fire of artillery.	[illegible]
"		12.8 am	"Retard" 30 mins was received from Infantry and immediately passed to all Btys	
"	"	12.20 am	"Retard" a further 15 mins was received	
"	"	12.55 am	"Retard" a further 30 minutes received	
"	"	1.45 am	Guns opened at B.F. 5 secs using A.X. 18pdrs	
"	"	1.48	18pdrs reduced rate of fire to B.F. 10 sec using $\frac{1}{3}$ A $\frac{2}{3}$ AX.	

1875 Wt. W593/826 1,000,000 4/15 J.B.C. & A. A.D.S.S./Forms/C. 2118.

Instructions regarding War Diaries and Intelligence Summaries are contained in F. S. Regs., Part II. and the Staff Manual respectively. Title Pages will be prepared in manuscript.

WAR DIARY
or
INTELLIGENCE SUMMARY
(Erase heading not required.)

Army Form C. 2118

Place	Date	Hour	Summary of Events and Information	Remarks and references to Appendices
HULLUCH SECTOR	5/8/16	2.13 AM	Message received from Col Askwith, that the 18pdr. Btys were to continue firing, this in view of the fact that our fire was to be stopped at 2.25, 40 mins after zero time.	
"	5/8/16	2.38 AM	Message received to stop C/182, B/182, and 32nd Bty of 8th D.A. These Btys were covering extreme left of front approximately from G.12 a ½. 3½ to G12 d. 6. 3.	[signature]
"	5/8/16	2.59 am	Orders for Centre Btys to stop firing. G12 d 6. 3 to A13 d 4. 6. The extreme right btys continued firing the parties not having returned.	
"	5/8/16	3.2 am	All Btys stopped, (Extreme Rt zone Btys) Everything quiet and all parties in. The hostile retaliation was very light. T.M's rather active, a few 4.2s and 5.9s fell on our front and support line	
"	5/8/16	—	The enemy activity today rather above normal, our reserve trenches being rather heavily shelled with 4.2" and 77 mm during the day. We retaliated at various times, and also engaged hostile T.M's. The Inf. Brigadier sent a message congratulating the artillery on the good shooting on raid	
"	6/8/16	—	Normal. Nothing to report. The enemy very quiet. The 16th Div are extending its right and withdrawing it left. The 8th D.A. relieve ~~[illegible]~~ 182nd Bde R.F.A. and sections of former D.A. relieved sections of A. B. C. D. Btys 182nd who withdrew to wagon lines, First nights relief completed 10.30 pm	[signature]
"	7/8/16	—	Very quiet day. nothing to report. The relief of ~~[illegible]~~ 182nd Bde R.F.A by 8th Div Btys completed 10.30 pm. Sections withdrew to wagon line.	[signature]

1875 Wt. W593/826 1,000,000 4/15 J.B.C. & A. A.D.S.S./Forms/C. 2118.

Instructions regarding War Diaries and Intelligence Summaries are contained in F. S. Regs., Part II. and the Staff Manual respectively. Title Pages will be prepared in manuscript.

WAR DIARY
or
INTELLIGENCE SUMMARY
(Erase heading not required.)

Army Form C. 2118

Place	Date	Hour	Summary of Events and Information	Remarks and references to Appendices
HULLUCH SECTOR	8/8/16	10 am	182nd Bde H.Q's moved back to MAZINGARBE AVENUE. L23.d.1.7.	
		9.30 pm	Sections of A.B.C.D Btys relieved sections of 40th DIV ARTY, at following places. A/182 at M2b. 25.50 B/182, G26.c.45.55. C/182. G26 d. 35.25 D/182 M2c.25.05. All reliefs completed by 11.30 pm.	[signature]
LOOS SECTOR	8/8/16			
"	9/8/16	9.30 pm	Second section of 182nd Btys relieved 40th D.A. Btys. Relief completed by 11 pm. Rt Group now responsible for front taken over from 40th D.A.	
"	10/8/16		Col Askwith C.M.G. Cmdg 182nd Bde R.F.A. is now O.C. Rt Group. R.F.A. covering the 47th Inf. Bde. whose front extends from H31.c.55.13 to M5.d.4½.9½. D/180 How Bty. and B/77 18pdr Bty join the Group. Very quiet day. Registrations carried out.	[signature]
"	11/8/16	—	Registrations & retaliation carried out. Very little hostile shelling. T.M's rather active	[signature]
"	12/8/16	—	Infantry have given us maps with names of Hostile T.M Btys shown thereon. i.e.— DAISY. MAGGIE. ZENA etc. Code words arranged "MEDIUM DAISY NASTY" means Medium T.M active from emplacement named DAISY. Medium Daisy NODS — means Medium T.M " " DAISY situation in hand, Arty stand by. DAISY QUIET — means, T.M. ceased firing. Retaliations carried out during the day for hostile T.M's.	[signature]
"	13/8/16	—	Hostile fire rather above normal, particularly T.M's. These were engaged by us	[signature]
"	14/8/16	—	Hostile T.M's again very active our front and support lines around HARTS and HARRISONS craters being shelled during the day. Observation conditions poor owing to mist	[signature]

1875 Wt. W593/826 1,000,000 4/15 J.B.C. & A. A.D.S.S./Forms/C. 2118.

Instructions regarding War Diaries and Intelligence Summaries are contained in F. S. Regs., Part II. and the Staff Manual respectively. Title Pages will be prepared in manuscript.

WAR DIARY
or
INTELLIGENCE SUMMARY
(Erase heading not required.)

Army Form C. 2118

Place	Date	Hour	Summary of Events and Information	Remarks and references to Appendices
LOOS SECTOR.	14/8/16	—	T. M's again very active, our front and support line being shelled throughout the day. We retaliated. Working parties also fired on.	
"	15/8/16	—	Hostile T.M's active all day. We retaliated heavily. MAZINGARBE was shelled during the evening by a 4'2" High Velocity gun from direction of LENS. We retaliated by fired into CITE ST. LAURENT.	
"	16/8/16	—	Enemy shelled fosse 7 with 5.9" from direction of PONT A VENDIN 39 rds in all being fired. LOOS Enclosure also shelled with 4.2". We retaliated.	
		4.30.	A. B/182 carried out a small shoot in conjunction with ~~Hot~~ T.M's on four selected "soft spots". Each target was engaged for 7 mins with 5 min intervals between each. Rate of fire B.F. 10 sec. ½ A + ½ AX being used.	
"	17/8/16	—	Enemy much quieter today. Nothing to report.	
"	18/8/16	—	Enemy activity solely confined to T.M's. Normal	
"	19/8/16	—	Extremely quiet day. Working parties on Hill 70 fired on & dispersed	
		3-45 pm	We carried out a small bombardment as on 16th inst in conjunction with T.M's 6 soft spots being engaged for 5 mins each.	
"	20/8/16	—	Very quiet day, enemy activity practically nil.	
"	21/8/16	2 am.	A raid was carried out by the 6th R. I. Rifles, a mine being blown east of HARRISONS CRATER (M6.c.4.4). Rt Group Btys excluding B/77 opened a box barrage	

1875 Wt. W593/826 1,000,000 4/15 J.B.C. & A. A.D.S.S./Forms/C. 2118.

Instructions regarding War Diaries and Intelligence Summaries are contained in F. S. Regs., Part II. and the Staff Manual respectively. Title Pages will be prepared in manuscript.

WAR DIARY
or
INTELLIGENCE SUMMARY
(Erase heading not required.)

Army Form C. 2118

Place	Date	Hour	Summary of Events and Information	Remarks and references to Appendices
LOOS SECTOR	21/8/16	2.0 am	Rate of fire B.F. 5 secs for 5 mins, then slackening to BTY.F. 10 secs for 45 mins, when	
		2.40	Btys stopped fire. Liaison officer sent through for A/182 to open fire on night lines, S of Harrison Crater. This was done.	
		3.0 am	All Quiet. Lamps were successfully used for signalling from front line to MAROC.	
"	22/8/16	—	Very un-eventful day. Nothing to report	
"	23/8/16	—	Hostile TM's rather active again. We retaliated	
"	23/8/16	11.45 am	16th D.A. order No 11 received, conveying information that 16th DIV were to withdraw from the line, and to commence entraining on the 28th inst. Btys of Rt Group being relieved by 40th D.A. relieve by sections on nights of 25-26th and 26th-27th.	
"	"	10 pm	DIV. R.A. orders received ~~new~~ re new formation of the DIV ARTY, which takes place immediately on the Arty's arrival in rest billets. This Bde 182nd then becomes the 180th Bde, billeted at AMES.	

1875 Wt. W593/826 1,000,000 4/15 J.B.C. & A. A.D.S.S./Forms/C. 2118.

Army Form C. 2118

Instructions regarding War Diaries and Intelligence Summaries are contained in F. S. Regs., Part II. and the Staff Manual respectively. Title Pages will be prepared in manuscript.

WAR DIARY
or
INTELLIGENCE SUMMARY
(Erase heading not required.)

Place	Date	Hour	Summary of Events and Information	Remarks and references to Appendices
LOOS SECTOR	24/8/16	—	16th D.A. orders 12 + 13 received having reference to move of Btys to reserve area. Very quiet on front. 16th D.A. Btys now under command of 40th D.A.	[signature]
	25/8/16	—	Bty position of B/182, C/182, D/180 taken over by 40th D.A. Btys, section relief took place, the sections withdrawing to wagon lines.	[signature]
"	"	11. pm	Section relief complete.	
"	26/8/16		Second sections relieved, and A/182, D/182 and B/77 withdrew to wagon lines complete.	
"	"	11am	Complete relief by 40th D.A. The Grp H.Q. handed over to Col Robertson 40th D.A. Rt Group 16th D.A. moved to AMES as per instructions. The whole Bde 182nd moved to AMES via Bethune, Chogues, and Lillers	[signature]
AMES.	27/8/16	—	The 182nd Bde R.F.A. now becomes 180th Bde R.F.A. Btys being commanded as follows. A/180. Capt Maxwell, B/180. Major Stebbing, C/180 Major Digby D.S.O. D/180 Capt Spencer. The Bde is commanded by Col. H. F. Askwith C.M.G. Adjutant – Lt A. J. MacDuff. The Bde is composed as follows A/180 complete and 1 section of A/182, B/180 complete and 1 section C/182, C/180 complete and 1 section C/182. D/180 complete. ∴ 3 – 6 gun Btys 18 pdrs and 1 – 4 gun Bty 4.5" Hows	[signature]

1875 Wt. W593/826 1,000,000 4/15 J.B.C. & A. A.D.S.S./Forms/C. 2118.

Instructions regarding War Diaries and Intelligence Summaries are contained in F. S. Regs., Part II. and the Staff Manual respectively. Title Pages will be prepared in manuscript.

WAR DIARY
or
INTELLIGENCE SUMMARY
(Erase heading not required.)

Army Form C. 2118

Place	Date	Hour	Summary of Events and Information	Remarks and references to Appendices
AMES.	28/8/16	–	All surplus officers, ORs, vehicles etc. to be evacuated tomorrow. Each Bty made up to full strength.	[initials]
AMES.	29/8/16	–	All surplus Officers & ORs evacuated. Billeting officer sent on ahead to SALEUX.	
"	"	11 pm	According to orders, H.Q and D/180 arrived at LILLERS STATION, and began entraining, prior to moving off by train due to leave at 2.1 am 30th inst. Entrained satisfactorily moving off at 2.54 am 30th.	[initials]
"	30/8/16	2.57 am	H.Q. and D/180 moved to SALEUX by train.	
"	"	5.1 am	B/180 moved off by train to SALEUX } Each Bty arrived at LILLERS STATION 3 hours before departure of train.	[initials]
"	"	8.1 am	C/180 " " " " "	
"		10.31 am	A/180 " " " " "	
"		12 noon	H.Q. D/180 arrived SALEUX and proceeded to DOEUR, where they were billeted, followed at intervals by A. B & C Btys.	[initials]
DOEUR.	31/8/16	–	All Btys reported to 16th D.A. in complete.	

H. T. G. Kenth[?]
Col R.A.
O C 180 Bde R F A

1875 Wt. W593/826 1,000,000 4/15 J.B.C. & A. A.D.S.S./Forms/C. 2118.

NEW FORMATION.

180 Brigade R.F.A.

Colonel H.F. Askwith C.M.G.
Adjutant Lieut: A.J. MacDuff.
Orderly Officer 2/Lt. B.H. Walker.

"A" BATTERY.

Captain E.B. Maxwell.
2/Lt. A.L. Perry.
" H. Brocker.
" C. Steven.
" A.R. Lister

"B" BATTERY.

Major F.A. Stebbing.
Captain R.M. McConnel.
2/Lt. R. Hinxman
Lieut. G.R.T.G. Lynch.
" J.R.D. Martin.

"C" BATTERY.

Major A.K. Digby D.S.O.
Captain D.L.W. Tivy.

2/Lt. K.W. Tilley
" J.R. Kent.
" A.B. Weekes.

"D" BATTERY

Captain R.A. Spencer.
Lieut: R. Allhusen.
2/Lt. J.W. Hughes.
" T.C. Hipwell.
" J. Miller.

W A R   D I A R Y

180th Brigade Royal Field Artillery

FOR MONTH OF SEPTEMBER, 1916.

VOLUME 8

Vol 8

16th Div

Instructions regarding War Diaries and Intelligence Summaries are contained in F. S. Regs., Part II. and the Staff Manual respectively. Title Pages will be prepared in manuscript.

WAR DIARY
or
INTELLIGENCE SUMMARY
(Erase heading not required.)

Army Form C. 2118

Place	Date	Hour	Summary of Events and Information	Remarks and references to Appendices
DAOURS	1/9/16	9.5 am	Orders received from D.A. H.Q. for the Bde to move immediately to vicinity of 3rd D.A.C. wagon lines L 9 cent. Sheet 1/40000 Albert. Btys arrived at 6.30 pm, and bivouaced fornight	[signature]
		8 pm	1 gun per Bty went up to forward position A5d to registered LEUZE WOOD.	
L.9 central	2/9/16	—	Officers Cmdg Btys proceeded to Bty positions of Btys of 40th Bde R.F.A. they were relieving registration of front of LEUZE WOOD carried out. Capt Maxwell Cmdg A/180 wounded.	[signature]
"	3/9/16	— 4.0 pm	Orders received for Btys to proceed immediately to forward positions.	[signature]
"	4/9/16	1.0 am	All Btys reported in action.	
"	"	3.10 pm	5th Div attacked FALFEMONT FARM.	
		5.55 pm	Btys opened fire in front of LEUZE WOOD.	
"		6.45 pm	Stop firing. 111362 Dr Brown S. and 35954 Gr Gill were wounded.	[signature]
	5/9/16	10.20 am	S.O.S. line given at T27c.0.7 to T27.c.9.0.	
		10.48	Btys opened fire on S.O.S. line SF fire 3 min and stopped at 11.30 am	
"		4.0 pm	Btys opened Barrage on T21d.1.6. to T27b.9.9. S.F. 1 min 50% HE	
		6.37 pm	Stopped firing	
"		7.40 pm	Btys opened barrage T21d 7.8 to T28a. 1.8. S.F. 2 mins	[signature]
"		8.15 pm	Lifted Barrage 100x and continued firing all night.	
		11.30 pm	S.O.S line now T21d. 7.8. to T28a. 1.8.	
			Btys took over from 40th Bde down to 300 rds per gun	

1875 Wt. W593/826 1,000,000 4/15 J.B.C. & A. A.D.S.S./Forms/C. 2118.

Instructions regarding War Diaries and Intelligence Summaries are contained in F. S. Regs., Part II. and the Staff Manual respectively. Title Pages will be prepared in manuscript.

WAR DIARY
or
INTELLIGENCE SUMMARY
(Erase heading not required.)

Army Form C. 2118

Place	Date	Hour	Summary of Events and Information	Remarks and references to Appendices
	6/9/16	7.45 am	Btys opened on Barrage line from T21d 3.6 to T27.b.6.7. S.F. 2 mins and continued all day with slight alterations	[signature]
	"	8.5 pm	Opened on S.O.S line and continued through the night.	
	"		47106 Gr Wesley. C killed 36292 Gr Ellis. J. 13457 Gr Barry J and Gr Biss. J. wounded.	
	7/9/16	9.0 am	Bty wagon lines moved to A14c. from L.9. cent.	
	"	10.30 am	New Barrage line given T21b 3.6. to T21.b.7.1. and then to T21.d.4.3.	
	"	2.15 pm	S.O.S line given as T21a.5.1 to T21.b.5.0.	
			Firing on barrage line continued throughout the day.	[signature]
	"	8.30 pm	Btys firing on tracks and approaches to German trenches throughout the night, 30 rds per Bty	
	"	11.5 pm	S.O.S. received. Opened fire at S.F. 20 sec. but slackened to S.F. 30 sec and stopped 11.50 pm and returned to original barrage	
	"		Gr Moor E. T. H wounded 6836 Sgt W. Nugent wounded. 91277 Cpl. Brereton W. A. Killed 46570 Gr Larman slightly wounded remaining at duty.	
	8/9/16	–	Firing on tracks around German trenches continued	
	"	8.30 pm	Points selected for night firing at rate of 20 rds per Bty per hr.	[signature]
		–	Orders received from D.A. re preliminary bombardment for 9th and passed to Btys.	
			36024. Gr W. H. LUCAS wounded, 39307 Dr PARKINS wounded.	
	9/9/16	–	16th D.A.C. moved to A19a.	
	"	7.0 am	18 pdr Btys opened intense fire on enemy trenches. The Hows barraging centre of Bouleaux Wood This was kept up until Zero time. Order re How shooting "Stink" shell cancelled.	

1875 Wt. W593/826 1,000,000 4/15 J.B.C. & A. A.D.S.S./Forms/C. 2118.

Instructions regarding War Diaries and Intelligence Summaries are contained in F. S. Regs., Part II. and the Staff Manual respectively. Title Pages will be prepared in manuscript.

WAR DIARY
or
INTELLIGENCE SUMMARY
(Erase heading not required.)

Army Form C. 2118

Place	Date	Hour	Summary of Events and Information	Remarks and references to Appendices
	9/9/16	4.45 pm	56th Div opened attack Zero time. Btys opened on rolling and stationery barrage, Rolling barrage being from T20d to N corner T21c and onto T21d. stationary barrage opened T20 d. T20 b. T21 a. T21 d. Rolling barrage moved at +40 towards 3rd Stationery barrage Line, the rolling barrage moving at 50yds a minute.	
	"	7.57	Btys opened barrage on Trench T15d. to T21.b.3.0	
	"	7.15	Col H.F Askwith Cmdg this Bde acted as Liaison officer with 169th Bde Inf and sent through for Btys to open T21, d & T21b, as it was reported the Enemy were counter attacking	
	"		D/180 How Bty barraged N.E Corner of Bouleaux Wood with H.E. 5mins intense and 25 mins slow	
	"		This barrage continued all night.	
	"		38929 Gr Smith J. (Died) heart failure, 36132 Gr Anstey W, admitted to hospital shell shock. 2/Lt H Brookes admitted hospital with fever.	
	10/9/16	—	Information sent in by F.O.O states, L.R.B failed to get objective T21d to T27b. S.E edge of Leuze wood still strongly held by Huns	
		6.35 am	Col Askwith sent through for Btys to open T21 d. 6.3 to T21 d. 3. 6. 3mins intense fire. then lift 20yds at ordinary rate for 20mins	
		1.10pm	Information received enemy massing in Bouleaux Wood. 18pdrs opened on centre at intense rate, the How Bty shooting stuck shell into valley at end of wood. N E Corner	
		1.30pm	Normal, slacken to slow rate.	
			S.O.S line now T15d. 5. 5 to T21d 7.1. Hows as before.	
			Btys continued firing on enemy trenches all day	
		8.15	S.O.S line now T15d. 2 0. to T21 b. 6.0	

1875 Wt. W593/826 1,000,000 4/15 J.B.C. & A. A.D.S.S./Forms/C. 2118.

Instructions regarding War Diaries and Intelligence Summaries are contained in F. S. Regs., Part II. and the Staff Manual respectively. Title Pages will be prepared in manuscript.

WAR DIARY
or
INTELLIGENCE SUMMARY
(Erase heading not required.)

Army Form C. 2118

Place	Date	Hour	Summary of Events and Information	Remarks and references to Appendices
	10/9/16	—	No casualties in Bde.	
	11/9/16	—	Normal. Btys barraged Bouleux wood and enemy trenches during the day.	
		5.10 pm	False S.O.S received. Btys opened but returned to trench Barrage again.	
		11.45 pm	A/180 commenced a rolling barrage from T15.c.2.0 to T 21a.0.8. rolling to line T4d.9.5 – T4d.8.1½.	
		12.0 midnight	Stop firing received.	
	12/9/16	7.50 am	S.O.S received, Btys opened on line but stopped at 8.40am false alarm, firing carried out during the day, Bouleaux wood receiving attention owing to enemy reported in the wood. Normal day 18404 B.S.M. Dutton. C. slightly wounded Remained at duty.	
	13/9/16	Morning & Afternoon	Firing carried out, enemy trenches and woods. Nothing particular on hand	
		6.0. pm	Btys fired N W edge of Bouleaux wood for 10 mins intense & 10 mins ordinary	
	14/9/16	Dawn	Btys of 180th Bde moved to positions in T25d and carried out necessary registration. The 180th Bde and 2nd Bde R.F.A. 6th D.A. now come under the command of Col Askwith CMG R.A. and becomes Right Group of 6th D.A. Cmd by Bd Gen Cleeve. Group H.Q. A.3.c 1000 Maricourt area	

1875 Wt. W593/826 1,000,000 4/15 J.B.C. & A. A.D.S.S./Forms/C. 2118.

Instructions regarding War Diaries and Intelligence Summaries are contained in F. S. Regs., Part II. and the Staff Manual respectively. Title Pages will be prepared in manuscript.

WAR DIARY
or
INTELLIGENCE SUMMARY
(Erase heading not required.)

Army Form C. 2118

Place	Date	Hour	Summary of Events and Information	Remarks and references to Appendices
T.25d. 1/10000 LONGUEVAL	14/9/16	—	30232 A/BDR E LOOP KILLED 44966 A/BRD H. PENNY wounded. 36202 Gr A.W CARTER wounded. 2/Lt R. HINXMAN admitted Hospital Sick.	[initials]
"	15/9/16	—	The 4th Army attacked the line FLERS–LESBOEUFS–MORVAL.	
		6.20 am	Zero time. Btys opened fire on creeping & stationery barrages T15d.0.8 to T15d.4.0 1/20000 LONGUEVAL. 13/180 did creeping barrage and opened 100x in front of above line creeping at rate of 50yds a minute. Stationery Barrage 2nd Bde fired on above line until creeping barrage reached Second objective. T10.c. T16a.	
		8.10 am	Btys opened fire on 2nd objective.	
		9.50	Btys firing on 2nd objective. The creeping barrage moving forward to 3rd objective	
		10.40	" " " 3rd and creeping & stationery barrages remain here.	
		12.20 pm	Owing to failure of Inf to take QUADRILATERAL, Btys will barrage there from 1.15pm to 1.45pm	[initials]
		1.15pm	This order cancelled.	
		3.20pm	Infantry German reported massing. 2nd Bde R.F.A opened barrage immediately, also 180th Bde.	
		4.30pm	Stop firing on above, 2 Hows to shoot QUADRILATERAL and 18pdrs to cut wire on MORVAL LINE. Barrages Continue various barrage during early Evening	
		9.0pm	50% of guns only shooting	
		11.0	Stop shooting for night.	

1875 Wt. W593/826 1,000,000 4/15 J.B.C. & A. A.D.S.S./Forms/C. 2118.

Instructions regarding War Diaries and Intelligence Summaries are contained in F. S. Regs., Part II. and the Staff Manual respectively. Title Pages will be prepared in manuscript.

WAR DIARY
or
INTELLIGENCE SUMMARY
(Erase heading not required.)

Army Form C. 2118

Place	Date	Hour	Summary of Events and Information	Remarks and references to Appendices
T25d. 1/10000	16/9/16	6.0am	Btys continued wire cutting.	
		9.25 am	Zero time Attack resumed. Btys opened on Trench at Intense rate of fire	
			How Bty turned on to sunken Rd T10c. 8.8 to T16a. 8.6.	
		11.15.	Barrage continued at slow rate.	[illegible initials]
		1.15pm	All 18 pdrs started cutting wire on Morval Line.	
			Dumps reduced to 500-600 rds per gun from 1000 rds	
		6.30pm	S.O.S line is now T15c. 4 6 to T15a. 2½.6.	
		7.0pm	S.O.S received, supposed attack on left flank	
			Night firing tracks & trenches around Morval.	
"			2/Lt T.G KEY wounded.	
	17/9/16	–	Btys continued wire cutting on trench in front of Morval	
		3.20pm	All Btys carefully registered QUADRILATERAL from Arrow Head Copse.	[illegible initials]
		7.30pm	All Btys shooting quadrilateral, and Hows shooting road leading to it.	
			Night firing as last night.	
	18/9/16	5.50 am	34908 Gr PINNOCK accidently injured	
			Zero time. Attack on QUADRILATERAL by 6th DIV.	
			All faces of QUAD heavily bombarded, and rds and cuttings leading to it.	
		+30min	Intense fire	
		7.30 am	QUAD taken together with 300 prisoners.	
		2.30 pm	Enemy reporting massing near Morval Mill, all Btys turned on to this and surrounding district.	
		3.30 pm	Btys turned on to Morval.	

1875 Wt. W593/826 1,000,000 [illegible] I.R.C. & A. A.D.S.S./Forms/C. 2118.

Army Form C. 2118

Instructions regarding War Diaries and Intelligence Summaries are contained in F. S. Regs., Part II. and the Staff Manual respectively. Title Pages will be prepared in manuscript.

WAR DIARY
or
INTELLIGENCE SUMMARY
(Erase heading not required.)

Place	Date	Hour	Summary of Events and Information	Remarks and references to Appendices
T25d.	18th	5.30 pm	S.O.S line now T16c.0.0 to T15b.7.3½. Btys opened at slow rate on S.O.S line and Hows on road leading to Morval from the North.	[signature]
		7.30 pm	Btys stop shooting S.O.S line and start night firing on Tracks and Trenches around Morval.	
"	19/9/16	9.5 am	S.O.S line is now T16c 4.2 to T16a 0.2.	
		10 am	Infantry reported large bodies of enemy seen in front of Morval. Btys informed & opened fire. Btys of 2nd Bde proceeded to cut wire from T16a.7.5½ to T10c. 2½.2½. Usual daily barrage nothing of interest to report.	[signature]
		6pm	The Rt Group was joined by 281st Bde R.F.A. 56th D.A. and came under the orders of Col. H.F. Askwith. 38809 Dr Richards. G. wounded. Night firing. Tracks and Trenches around MORVAL. 2 Bty of 2nd Bde went to forward position near Leuzewood to cut wire.	
	20/9/16		Enemy reported to have made new trenches. T16b 5.8 to T16b.9.2. T17c T11a T12b. Btys instructed to keep these trenches under fire day & night. Btys continued wire cutting at above points also Western side of Morval, Inf report fire very effective. S.O.S line T16c. 6.4 to T16a 3½.4½.	
	21/9/16	—	Forward Btys continued to cut wire, and made good progress. Btys instructed to keep up to 300 rds per gun	

1875 Wt. W593/826 1,000,000 4/15 J.B.C. & A. A.D.S.S./Forms/C. 2118/

Instructions regarding War Diaries and Intelligence Summaries are contained in F. S. Regs., Part II. and the Staff Manual respectively. Title Pages will be prepared in manuscript.

WAR DIARY
or
INTELLIGENCE SUMMARY
(Erase heading not required.)

Army Form C. 2118

Place	Date	Hour	Summary of Events and Information	Remarks and references to Appendices
T25 d.	21/9/16	2–4 pm	Btys 180th Bde very heavily shelled, all communications cut. 5 men being killed and 9 wounded. Night firing the tracks and roads around Morval.	
T25 d.	22/9/16	9.0 am	The Div Arty is now rearranged the Rt Group becoming Left Group, and the 281st Bde attached rejoining their own Div. Barrage line is now T16a 3½.5 to. 2nd Bde Btys continued wire cutting successfully. Night firing tracks and trenchs round MORVAL. 18pdr to expend 200rds per Btys.	
T25d	23/9/16	—	Orders received re renewed attack to take place on 25th inst. Btys continued wire cutting. Orders received to get up every available round 18/pdr ammunition. 2nd Bde R.F.A report Btys have cut two clean gaps, and badly damaged wire all along zone. S.O.S line for night T16a.5.8 to T10c.0.9. Btys continued night firing 200rds per 18pdr gun streets and road round Morval. 4. O.R. wounded.	
T25d	24/9/16	—	New trench reported T11.b.8.3 – T11.b.5.8. Hows registered this trench, and kept it under fire day and night. Btys continued wire cutting. Bty kept suspected M.G and strong points under fire. Night firing as 23rd. Ordered to increase gun dumps to 1000rds per gun. Btys report wire cutting satisfactory.	
T25d	25/9/16	—	Wire cutting Btys continued wire cutting.	

1875 Wt. W593/826 1,000,000 4/15 J.B.C. & A. A.D.S.S./Forms/C. 2118.

Army Form C. 2118

WAR DIARY
or
INTELLIGENCE SUMMARY
(Erase heading not required.)

Instructions regarding War Diaries and Intelligence Summaries are contained in F. S. Regs., Part II. and the Staff Manual respectively. Title Pages will be prepared in manuscript.

Place	Date	Hour	Summary of Events and Information	Remarks and references to Appendices
T25.d.	25/9/16	12.35 pm.	Zero time. Right Centre A. O.O No 1 copy 6 is attached herewith. The 2nd & 180th Bdes Comprising Left Group. The 180th Bde undertook the creeping & 2nd Bde the stationary barrage and were covering the Left Inf. Bde.	
..	..	1.15 pm	F.O.O reported that the Sunken road had been taken, with little resistance. Arty barrage reported by F.O.O. to be very satisfactory.	
..	..	1.50 pm	Our infantry continued to push on and took the Brown line, (see maps), the enemy making no effort to stop them	[signature]
..	..	2.55 pm	F.O.O reports our infantry now in N end of Morval, and pushing on towards LESBOEUFS Prisoners coming in freely.	
..	..	3.40 pm	Infantry report all objectives taken, and digging in on Eastern edge of village	
..	..	5.18 pm	Orders to reduce rate of fire to 2 rds a Bty a minute	
..	..	6.0 pm	Btys lifted to enemy trench T11.b. 7.6 to T12c 4.2 to T17.b.9.6 to enable Inf patrols to go out.	
..	..	8.7 pm	Infantry reported digging in T11 a & c.	
..	..	8.20 pm	Barrage lifted 100yds.	
..	..		Btys fired all night, 18pdr 300rds per gun on lines T17.b. 7.2½ to T18.a. 3.9 to T12c 6.2 to T12a 6.5, Hows on roads beyond.	
..	26/9/16	9.15 am	Reported normal on front. Information received that 2 Btys of 2nd Bde & all Btys	

Army Form C. 2118

WAR DIARY
or
INTELLIGENCE SUMMARY
(Erase heading not required.)

Instructions regarding War Diaries and Intelligence Summaries are contained in F. S. Regs., Part II. and the Staff Manual respectively. Title Pages will be prepared in manuscript.

Place	Date	Hour	Summary of Events and Information	Remarks and references to Appendices
T25d.	26/9/16	—	180th Bde to be ready to move to valley West of MORVAL.	
		Morn	Btys fired all the morning at slow rate of fire on roads East of Morval.	
	"	2.6 pm	F.O.O. reports our infantry line runs approximately T11b. ½. 1 to T12a. 0.3 to T12c. 5.0.	[signature]
	"		Bty Cmds went forward and selected Bty positions in above valley and working parties endeavoured to make track for Btys to pass along.	
"	"		Night firing tonight about 500 yds East of Morval T12c.	
"	27/9/16	—	Gen Stone. R.A. Cmdg Corps Arty congratulated all ranks on splendid work done on 25th. Advance parties sent forward to proposed new positions in Valley W of MORVAL where pits were dug.	
"	"	11 am	Order received for Btys of 180th Bde & 2 Btys 2nd Bde to move to positions at bottom of valley in T16.a.	[signature]
T16a.	"	3pm–6pm	Btys drew out of old positions & went to above.	
"	"	11pm	All Btys now in position.	
"	28/9/16		From 6pm last night 2nd & 180th Bde became Centre Group of Rt Arty, and covered the French who took over line.	
"	"		Btys registered trench front of LA TRANSLOY T36a. 4.9. and T36d. 6. 8 and continued shooting on same.	
"	"	12.30 pm	Rt Arty O.O No 1 received, and instructions passed to 180th Bde to fire day & night on trench T36.b.0.5 to T36b. 1.7½. 2nd Bde to keep under fire enemy gun pits in T36.c. & T5b. Btys fired on above all day & night. S.O.S line given as T12c. 5.3 to T12a. 2. 8. Normal on front all day. Bde H.Q. 180th moved to A5d. 4. 2.	[signature]

1875 Wt. W593/826 1,000,000 ... I.R.C. & A. A.D.S.S./Forms/C. 2118.

Army Form C. 2118

Instructions regarding War Diaries and Intelligence Summaries are contained in F. S. Regs., Part II. and the Staff Manual respectively. Title Pages will be prepared in manuscript.

WAR DIARY
or
INTELLIGENCE SUMMARY
(Erase heading not required.)

Place	Date	Hour	Summary of Events and Information	Remarks and references to Appendices
T16 a	29/9/16	noon / afternoon	Btys continued firing on same points as yesterday.	
		1 pm	Instructions received that Btys of 180th, 2nd Bde R.F.A would move to their wagon lines after dusk. This was done, all ammunition being handed over to 56th D.A. Btys to march out full wagon lines were refilled.	[illegible]
	"	7 am	Btys withdrew to wagon lines. C/180 suffered casualties 2 men killed and 9 wounded while withdrawing A/180, 2 wounded & D/180 1 wounded.	
	30/9/16	11 am	Bde H.Q. withdrew to wagon line.	
		6 pm	Orders received re moving 1st Oct. 16.	

H. T. Ackworth Col RA
O.C. 180th Bde R.F.A.

1875 Wt. W593/826 1,000,000 4/15 J.B.C. & A. A.D.S.S./Forms/C. 2118.

Copy No. 6

Right-Centre Artillery Operation Order No. 1.

Reference. LONGUEVAL and COMBLES Sheets. 1/10,000.

23th September, 1916.

1. The Fourth Army will renew the attack on 25th instant in combination with the attack of the French to the South and of the Reserve Army to the North.

2. The objective of the XIV Corps includes the villages of MORVAL and LESBOEUFS, and that of the XV Corps GUEUDECOURT.

3. The attack will be carried out by 5th Division on the Right, the 6th Division in the Centre, and the Guards Division on the Left, the 56th Division forming a protective flank facing South.

4. The main attack of the Corps will be made in 3 stages.

5. The Right-Centre Artillery will cover the attack of the 5th Division, which will be made by the 95th Infantry Brigade on the Right and the 15th Infantry Brigade on the Left.

The attacks of the Infantry Brigades must be treated as separate operations.

6. The 95th Infantry Brigade leaves its departure trenches at Zero, and at the same time the Standing Barrage is put down on the 1st Objective - T.10.c.5½.0. - cross-roads T.16.a.8.6½. - thence on new trench running to T.16.c.4½.8.8. The Creeping Barrage will be put down at Zero on a line in front of our Infantry - this line will be notified later, and will depend upon the actual position of the departure trenches - and will start creeping by 50 yards a minute at plus 3 minutes till it reaches the dotted bright GREEN line where it will halt till plus 1 hour 2 minutes. It then lifts to the BROWN dotted line direct, and remains there till plus 2 hours 2 mins.

At plus 2 hours 2 mins. it starts creeping forward at the same pace till the dotted BLUE line is reached.

At plus 2 hours 38 minutes it creeps forward to the dotted RED line.

At plus 3 hours 12 mins. it creeps forward again to the SAGE GREEN line.

At plus 3 hours 46 mins. it creeps forward again to the YELLOW (final) line.

All lifts at 50 yards a minute.

Times of lifts are also shown on the attached tracing.

The Standing Barrage lifts to the BROWN line from the bright GREEN line as the Creeping Barrage reaches that line.

It lifts again to the dotted BLUE line at plus 1 hour 2 mins.

At plus 2 hours 2 mins. it lifts to the continuous BLUE line.

At plus 2 hours 26 mins. it lifts to the SAGE GREEN line.

At plus 3 hours it lifts to the YELLOW line.

At plus 3 hours 38 mins. it lifts to the RED and BLUE line.

The Standing Barrage drops a defensive barrage on the right flank as it goes as shown in the diagram

7.

P. T. O.

7. The procodure in the case of 15th Infantry Brigade is the same till the dotted BLUE line is reached by the Standing Barrage and the dotted BROWN line by the Creeping Barrage.

The Creeping Barrage then commences to creep forward at plus 2 hours 2 mins. at 50 yards a minute till the dotted YELLOW (final) line is reached.

The Standing Barrage lifts to the continuous BLUE line at plus 2 hours 2 mins., to the RED line (including the right flank barrage) at plus 2 hours 5 mins., and to the SAGE GREEN line at plus 2 hours 12 mins.

The Right Flank Barrage shortens up as the 95th Infantry Brigade advances, i.e., it ceases between the 95th Infantry Brigade BLUE and SAGE GREEN Standing Barrage lines at plus 2 hours 26 mins., between the SAGE GREEN and YELLOW at plus 3 hours, and is taken off altogether at plus 3 hours 38 mins.

8. At plus 4 hours the whole Creeping and Standing Barrages, which have then halted on the final line, will be re distributed as follows:-

RIGHT GROUP. T.16.d.2.8. to T.17.b.1.8.

LEFT GROUP. T.17.b.1.8. to T.11.a.6½.3½.

9. After the Infantry are established on the Eastern boundary of the village of MORVAL, patrols will be pushed forward to establish posts on the spur running into T.12.a. & c.

Orders for lifts of the barrage to cover these patrols will be issued during the action.

10. Great care must be exercised by the guns and howitzers shooting on the right flank of the Left Infantry Brigade not to shoot too far North. There must be no firing by those guns and howitzers North of the houses on the North side of the road running into MORVAL from GINCHY.

The right boundary of the Left Infantry Brigade is the road running from T.10.c.8.½. to T.11.c.2½.5., and though the flank barrage must try to keep down fire from the houses it must avoid hitting our own troops.

11. There must be no barrage within a good 100 yards of point T.9.d.6.8. which is held by our troops.

12. RATES OF FIRE:-

RIGHT GROUP. Intense between the following times.
Zero to plus 15 mins.
Plus 1 hour to plus 1 hour 15 mins.
Plus 2 hours to plus 2 hours 15 mins.
Plus 2 hours 36 mins to plus 2 hours 50 mins.
Plus 3 hours 10 mins to plus 3 hours 24 mins.
Plus 3 hours 44 mins. to plus 3 hours 59 mins.

At other times Ordinary.

LEFT GROUP. Intense between the following hours.
Zero to plus 15 mins.
Plus 1 hour to plus 1 hour 15 mins.
Plus 2 hours to plus 2 hours 30 mins.

13. The 4.5" Howitzer Programme and diagram is attached.

14. A steady bombardment by Heavy Artillery will commence at 7-0 a.m. on 24th September, and continue till 6-30 p.m. that day.
It will re-commenced at 6-30 a.m. on 25th September and continue till Zero hour.
The ground in front and in rear of the German trenches, including roads leading into MORVAL not specially detailed for treatment by 4.5" Howitzers, will be searched occasionally with 18-pounder Shrapnel and High Explosive Shell.

15. Night firing will be carried out nightly between the hours of 6-30 p.m. and 6-30 a.m.

16. There will be no intensive fire before Zero, except where poison shell is fired and specific orders are given as to Rate of Fire.

17. The Boundaries of the Division and between Groups are shown on the Barrage tracings.

18. 56th Division will form a defensive flank on the right of 5th Division and eventually obtain a junction with it at T.16.c.4½.7.

19. A Smoke Barrage will be established by 56th Division on the Right.

20. Intensive fire for 18-pounders will not exceed 4 rounds a gun a minute, nor will it be less than 3 rounds a gun a minute.
For 4.5" Howitzers it will be 2 rounds a Howitzer a minute.

Ordinary fire will be 1 round a gun a minute for both natures.

Slow fire will be 1 round a battery a minute for both natures.

21. During the preliminary bombardment the following targets will be kept under fire by 4.5" Howitzers:-

RIGHT GROUP.

1 Battery. New trench on W. and S.W. Edge of MORVAL village, and the street from T.16.b.4.9. to T.11.c.3.2.

1 Battery. The street T.17.a.6.6. to T.11.c.3.3. and the Road T.11.c.3½.½. - T.17.b.8.9½.

1 Battery. The ORCHARD T.16.b.6.4. and trench in its immediate vicinity.

LEFT GROUP.

1 Battery. Sunken Road T.16.a.8.6. to T.10.c.7½.8.

1 Battery. The street in MORVAL T.11.c.3.3. to T.11.a.0.3.

The above targets will be kept under fire day and night.

22. Rates of fire during the Preliminary Bombardment:-

	By day.	By night.
4.5" Howitzers.	15 rounds per Howitzer per hour.	20 rounds per battery per hour.
18-pounders.	As required.	200 rounds per battery per night.

23. The Right Group will detail one Senior Officer as Liaison Officer with 95th Infantry Brigade, and one Subaltern as Liaison Officer with each Battalion in front line on 25th instant.
The Left Group will detail similar Liaison Officers with 15th Infantry Brigade on 25th instant.

The Right Group will cover 95th and the Left Group the 15th Infantry Brigade.

24. Flares will be lit on obtaining each objective, and also at 6-0 p.m., September, 25th.

25. ACKNOWLEDGE.

L. Wy Savile

Major, R. A.

Brigade Major, Right-Centre Artillery.

Issued at 6.15 p.m.

Copies to:-

Right Group. (5).
Left Group. (3).
5th Division "G". (4).
R.A., XIV Corps.
H.A., XIV Corps.
Right Artillery.
Left-Centre Artillery.
Liaison Officer, H.A., 5th Div.
French Liaison Officer, 5th Div. (2).
Staff Captain, 5th Div. Arty.

Issued with Operation Order No. 1.

RIGHT CENTRE ARTILLERY.

4.5" Howitzer Programme from Zero, 25th September, 1916.

RIGHT GROUP.

1 Section. From Zero onwards. On road T.16.Central to road-junction T.16.d.2.8. to T.16.b.4.0.

1 Battery and 1 Section.

Zero to plus 2 hours 2 mins. The ORCHARD T.16.b.6.3½. and trench T.16.b.4.5. to 7.2½.

Plus 2 hours 2 mins. to plus 3 hours 12 mins. Street and Orchards T.17.a.3.5. to T.11.c.2.½.

Plus 3 hours 12 mins. to plus 3 hours 46 mins. Street T.17.a.7.5. to T.17.a.4½.8½.

Plus 3 hours 46 mins. onwards. The Battery lifts to road T.17.d.2½.7½. to T.17.a.9.1., and the Section to road T.16.b.8½.7. to T.17.a.½.0.

1 Battery.

Zero to plus 2 hours 2 mins. Trenches T.17.a.0.7. - T.10.d.4½.1½.

Plus 2 hours 2 mins. to plus 2 hours 38 mins. Houses in street T.10.d.6½.1. - T.11.c.3.2½.

Plus 2 hours 38 mins. to plus 3 hours 12 mins. T.10.d.9.1½.- T.11.c.4.2½.

Plus 3 hours 12 mins. to plus 3 hours 40 mins. Street T.17.a.4½.8½. - T.11.c.3½.2.

Plus 3 hours 40 mins. onwards. Road T.17.b.2.9½. to 8½.9½.

LEFT GROUP.

1 Battery.

Zero to plus 2 hours. New trench T.10.d.3½.2½. - T.10.b.6.1.

Plus 2 hours to plus 2 hours 10 mins. Street T.11.c.3½.2. - 2½.6.

Plus 2 hours 10 mins onwards. Road T.11.d.3½.6½. - 8.8.

1 Battery.

Zero to plus 1 hour. Sunken Road T.10.c.8.2. - T.10.a.7½.0.

Plus 1 hour to plus 2 hours 7 mins. Street T.11.c.2½.6. - T.11.a.1.2.

Plus 2 hours 7 mins onwards. Road T.11.b.2.3½. - 7.6.

ADDENDUM to RIGHT CENTRE ARTILLERY Operation Order No. 1.

50% of 18-pounders will form the Creeping Barrage, and 50% the Standing Barrage in each Group.

L. Mc Savile. Major, R. A.

23/9/16. Brigade Major, Right Centre Artillery.

SECRET

No. [illegible] 930/[illegible].

MEMORANDUM.

Reference para. 8, Right Centre Artillery Operation Order No. 1, the Creeping Barrage will open on the line T.16.a.1¼.1¼. to 3.5½. to T.[illegible]9.d.7½.7.

It will start creeping at Zero plus 3 mins. and halt on the dotted Bright GREEN line.

The Standing barrage will lift as the Creeping Barrage reaches it, i.e., at plus 5 minutes on left and at plus 7 mins. on the right.

[illegible] Major, R. A.

24/9/16. Brigade Major, Right-Centre Artillery.

Distribution as for Operation Order No. 1.

SECRET.

No. B.M. 930/4.

Amendments to Right-Centre Artillery Operation Order No. 1.

1. The Northern boundary of the Division is a line running as follows:-

T.9.d.7.8. - Road junction T.10.c.$7\frac{1}{2}$.$8\frac{1}{2}$. - Northern house in MORVAL T.11.a.1.$\frac{3}{4}$. - T.11.b.0.4.

All barrage and Howitzer diagrams will be amended accordingly, and there is to be no firing North of this line.

2. In 4.5" Howitzer Programme, last line but two, <u>for</u> "Plus 1 hour to plus 2 hours 9 mins." <u>read</u> "Plus 1 hour to plus 2 hours 7 mins", and in last line, <u>for</u> "Plus 2 hours 9 mins." <u>read</u> "Plus 2 hours 7 mins".

Also amend all tasks on the left to come within the boundary mentioned in para. 1.

L. M. Saville.
Major, R. A.
Brigade Major, Right-Centre Artillery.

24/9/16.

Distribution as for Operation Order No. 1.

SECRET

MEMORANDUM.

The following will be substituted for the 4.5" Howitzer Programme, issued with Operation Order No. 1:-

RIGHT CENTRE ARTILLERY.

4.5" Howitzer Programme from Zero, 25th September, 1916.

RIGHT GROUP.

1 Section.

From Zero onwards. On road T.16.Central to road-junction T.16.d.2.8. to T.16.b.4.0.

1 Battery and 1 Section.

Zero to plus 2 hours 2 mins. The ORCHARD T.16.b.6.3½. and trench T.16.b.4.5. to 7.2½.

Plus 2 hours 2 mins. to plus 2 hours 40 mins. Street and Orchards T.17.a.3.5. to T.11.c.2.½.

Plus 2 hours 40 mins. to plus 3 hours 12 mins. Street T.17.a.7.5. to T.17.a.4½.8½.

Plus 3 hours 12 mins onwards. The Battery lifts to road T.17.d.2½.7½. to T.17.a.9.1., and the Section to road T.16.d.8½.7. to T.17.a.½.0.

1 Battery.

Zero to plus 2 hours 2 mins. Trenches T.17.a.0.7. - T.10.d.4½.1½.

Plus 2 hours 2 mins. to plus 2 hours 38 mins. Houses in street T.10.d.8½.1½. - T.11.c.3.2½.

Plus 2 hours 38 mins. to plus 3 hours 12 mins. Street T.17.a.4½.8½. - T.11.c.3½.2.

Plus 3 hours 12 mins. onwards. Road T.17.b.2.9½. to 8½.9½.

LEFT GROUP.

1 Battery.

Zero to plus 2 hours. New trench T.10.d.3½.2½. - T.10.b.6.1.

Plus 2 hours to plus 2 hours 8 mins. Street T.11.c.3½.2. - 2½.6.

Plus 2 hours 8 mins onwards. Road T.11.d.3½.6½. - 8.8.

1 Battery.

Zero to plus 1 hour. Sunken Road T.10.c.8.2. - T.10.a.7½.0.

Plus 1 hour to plus 2 hours 7 mins. Street T.11.c.2½.6. - T.11.a.1.2.

Plus 2 hours 7 mins. onwards. Road T.11.b.2.3½. - 7.6.

L. Mew Savile.

Major, R. A.

24/9/16.
8-50 p.m.

Brigade Major, Right Centre Artillery.

Distribution as O.O. No. 1.

Identification Trace for use with Artillery Maps.

25/9/16

NOTE.—(1). These traces are intended to facilitate the communication of information as to the position of targets, which have been located on a squared map.

(2). The squares on this trace are 500 yards in length on the 1/10,000 scale, 1,000 yards in length on the 1/20,000 scale, and 2,000 yards in length on the 1/40,000 scale.

(3). The squares on the trace are fitted to the squares of the map showing the targets, which are then drawn on the trace. Sufficient letters and numbers must also be added to enable the recipient to place the trace in the correct position on his own map. A little detail may also be traced, but this is not essential. The name and scale of the map to which the trace refers must be always given. The trace can be used for the 1/10,000, 1/20,000, or 1/40,000 scale.

G.S.G.S. 3025.

Tracing taken from Sheet ....

of the 1: .... *map of* ....

Signature .... *Date* ....

Identification Trace for use with Artillery Maps.

NOTE.—(1). These traces are intended to facilitate the communication of information as to the position of targets, which have been located on a squared map.

(2). The squares on this trace are 500 yards in length on the 1/10,000 scale, 1,000 yards in length on the 1/20,000 scale, and 2,000 yards in length on the 1/40,000 scale.

(3). The squares on the trace are fitted to the squares of the map showing the targets, which are then drawn on the trace. Sufficient letters and numbers must also be added to enable the recipient to place the trace in the correct position on his own map. A little detail may also be traced, but this is not essential. The name and scale of the map to which the trace refers must be always given. The trace can be used for the 1/10,000, 1/20,000, or 1/40,000 scale.

G.S.G.S. 3025.

Tracing taken from Sheet ....

of the 1: .... *map of* ....

Signature .... *Date* ....

Trace for use with Artillery Maps.

25/9/16

1 Sect. Rt Group
1 Bty + 1 Sect. Rt Group
Bty Rt Group
1 Bty Left Group
1 Bty Left Group

...sition of targets, which have been located on a squared map. ...ds in length on the 1/20,000 scale, and 2,000 yards in length

...targets, which are then drawn on the trace. Sufficient ... the correct position on his own map. A little detail ...hich the trace refers must be always given. The trace

Tracing taken from Sheet [illegible]

of the 1: [illegible] *map of* FRANCE

Signature [illegible] Maj *Date* [illegible]

W A R   D I A R Y

MONTH   OF   OCTOBER,   1916.

VOLUME 9

180th Brigade R.F.A.

Instructions regarding War Diaries and Intelligence Summaries are contained in F. S. Regs., Part II. and the Staff Manual respectively. Title Pages will be prepared in manuscript.

WAR DIARY
or
INTELLIGENCE SUMMARY
(Erase heading not required.)

180th Bde R.F.A.
No 9.

Army Form C. 2118

Place	Date	Hour	Summary of Events and Information	Remarks and references to Appendices
CARNOY	Oct 1	5am	The Division marches from Wagon Lines to TALMAS. 180th Bde leading. Beautiful weather.	E.H.W.
AUTHIEULE.	2	2pm	Continued March to AUTHIEULE on the AUTHIE RIVER nr DOULLENS – a pouring wet day.	E.H.W.
BOUBERS	3.	6am.	Continued March to BOUBERS-sur-chance – still wet	E.H.W.
PREDEFIN.	4	6.30am	Continued march PREDEFIN – still wet	
ECQUES.	5.	4.30am	" " to ECQUES – very wet to start with. an early march with long halt at ESTREE-BLANCHE. to enable 8th Div Q. to be clear of the road.	E.H.W. E.H.W.
COQ-de-PAILLE.	6.		Continued march to area in vicinity of COQ-de-PAILLE. – fair weather.	E.H.W.
	7.		Billeted in area COQ-de-PAILLE. B.C. attended Conference at WESTOUTRE. HQ. 16th DA	E.H.W.
	8.		Billeted in the same area. Brig Com. Signal officer and BCs reconnoitred Gun Positions near VIERSTRAAT. occupied by A/173 36th Div. Artillery	E.H.W.
HALLEBAST	9.		Brigade marched to Wagon Lines in vicinity of Md.10. MD11. one section A and B and D complete moved into new positions West of VIERSTRAAT at Farm KLEIN VIERSTRAAT.	E.H.W. E.H.W.
	10		Registration carried out by Sections already in position One section A and B moved into new positions.	E.H.W.

1875 Wt. W593/826 1,000,000 ... I.B.C. & A. A.D.S.S./Forms/C. 2118.

Army Form C.-2118

Instructions regarding War Diaries and Intelligence Summaries are contained in F. S. Regs., Part II. and the Staff Manual respectively. Title Pages will be prepared in manuscript.

WAR DIARY
or
INTELLIGENCE SUMMARY
(*Erase heading not required.*)

Place	Date	Hour	Summary of Events and Information	Remarks and references to Appendices
HALLEBAST	11		Carried out further registration. Very quiet day.	E.H.W.
	12.		Registration + Retaliation for T.M.	E.H.W.
	13		" for T.M.	
	14.		TEST S.O.S. 9.28 pm and 11.51 pm RDS got off within 30 secs of infantry call.	E.H.W.
	15		Received orders that Bde will be withdrawn and attached to I ANZAC Corps as from 20th inst.	E.H.W.
	16.		1 section A/180 + one section B/180 were relieved by 2 sections of B/177. One section of A/180 relieved by one section of C/177. Relieved sections removed to Wagon Line. Col. H.F. Askwith CMG was to-day admitted to No 2 C.C.S. Major N.A. Stebbing became O.C. Brigade.	E.H.W.
	17		Bde withdrew complete to the Wagon Line	E.H.W.
WIPPENHOEK	18		The Brigade marched from Wagon Line to L25a 9.5. O.C. Bde + B.C.s reconnoitred Battery positions at YPRES. At 12 noon the Bde passed under the command of the 2nd Div. I ANZAC Corps.	E.H.W.

1875 Wt. W593/826 1,000,000 4/17 J.B.C. & A. A.D.S.S./Forms/C. 2118.

Instructions regarding War Diaries and Intelligence Summaries are contained in F. S. Regs., Part II. and the Staff Manual respectively. Title Pages will be prepared in manuscript.

WAR DIARY
or
INTELLIGENCE SUMMARY
(Erase heading not required.)

Army Form C. 2118

Place	Date	Hour	Summary of Events and Information	Remarks and references to Appendices
WIPPENHOEK	19th		O.C. Bde reconnoitred Wagon Lines. Two sections of A and one section of B.C. and D. relieved sections of 22nd Australian Bde – 13th 19th 20th & 21st Batteries A.F.A.	E.H.W.
YPRES.	20.		Relief of 22nd A.F.A. Bde completed. O.C. Bde reconnoitres O.P. Registrations were carried out. Covering 23rd Div.	E.H.W.
	21		Checking registration of night lines	E.H.W.
	22.		Working party dispersed by fire of C/180.	E.H.W.
	23.		Bde passed into the control of 47th Div for all purposes. Bde is named officially 23rd Div. Arty Group.	E.H.W.
	25.		C/180 passed at noon under the Command of the Rt. GROUP for tactics. S.O.S. lines were altered so that 18pdr shells will fire 100 yds the side of the HUN FRONT LINE – 4.5" Hows on Front Line.	E.H.W.
	26		A considerable amount of T.M. activity to the Right of our zone	E.H.W.
	27		T.Ms again active on the Right of our zone	E.H.W.
	28		At 12.30 pm A/180 Bty position was shelled with 4.2s Killing 63961 Sgt Bloss and wounded 63392 Sgt Eagle	E.H.W.

1875 Wt. W593/826 1,000,000 ... I.B.C. & A. A.D.S.S./Forms/C. 2118.

Instructions regarding War Diaries and Intelligence Summaries are contained in F. S. Regs., Part II. and the Staff Manual respectively. Title Pages will be prepared in manuscript.

WAR DIARY
or
INTELLIGENCE SUMMARY
(Erase heading not required.)

Army Form C. 2118

Place	Date	Hour	Summary of Events and Information	Remarks and references to Appendices
YPRES	28		42104 Cpl Holland 36133 Gnr. Baker. 13501 Gnr Massey	G.H.W.
	29		Quiet day, usual routine. Test S.O.S.	G.H.W.
	30		Routine Test S.O.S.	
	31	7.24pm	Small raid made on the "Cul rost", by the Enemy, we opened fire with one 18 pdr Bty and one How. until the situation was cleared up. at 9 25 pm.	G.H.W.

1875 Wt. W593/826 1,000,000 ... L.R.C. & A. A.D.S.S./Forms/C. 2118.

W A R D I A R Y .

F O R

MONTH OF NOVEMBER, 1916.

VOLUME 10

180th Brigade R.F.A.

Vol 10

Instructions regarding War Diaries and Intelligence Summaries are contained in F. S. Regs., Part II. and the Staff Manual respectively. Title Pages will be prepared in manuscript.

WAR DIARY
or
INTELLIGENCE SUMMARY
(Erase heading not required.)

Army Form C. 2118

180 Bde. R.F.A.
No. 10.

Place	Date	Hour	Summary of Events and Information	Remarks and references to Appendices
YPRES	1st		Brigade still in action at YPRES. Batteries are busy repairing the gun + wagon lines. Situation quiet.	
"	2nd		D/180 Registered a point on "FORRESTERS LANE", at the request of the Infantry.	
"	4th		The C.O. reconnoitred the "Withdrawal Positions" in the area.	
"	5th		The O.C. Reported on O.P's	
"	6th		Colonel H.F. Askwith returning from leave, resumed command of the Brigade	
"	7th		O.C. reconnoitred O.P's for Withdrawal Position on the G.H.Q. Line.	
"	8th		O.C. reconnoitred position for Brigade H.Q. on withdrawal to G.H.Q. Line arranged with 70th Infy Brigade to use the available to barrage only in places likely to be attacked, leaving the rest of the line to machine guns. New Night Lines considered with reference to air photographs.	
"	11th		Colonel Askwith ordered to report to 16th Div. Major N.A. Stebbing assumed command. New Night Lines registered by "A" + "D" Batteries from O.P. in "LOVERS WALK"	
"	12th	9am	New Night Lines come into operation at.	
"	13th	10.15am 1.45pm	"A" Battery fired 70 Rounds in bursts of fire in NEW GERMAN SAPS front line in I.19.a no retaliation that night.	
"	14th		YPRES Shelled with 5.9's intermittently during the forenoon No 34894 Br. P. Marsh wounded by Shrapnel. Night firing last night, reported satisfactory. Trenches considerably damaged. "D" Batty Shelled a trench with new work in it, + destroyed it.	

1875 Wt. W593/826 1,000,000 4/15 J.B.C. & A. A.D.S.S./Forms/C. 2118.

Instructions regarding War Diaries and Intelligence Summaries are contained in F. S. Regs., Part II. and the Staff Manual respectively. Title Pages will be prepared in manuscript.

WAR DIARY
or
INTELLIGENCE SUMMARY
(Erase heading not required.)

Army Form C. 2118

180th Brigade R.F.A.
No 10.

Place	Date	Hour	Summary of Events and Information	Remarks and references to Appendices
YPRES	15th		Night firing last night, to prevent enemy working on his front line. This morning O.C. "A" Battery reports that this proved effective.	
"	16th		Night firing again last night on enemy front line, which again caused him to cease work. Some damage done to his parapet. Received from GROUP H.Q. a scheme of Bombardment of Trench Mortars.	
"	17th		Enemy work on front line again stopped last night by "A" Battery which kept up intermittent firing from 11pm till 4am. A half hour's bombardment was carried out by one section of "D" Battery (How) & one section "B" Battery (18pr) in conjunction with 55th Division on our left, which carried out a raid.	
"	20th		Registrations on Co-ordinates in conjunction with T.M. Schemes, carried out by batteries from "LOVERS LANE" in front line. Four guns of "A" Battery were lent to Right Group to assist in raid carried out by them.	
"	21st		Further registration as above	
"	23	12.10 – 12.20	Scheme II (Bombardment of TM's) carried out by order of LOWES GROUP	
"	24th	4.30 – 4.40	Scheme II again carried out by order of LOWES GROUP – Retaliation for enemy 4.2s	
"	29th	4.50pm – 5.50pm	"D" Battery fired 79 Rounds on Enemy front line + M.G emplacements. "A" Battery fired on German Working Parties	

1875 Wt. W593/826 1,000,000 ... I.R.C. & A. A.D.S.S./Forms/C. 2118.

3.12.16

D Mackay Lt R.A.
A. 180th Bde R.F.A.

WAR DIARY FOR MONTH OF DECEMBER, 1916.

VOLUME 11

180th Brigade R.F.A.

Vol XI

Instructions regarding War Diaries and Intelligence Summaries are contained in F. S. Regs., Part II. and the Staff Manual respectively. Title Pages will be prepared in manuscript.

WAR DIARY
or
INTELLIGENCE SUMMARY
(Erase heading not required.)

Army Form C. 2118

180th Bde R.F.A.

No 11.

Place	Date	Hour	Summary of Events and Information	Remarks and references to Appendices
YPRES	1.		Brigade still in action at YPRES	
	2.		D/180 with one section at RT Bde disposal fired 30 rds in connection with a raid	
	3.	6.12 pm	Test BELLEWAARDE (a mutual support barrage) is carried out by B and D/180.	
		6.25 6.40	Bursts of fire by "B" battery on new work.	
	4		A battery dispersed working party at J13c 3½ 0.	
	5.		No 42784 Gnr Smith JP Killed	
			No 27242 Gnr Wyatt H. Wounded.	
	5.		Small German mine went up on left: no action followed.	
	6.		T.M. Scheme II put into operation by order of DA. Complaint of shorts by guns and howitzers	
	7.		Undermentioned officers have been posted to the brigade with effect from the 5th 2nd Lieut W.H. Hurstbourne to D/180 Lt R Sapsole to B/180. In view of reported "shorts" batteries reregistered their points for Scheme II. Registrations found correct.	

1875 Wt. W593/826 1,000,000 4/15 J.B.C. & A. A.D.S.S./Forms/C. 2118.

Army Form C. 2118

Instructions regarding War Diaries and Intelligence Summaries are contained in F. S. Regs., Part II. and the Staff Manual respectively. Title Pages will be prepared in manuscript.

WAR DIARY
or
INTELLIGENCE SUMMARY
(Erase heading not required.)

180th Bde R.F.A. No 11.

Place	Date	Hour	Summary of Events and Information	Remarks and references to Appendices
YPRES	8th		Scheme II again in operation against hostile TMs - time 2.45pm Complaint of some "shorts"	
	9		Scheme II again reregistered by Batteries in presence of Brig Commander. Ranges found correct & safe.	
	11		Authority to wear badges of acting rank have been granted under CRO 3824a Sect 3 to the following officers Major A Mason A/180 Capt A.L. Perry A/180 Capt G.T. Lynch B/180 G.O.C.R.A. Xth Corps visited Bde, went thoroughly into D/180's ranges & Calculations & found everything in order.	
	12		Capt A.L. Perry assumed Command of A/180 R.F.A. Sec Lieut A.E.N Clark posted to Brigade with effect from 16th & is posted to C/180. Army Commander visited batteries of the Brigade. Capt H.G. Glendinning (posted but not joined) struck off off the strength	
	13		Capt Lynch assumed command of B/180 on return from BC's Course. T.M. Scheme again in operation	

1875 Wt. W593/826 1,000,000 4/15 J.B.C. & A. A.D.S.S./Forms/C. 2118.

Instructions regarding War Diaries and Intelligence Summaries are contained in F. S. Regs., Part II. and the Staff Manual respectively. Title Pages will be prepared in manuscript.

WAR DIARY
or
INTELLIGENCE SUMMARY
(Erase heading not required.)

Army Form C. 2118.

180th Bde RFA
No 11 (cont).

Place	Date	Hour	Summary of Events and Information	Remarks and references to Appendices
YPRES	15th		No 40016 Gnr Hollocks A.W. wounded.	
	16		Lt H.A. Goodall joined the Brigade & is posted to A/180	
	"		Lt J.A. Hobday transferred to 77th Bde RFA.	
	19		Lt R.S. Mearman joined brigade today posted to C/180	
	20.		Trench Mortar Retaliation Scheme came into operation thrice in the forenoon	
	21.		2nd Lieut. R.A. Smith transferred from C/180 to B/180 D/180 RFA shelled Sterling Castle several times in reply to 4.2" How shelling of YPRES	
	22 23 24 25		Hostile Artillery quiet.	
	26.		One section A.B.C.D/180 RFA relieved one section ~~each~~ A.B.C.D/102 RFA 28th Divl Arty. 180th Bde RFA wagon lines moved to their position in the 16th Divl Area	
	27		Relief of 180th Bde. by 102 Bde RFA. was completed by 7 pm. One section A.B.C.D/180 relieved corresponding sections of 173rd Bde RFA in the Spanbrock Section 16th Div front	

2449 Wt. W14957/M90 750,000 1/16 J.B.C. & A. Forms/C.2118/12.

Instructions regarding War Diaries and Intelligence Summaries are contained in F. S. Regs., Part II. and the Staff Manual respectively. Title Pages will be prepared in manuscript.

WAR DIARY
or
INTELLIGENCE SUMMARY

(Erase heading not required.)

Army Form C. 2118.

Place	Date	Hour	Summary of Events and Information	Remarks and references to Appendices
DRANOUTRE	28th		Lt R Allhusen D/180 RFA struck off the strength. Relief of 173rd Bde completed. Headquarters of 180th Bde stationed at DRANOUTRE.	
	29th		Batteries registered their points – high wind & poor visibility.	
	30th		Batteries registered their points – S.O.S. Night-lines.	
	31		Quiet day – further registration.	

M. Stebbing Major RFA
Comdg 180th Bde RFA

2449 Wt. W14957/M90 750,000 1/16 J.B.C. & A. Forms/C.2118/12.

WAR DIARY for month of JANUARY, 1917.

VOLUME 12

180th Brigade R. F. A.

Vol 12

Instructions regarding War Diaries and Intelligence Summaries are contained in F. S. Regs., Part II. and the Staff Manual respectively. Title pages will be prepared in manuscript.

WAR DIARY
or
INTELLIGENCE SUMMARY.
(Erase heading not required.)

Army Form C. 2118.

180TH BRIGADE R.F.A. No. 12

180th BRIGADE R.F.A. S/621 1.2.17

Place	Date 1917	Hour	Summary of Events and Information	Remarks and references to Appendices
	Jany			
DRANOUTRE	1		2Ls Ormond Stevens A/180. J.W. Hughes D/180. D Mackay a/Adjutant promoted Lieutenants as from 4th Oct 1916. Temp. Lieut A Mason promoted Temporary Captain Gazette 28th Dec. In New Years honours list Major N.A. STEBBING received the D.S.O.	
	2		Col. H.F. ASKWITH C.M.G, Lieut D. Mackay, 34760 Gunner Murray P, Corporal Jeffery Smith L.B. "Mentioned in New Years dispatch.	
	5.		Lt. F.H. Smith slightly wounded (at duty). 24269 Sergt. Atkinson died of wounds.	
	9.		Intimated that G.O.C. had granted Military Medal to Fitter Corporal Abrathat 36234	
	12.		2Lt. G.H. Hinds joined Brigade and posted to A/180. B and C/180 bombarded front and communication trenches between N.30.d.25.15 and N.30.c.10.65. for raid made by 49th Bde.	
	14.		C.R.A. inspected wagon lines. No shelling theirs or ours reported yesterday. Visibility 50 yards.	
	15.		Army Commander General Sir H. Plumer inspected wagon lines of 180 Brigade. One section C/180 withdrew to wagon line. 2Lieut. A.L. Perry ceases to be acting Captain, on becoming Adjutant VIERSTRAAT GROUP.	
	16.		Remaining two sections C/180 withdrew to wagon line and passed under the command of O.C. 77 Brigade from 6.0 pm.	

2353 Wt. W2544/1454 700,000 5/15 D. D. & L. A.D.S.S./Forms/C. 2118.

Instructions regarding War Diaries and Intelligence Summaries are contained in F. S. Regs., Part II. and the Staff Manual respectively. Title pages will be prepared in manuscript.

WAR DIARY
or
INTELLIGENCE SUMMARY.
(Erase heading not required.)

Army Form C. 2118.

180TH BRIGADE R.F.A. No. 12.

Place	Date	Hour	Summary of Events and Information	Remarks and references to Appendices
	Jany.			
DRANOUTRE.	17.		Lieut-Col. L. E. S. Ward. D.S.O. joined 180 Brigade and took over command.	
	18.		Lieut J. W. Hughes proceeds to England to attend Battery Commanders course.	
	19.		The officer of the detached section (A/180) O.P. observed the detachment of SIDNEY in action and dispersed it.	
	21.		Trench Mortar activity only on our front.	
	25.		2/Lieuts J. W. Hewitt and F. E. Davey joined the 180 Brigade. 2/Lt. Hewitt posted to "D" Battery 2/Lt. Davey to "B" Battery. Brigade co-operated with group on left, shelling trenches during enemys suspected relief.	
	26.		Col. H. F. Askwith C.M.G. struck off strength.	
	28.		DUCHESS, Heavy T.M. engaged SIDNEY SATAN and SYBIL covered by the fire of Howitzers and 18 pdrs. of this group on Enemy O.Ps. 6", 2" and Stokes Mortars co-operated.	Appendix 1. O.O.2. d.27.1.17.
	29.		SPANBROEK GROUP removed Headquarters to Little Kemmel on re-organisation of Div: front into a two Brigade front. Command passed at 12 noon.	
LITTLE KEMMEL.	30.		Wire cutting in front of SPANBROEK MOLEN was done by C/177, the object being to give the enemy the impression we were to attack him. Arrangements were made for A/180 and B/180 to continue the wire cutting. This was cancelled.	

2353 Wt. W2544/1454 700,000 5/15 D. D. & L. A.D.S.S./Forms/C. 2118.

Army Form C. 2118.

WAR DIARY
or
INTELLIGENCE SUMMARY.
(Erase heading not required.)

Instructions regarding War Diaries and Intelligence Summaries are contained in F. S. Regs., Part II. and the Staff Manual respectively. Title pages will be prepared in manuscript.

180TH BRIGADE R.F.A. No. 12.

Place	Date	Hour	Summary of Events and Information	Remarks and references to Appendices
LITTLE KEMMEL	31.		Howitzers engaged enemy O.Ps. at SKIP POINT, JUMP POINT and L'ENFER RIDGE re-inforced by 18 pdr. shrapnel fire while Heavy T.M. named the "DUCHESS" engaged the T.M. SIDNEY. 18 pdr. section of B/180 sprinkled SPANBROEK MOLEN. Shoot was successful.	Appendix 2 O.O. No. 4. d. 30.1.17.

L. E. S. Ward Lieut-Col
Comdg 180th Bde R.F.A.

2353 Wt. W2544/1454 700,000 5/15 D. D. & L. A.D.S.S. Forms/C. 2118.

COPY NO. 12.

OPERATION ORDER NO. 2.

by

Lieut. Col. L. R. S. WARD. D.S.O. R.F.A.

Commanding SPANBROEK Group. R.F.A.

::

27-1-17.

Ref. Map: WYTSCHAETE 1:10,000. edition 3B.

(1). On 28th instant, the Heavy Trench Mortar "DUCHESS" will engage Hostile Trench Mortars :-

"SYBIL" N.36.b.41.50.

"SIDNEY" N.36.b.35.70.

"SARAH" N.36.b.30.62.

with a view to destroying their emplacements and damaging the tramline and trenches in their vicinity.

(2). The following Batteries will take part in the operation.

A/180 18-pdr. Battery.

B/180 do do

D/177 4.5" Howitzer Battery.

D/180 do do do

Howitzer Batteries will assist the Heavy T.M. with deliberate fire.

18-pdr. Batteries will give covering fire on likely places from which the enemy may observe.

A table of tasks is attached.

(3). Zero will be at 5-0 p.m.

(4). G.O.C. 47th Infantry Brigade is arranging for a preliminary bombardment with 2" Trench Mortars, 6" Stokes Mortars and 3" Stokes Mortars from five to ten minutes before zero in order to induce the enemy to man his own Trench Mortars.

(5) Trenches N.36.7., N.36.8., N.36.9., and N.36.10. (inclusive) and corresponding communication and support trenches, are being cleared under arrangements by G.O.C.

47th Infantry Brigade.

(6). Watches will be synchronised from SPANBROEK GROUP Headquarters at 1-30 p.m.

(7). O.C. Group will be at SPANBROEK GROUP H.Q. during the operation.

(8). A C K N O W L E D G E .

Lieut. R.F.A.

27-1-17. Adjt. 180 Brigade, R.F.A.

Copies to :-

A/180 Bde.
do (Detached Section).
B/180 Bde.
D/180 Bde.
D/177 Bde.
16th Divl. Arty.
47th Inf. Bde.
D.Y.M.O.
O.C. V/16 T.M. Battery.
Left Group 36th Divn.
Centre Group 16th Divn.
File.
War Diary.

B A T T E R Y   T A S K S.

A/180 Battery (Detached Sec.).	Zero to Zero plus 60.	2 guns enfilade from :- N.30.c.96.43. to N.30.a.94.12.	30 rds. "AX"
A/180 Battery 4 guns.	-do-	Sweep Hostile Trench (SKIP POINT) from O.25.a.92.12. to O.25.a.42.60.	120 rds. "AX"
B/180 Battery	-do-	2 guns SPANBROEKMOLEN from N.30.c.30.60. to N.30.a.30.00. 4 guns sweep hostile trench (JUMP POINT) from O.25.b.15.50. to O.25.a.80.92.	180 rds. "AX"
D/180 Battery.	-do-	(1). O.25.d. 84.76 (House). (2). Trench from :- O.25.d.67.65. to O.25.d.72.62. (3). "SYBIL" N.36.b.41.50. (4). Trench Tramway Junction at N.36.b.4.55.	75 rds. "BX"
D/177 Battery.	-do-	Hostile T.M's. "SIDNEY" N.36.b.35.70. "SATAN" N.36.b.30.62. and tramway in vicinity.	75 rds. "BX"

The rates of fire for the above Battery Tasks, under Battery Commandere arrangements.

COPY NO. ____

S P A N B R O E K   O P E R A T I O N   O R D E R   N O. 4.

by

Lieut. Col. H. M. S. WARD. D.S.O. R.F.A.

Commanding SPANBROEK Group R.F.A.

:::::::::::::::::::::::::::::::::::::::

30-1-17.

Ref. Map - WYTSCHAETE, edition 3 B. 1/10,000.

(1). The two Howitzer Batteries will bombard the hostile defences at SKIP POINT and JUMP POINT on 31st instant, with a view to destroying hostile observation facilities at these points.

(2). <u>Ist operation.</u> SKIP POINT. Zero, 9-45 a.m. Duration of Bombardment 60 minutes.

<u>Battery Tasks.</u>

D/177. Hostile trenches from O.25.a.85.20. to O.25.a.62.40. and O.25.a.85.20. to O.25.b.00.34.

D/180. Hostile trenches from O.25.a.55.20. to O.25.a.94.10. and thence to O.25.b.08.20.

Ammunition 75 rounds per Battery.

(3). <u>2nd operation.</u> JUMP POINT. Zero, 11-0 a.m. Duration of bombardment 60 minutes.

<u>Battery Tasks.</u>

D/177. Hostile trenches from O.25.a.90.80. to O.19.c.85.03.

D/180. Hostile trenches from O.25.a.90.80. to O.25.b.10.62.

Ammunition 75 rounds per Battery.

(4). Watches will be synchronized from Group H.Q. at 9-15 a.m.

(5). A C K N O W L E D G E.

A Mackay
Lt. R.F.A.
Adjt. 180 Brigade. R.F.A.

Copies to :-
D/177 Battery.
D/180 Battery.
16th Divl. Arty.
47th Inf. Bde.
War Diary.
File.

W A R D I A R Y.

FOR MONTH OF FEBRUARY, 1917.

VOLUME 13

UNIT:- 180th Brigade R.F.A.

Vol 13

Instructions regarding War Diaries and Intelligence Summaries are contained in F. S. Regs., Part II. and the Staff Manual respectively. Title pages will be prepared in manuscript.

WAR DIARY
or
INTELLIGENCE SUMMARY.
(Erase heading not required.)

Army Form C. 2118.

180th Bde R.F.A. No 13.

Place	Date	Hour	Summary of Events and Information	Remarks and references to Appendices
Little Kemmel.	1.	5.10am.	Attempted Raid by the Enemy between SPANBROEKMOLEN and PECKHAM and at CLOCHER VALLEY. – Special report attached	Appendix 1.
	2.		No 34297. Gnr. WELLS. slightly wounded. A/180 R.F.A Battery Position heavily shelled by lachrymatory shells 5.9" How.	
	3.		Lone Pine on immediate right of Kingsclaere Wood knocked down	
	4.		500 Rounds fired on A/180 R.F.A. Battery Position. Following casualties sustained. Lt HINDS G.H. 36000 Gnr ANGLISS G 36034. Gnr WILSON. 122501 Gnr LOMAN H.L. – all slightly wounded 30436 Cpl KEELING. G.T. seriously wounded. 9947 Sergt. MEADOWS J. and 110649. Dvr PROSSER. wounded. 30 rounds fired between 5.30 and 8 pm to impede the Battery should it attempt to withdraw. B/180 moved ~~second~~ section in position N33a.88.	
	5		Hostile Trench Mortar activity.	
	6.		Lt V.G. Williams joined and was posted to A/180 R.F.A. ~~Heavy~~ Battery position near Headquarters shelled with about ~~100~~ 5.9" shells	

Army Form C. 2118.

WAR DIARY
or
INTELLIGENCE SUMMARY.
(Erase heading not required.)

Instructions regarding War Diaries and Intelligence Summaries are contained in F. S. Regs., Part II. and the Staff Manual respectively. Title pages will be prepared in manuscript.

Place	Date	Hour	Summary of Events and Information	Remarks and references to Appendices
Little Kemmel.	8		KEMMEL SHELTERS shelled with about 280 5.9" Hrs shells and 104 rounds into heavy battery position N20a40.27. 18pdr Batteries of 8PAN^c Group engaged tramways in N36b.03.12. 30 rounds per battery. Casualties were believed to have been inflicted.	
	9.		Concentrated fire of Group was brought to bear on dump at EARL FARM at 2.55 pm for 5 minutes, and trench tramways at 3.20 pm. Tramways were again engaged between 8 and 10 pm.	O.O. No 5.
	10.		Much hostile air activity which prevented a shoot by the Group on our left from cooperating in Corps H.A. Bombardment	
	11		A/150 heavily shelled during morning and afternoon. Major Mason slightly wounded. One gun knocked out of action. At 3.7 pm and 3.44 pm Group assisted by H.T.M. DUCHESS and 51st H.A.G. bombarded enemy TMs and O.P. areas. A/180 while under heavy shell	O.O. No 6.

2353 Wt. W2544/1454 700,000 5/15 D. D. & L. A.D.S.S./Forms/C. 2118.

Instructions regarding War Diaries and Intelligence Summaries are contained in F. S. Regs., Part II. and the Staff Manual respectively. Title pages will be prepared in manuscript.

WAR DIARY
or
INTELLIGENCE SUMMARY.
(Erase heading not required.)

Army Form C. 2118.

180th Bde RFA

Place	Date	Hour	Summary of Events and Information	Remarks and references to Appendices
Little Kemmel	11.		fire carried out its share of the programme.	
	13.		A/180 withdrew as a result of recent heavy shelling and came into action at N 10 b 35.85 and was handed over to VIERSTRAAT S.P. in exchange for A/177.	OO. No 7.
	14.		Registration carried out by aeroplane with some success B/177 and B/180 – STOP POINT as target.	
	15.		C/177 heavily shelled 50 or 60 universal 5.9 shells – two guns put out of action.	
	18.		Spanbroek S.P. cooperated with IXth Corps Heavies in a bombardment of enemy trenches near SPANBROEKMOLEN unsuccessful raid by 6th Inniskilling Rangers at 7.15 am	~~[illegible]~~ OO. No 8.
	19.		Mine went up somewhere north of our Sector about 4.45 pm.	
	23.		A/180 fired 200 rounds in support of VIERSTRAAT S.P. operations – assisting 41st Div. Raid preparations. ~~Raid by [illegible]~~	
	24.		A/180 again assisting 41st Div. Preparations. Raid began at 4.55 pm A/180 fired about 500 rounds. C/180 was employed along with one Hows of A/180 to neutralize a line.	

2353 Wt. W2544/1454 700,000 5/15 D. D. & L. A.D.S.S. Forms/C. 2118.

Army Form C. 2118.

WAR DIARY
or
INTELLIGENCE SUMMARY.
(Erase heading not required.)

180th Bde RFA

Instructions regarding War Diaries and Intelligence Summaries are contained in F. S. Regs., Part II. and the Staff Manual respectively. Title pages will be prepared in manuscript.

Place	Date	Hour	Summary of Events and Information	Remarks and references to Appendices
Little Kemmel	24.		gun on Wytschaete village. C/180 completed its relief of C/177 and on reorganization A/180 became a 6 how battery. During the Raid on our left Little Kemmel was shelled by 40 rounds 5.9" Hows. Some were lachrymatory shells.	O.O. No. 9.
	25.		Registration for coming bombardments.	
	26.		At 12 noon A/180 came back into this group and A/177 returned WULVERGHEM GROUP. The SPANBROEK GP is now wholly 180th Bde batteries.	OO No. 10.
	27.		Quiet.	
	28.		Very Quiet.	
			Group Defence Scheme attached	

L. E. S. Ward Lieut Col
Cm dg 180th Bde R.F.A.

SECRET M.S. 39.

Headquarters
6th D.A.

The following facts have been elicited from our LIAISON OFFICER. – Lt R.A. SMITH. B/180. with reference the operations of last night

At 7.15 am the Artillery opened "like one gun".
At 7.18 am the Left Party was reported back.
~~Two men were stated to have been shot by one of our own officers~~
At 7.23 am the Centre Party came back. and at 7.25 the Right Party returned.
The LIAISON OFFICER was not permitted to send the CODE WORD "COMING" to Group HQ. till 7.36 am. It was received at Group HQ. at 7.37 am.
The Artillery barrage is reported by everyone as being excellent and accurate. The "shorts" attributed to the Artillery during the late stages of the operation are now recognized as the work of the Stokes guns.
The casualties are reported to be about 40 of whom 15 were killed mainly by hostile rifle fire. About 3 machine guns are believed to have been used. Officer casualties are believed

to be as high as five – 2 killed and 3 wounded – of the latter one is a prisoner.
The enemy does not seem to have sent any "S.O.S." signal to his Artillery. His artillery did not open fire about 7.40am ~~when~~ as a result of our Field Guns and Howitzers (4.5") engaging SIDNEY, SATAN, etc. All was quiet at 8.14 am
The enemy was reported shelling the area SHAMUS FARM, DURHAM ROAD at 8.33 am. This Group retaliated with "Concentration A" for 5 minutes at the rate of 2 rds per gun per minute. All quiet again about 8.50 pm.
After this the enemy seems to have allowed our stretcher bearers to take in their dead and wounded.
The wire from FOO to Group HQ was the only one which remained intact all the time.

N. Stibbing Major RFA.

Comdg 180th Bde R.F.A.

SECRET. No 13 Appendix I

Headquarters, 16th Divl. Army.
-do- 47th Inf. Bde. (For information)
War Diary.
File.

Report on attempted Raid on the night 31st January-1st February 1917.

The first intimation of Hostile Enterprise received at SPANBROEK Group Headquarters, was the sound of intense Artillery fire at about 5-10 a.m.

About 5-20 a.m. a report was received from D/180 Battery that there was an intense Hostile Barrage of 77 mm. and 105 mm. on the Group Front.

Telephone call S.O.S. was received by C/177 Battery from Left Company Headquarters at 5-17 a.m.

At 5-25 a.m. the Rocket Picquet reported S.O.S. Rocket from the Left Company, Left Battalion.

Batteries opened fire on their Night Lines at the following times :-

A/180. at 5-15 a.m. (On B.C's. initiative).
B/180. at 5-30 a.m. (By order of Group).
D/180. at 5-27 a.m. -do- -do-
C/177. at 5-10 a.m. (Call for retaliation by Infantry)
D/177. at 5-27 a.m. (By order of Group).

At 5-35 a.m. I communicated with Brigade Major, 16th Divisional Artillery, requesting assistance from Left Group, 36th Divisional Artillery. VIERSTRAAT Group was already co-operating.

At this time the general situation was by no means clear, and conflicting reports were being received.

At 5-40 a.m. reports indicated that the main scene of operations was centring about our trenches N.29.3.

N.29.4., and N.30.3.

I switched two sections of B/180 Battery on to this front also directing A/180 Battery to switch inwards on to the front of B/180 Battery.

Batteries switched a section at a time.

At the same time I requested the VIERSTRAAT Group to strengthen my Barrage on this front.

About 5-55 a.m. the situation began to quieten down, but the Liaison Officer with Right Battalion reported that although no attack had been made, the infantry expected one on the Right.

I switched back A/180 and B/180 Batteries on to their original frontages and maintained a slow rate of fire pending developments on this front but ceased fire with the remaining Batteries.

At 6-10 a.m. as no further developments had occurred I sent out "Cease fire" to all Batteries in the Group and to neighbouring Groups.

As far as my information goes, the Hostile Artillery fire commenced North of my Zone and worked Southwards. A heavy Hostile Barrage was placed in rear of our trenches from "PICCADILLY" to "KITCHEN AVENUE". The Communication Trench "PALL MALL" was included in a "Box Barrage" and heavily shelled.

The O.C. Right Company, Left Battalion, whose telephonic communications were immediately cut, attempted to fire S.O.S. Rockets without success.

The S.O.S. Rocket reported by my Rocket Picquet was sent up by the Company Commander, Left Company, Left Battalion.

(3).

According to present reports, a Hostile Raiding Party issuing from SPANBROEKMOLEN about 0.30.a.10.05. attempted to enter our trenches at a point just North of "PICCADILLY" but were driven back.

Another party attacked "CLOGHER AVENUE" but also met with no success.

No casualties were incurred by the Left Battalion, but six men were reported to have been killed by shell fire in the Right Battalion.

A/180 and B/180 Batteries were heavily shelled with Lachrymatory Gas.

L. ? S. Ward. Lieut Col. R.F.A

1-2-17. Commdg. SPANBROEK Group R.F.A.

SECRET.   180th Brigade, R.F.A. No.S.[illegible]18/1.

Headquarters,

16th Divisional Artillery.

Reference your R/2649 dated 2nd inst.

Is is very difficult to fix precise times, as in the initial stages of the Hostile Raid there was considerable congestion on the Group Lines and none but verbal messages were possible.

The N.C.O. of the Rocket Picquet states that he saw the first Rocket at 5-22 a.m. and at once reported it. The actual moment at which it was received in the Group Office cannot be definately stated, but it was between 5-22 a.m. and 5-25 a.m..

C/177 Battery called up Group Headquarters between 5-15 a.m. and 5-20 a.m. and the telephonists on duty at Group Headquarters, state that at the time they were busy taking in messages and gave C/177 the "M Q" (Wait) signal, but subsequently took the message about 5-20 a.m.

The first report received in H.Q. Signal Office was about 5-15 a.m. and was to the effect that a heavy Hostile Bombardment of our trenches was in progress. This came from A/180 Battery.

The Lone Gun of C/177 Battery was in action with the remainder of the Battery and fired throughout the operation.

The detached section of A/180 Battery took no part in the action until 6 a.m., when I ordered them to open fire for five minutes at one round per gun per minute.

The failure of this section to take a more active

share was due to a misconception on my part. I was under the impression that it came in automatically with the rest of A/180 Battery for S.O.S. purposes.

I have taken steps to ensure this section being fully employed in future.

The paragraph of your R/2649 is duly noted for future guidance. I would however point out that I should not have asked for assistance from the Group on my Right any earlier, as until about 5-35 a.m. the situation had not sufficiently declared itself.

(Sd) L.E. Swan

Lieut. Col. R.F.A.

3-2-17. Commdg. SPANBROEK Group. R.F.A.

S E C R E T. Copy No. ____

S P A N B R O E K   O P E R A T I O N   O R D E R   No. 8.

by

Lieut-Col. L. H. S. WARD D.S.O., R.F.A.,

Commanding SPANBROEK Group. R.F.A.

Ref. Map.- WYTSCHAETE. Edition 4 a. 1/10,000.

1. The Spanbroek Group will shell hostile dumps during the afternoon 8th. February.

2. (a) From 2.50. p.m. to 2.55 p.m. A/180 Battery enfilade OCCULT AVENUE from O.25.d.10.22. to O.25.d.50.40. Thirty rounds.

B/180 Battery sweep ~~bridge~~ hedge in front of EARL FARM from O.25.d.30.33 to O.25.d.20.50. Thirty rounds.

C/177 Battery search ground N.E. of farm from O.25.d.60.44. to O.25.d.38.68. Thirty rounds.

D/177)
D/188) EARL FARM BUILDINGS.

20 rounds per battery.

(b) 3.20 p.m. to 3.25 p.m.

A/180 Battery search cutting from N.30.d.75.65. to N.30.d.88.92. Thirty rounds.

B/180 sweep trench from N.30.d.88.70 to N.30.d.90.62. Thirty rounds.

C/177 Enfilade trench tramway from N.30.b.51.30. to N.30.b.85.00. Thirty rounds.

D/177)
D/180) Destroy trench tramway in N.E. corner of N.30.d. (about N.30.d.90.90.)

20 rounds per battery.

3. Watches will be synchronized at 2.10 p.m.

Lieut., R.F.A.

Adjt., SPANBROEK GROUP.

9.2.17.

Copies to :-

A/180
B/180
D/180
C/177
D/177
16th. Div. Arty.
49th. Inf. Bde.
War Diary
File.

Copy No. 10

SPANBROEK OPERATION ORDER No. 6.

by

Lieut. Col. D. E. S. WARD. D.S.O., R.F.A.

Commanding SPANBROEK Group.R.F.A.

10.2.17.

Ref Map. WYTSCHAETE Edition 4 a 1/10,000.
PLOEGSTEERT " 4 a 1/10,000.

1. This Group will carry out a bombardment on 11th. February 1917 in conjunction with a bombardment by Light, Medium and Heavy Trench Mortars.

2. H.A. IX Corps will co-operate and will assist with Counter Batteries.

3. Zero time will be 3.7 p.m.

4. Watches will be synchronised with Group Headquarters at 2.30. p.m.

5. Batteries will be ready to reply to any retaliation at the end of the final bombardment out of the normal allotment of ammunition.

6. A Table of Tasks alloted to Batteries is attached.

7. ACKNOWLEDGE.

A Macnay Lieut., R.F.A.

Adjt.,SPANBROEK GROUP.

Copies to :-

1. A/190
2. B/190
3. D/190
4. C/177
5. D/177
6. Vierstraat Group.
7. Left Group 36th. D.A.
8. 16th. D.A.
9. 49th. Inf. Bde.
10. War Diary.
11. File.

TABLE OF BATTERY TASKS.

Battery.	Time.	Objective.	Ammunition.
D/180.	Zero to Zero plus 15 mins. Zero plus 37 to Zero plus 59 mins.	OCEAN TRENCH FROM SCOTT FARM to O.25.a.80.20.	100 rds. "BX"
D/177.	-do-	Cutting running N.E. along road from :- SCOTT FARM.	100 rds. "BX"
A/180. (Including Detached Section).	-do-	O.P. Area round SPANBROEKMOLEN.	25 rds. "A" 75 rds. "AX"
C/177.	-do-	O.P. Area round BOGAERT FARM (OCEAN CRESCENT).	25 rds. "A" 75 rds. "AX"
B/180.	-do-	O.P. Area enclosed by :- O.26.c.20.28. O.26.c.40.21. O.26.c.27.05.	25 rds. "A" 75 rds. "AX"

Rates of fire under Battery Commanders arrangements.

---------oOo---------

S E C R E T. COPY NO. 11

S P A N B R O E K   O P E R A T I O N   O R D E R   N O. 7.

by

Lieut-Col. L. H. S. WARD D.S.O., R.F.A.

Commanding SPANBROEK Group R.F.A.

Ref. Map. WYTSCHAETE - Edition 4 A - 1:10,000.

1. MOVES.

The following moves will take place on the dates specified :-

<u>February 12th.</u>

A/180 Battery will draw four guns from B/172 Battery and put them in position formerly occupied by B/77 Battery.

No tactical changes will take place on this date.

<u>February 13th.</u>

A/180 Battery will withdraw two guns from their present position at DAYLIGHT CORNER, putting ~~one in the position formerly occupied by the Lone Gun of C/177 Battery, and one gun~~ them into B/77 position.

The present Detached Section of A/180 Battery will pass to B/180 Battery, personnel only to be changed.

Battery Commanders concerned will arrange details.

B/180 Battery will hand over one gun to C/177 Battery. Details to be arranged by Battery Commanders.
A/177 take up Lone gun position

All moves to be carried out under cover of darkness, and to be completed by 10-0 p.m., 13th February.

2. RE-DISTRIBUTION of POSITIONS.

On the completion of moves, Batteries will stand as follows :-

A/177 (A/180) Battery - 6 guns in B/77 position.
1 gun in Lone Gun Position. (formerly of C/177).

B/180 Battery - 4 guns in their present position.
2 guns in Detached Section position. (formerly of A/180).

C/177 Battery - 6 guns in their present position.

3. TACTICAL RE-DISTRIBUTION. By 10-0 p.m., 13th February, the tactical situation will be as follows :-

Battery.	Position.	O.P.	ZONE.	Night Lines.
A/180. A/177 (5 guns).	N.15.b.35.85.	F.4. S.P.9. S.P.10.	N.30.c.08.76. to N.24.c.80.25.	N.30.c.06.85. N.30.a.15.05. N.30.a.35.27. N.30.a.42.59. N.24.c.70.15.
(1 gun).	N.34.a.75.05.			N.30.a.60.84.
B/180. (4 guns).	N.33.a.90.90.	K.3.8.	N.36.d.28.90. to N.36.a.54.76.	N.36.d.10.99. N.36.a.73.31. N.30.a.62.48. N.36.a.56.66.
(2 guns).	T.24.a.10.90.	T.3.a.		N.36.d.15.98. to N.36.a.90.16. and N.36.a.53.85. to N.30.c.48.28.
C/177. (6guns).	N.15.d.20.20.	K.18. F.K.8.	N.36.a.54.76. to N.30.c.08.76.	N.36.a.52.80. N.30.c.60.00. N.30.c.65.20. N.30.c.48.32. N.30.c.32.52. N.30.c.10.72.

4. MUTUAL SUPPORT. Reference SPANBROEK Defence Scheme, para 15.

(b). B/180 barrage from N.36.d.55.95.
to N.36.d.16.88.

x D/180. 1 gun on Trench Junction. N.36.d.35.65.

1 gun on Trench Junction. N.36.d.50.79.

x <u>Note.</u> Co-ordinates altered to agree with last edition of WYTSCHAETE Map. 1:10,000.

(d). C/177. One section enfilades from N.24.c.60.10.
to N.24.c.82.25.

One section enfilades from N.24.c.80.55.
to N.24.d.20.66.

A/177 A/180. Lone Gun enfilades salient N.24.c.77.47.

5 guns barrage from N.18.c.66.00.
to N.18.d.18.20.

D/180. No change.

5. COMMUNICATIONS. The Officer in charge of Group Signals will make the necessary alterations to comply with the new distribution.

B/180 will be connected with :-

Right Company, Right Battalion. (F O 6).

Right Battalion. (F M 3).

C/177 will be connected with :-

Left Company, Right Battalion. (F M 6).

Right Battalion. (F M 3).

A/177 A/180 will be connected with :-

Right Company, Left Battalion. (F M 10).

Left Company, Left Battalion. (F I 13).

Left Battalion. (F M 5).

O.P. and Group Communications will be adjusted in accordance with para 3.

6. CONCENTRATIONS. The following amendments come into force on re-distribution, reference SPANBROEK Defence Scheme, paras 13 and 14.

A/177 A/180 Battery takes up tasks as originally allotted to C/177 Battery.

B/180 Battery takes up tasks as originally allotted to A/180 Battery.

C/177 Battery takes up tasks as originally allotted to B/180 Battery.

Amended tables will be issued as soon as possible.

7. INTERIM DISTRIBUTION. The present tactical distribution will remain unchanged till 7-0 p.m., 13th February.

Between the hours of 7-0 p.m. and 10-0 p.m., 13th February, Batteries will distribute their fire on temporary Night Lines to cover the Group Front as follows :-

7. (Continued). B/180 Battery. 6 guns (including Detached Section) from N.36.d.28.90. to N.36.c.48.38.

C/177 Battery. 5 guns from N.30.c.48.38. to N.30.a. 45.53.

A/177 (A/180) Battery. 5 (4) guns from N.30.a.45.53. to N.24.c. 82.25.

At 10-0 p.m., 13th February, Batteries will lay on Night Lines as in para 3.

Officer in charge of Group Communications will arrange that temporary communications, between Batteries and Companies, remain in being to suit this interim distribution.

8. REGISTRATION. Battery Commanders will Register for the new tactical distribution (para 2), during the day, February 13th, as far as possible.

9. DEFENCE SCHEME. This order will be read in conjunction with the SPANBROEK Group Defence Scheme, to which it is supplementary.

Amendments to the Defence Scheme to suit the new distribution of Batteries will be issued shortly.

10. A C K N O W L E D G E.

L. E. S. Ward Lieut-Col. R.F.A

12-2-17. Commanding SPANBROEK Group. R.F.A.

COPIES TO:-

No.1. A/180.
" 2. B/180.
" 3. D/180.
" 4. C/177.
" 5. D/177.
" 6. 16th Div. Arty.
No. 7. 47th Inf. Bde.
" 8. VIERSTRAAT Group.
" 9. Left Group, 36th Div. Arty.
" 10. War Diary.
" 11. File.

S E C R E T.   COPY NO. 11

AMENDMENTS TO SPANBROEK OPERATION ORDER NO. 7.

The following amendments will be made to SPANBROEK Operation Order No. 7. :-

1\. MOVES.

A/180 Battery will withdraw two guns from their present position and put them into B/77 position.

The Detached Section of A/180 Battery will pass to B/180 Battery, personnel only being changed.

Battery Commanders will arrange details

A/180 Battery will be transferred to the VIERSTRAAT Group.

A/177 Battery will be transferred to the SPANBROEK Group.

Command will pass at 4-0 p.m., February 13th, with the exception of one Section of A/180 Battery, which will remain under the command of O.C. SPANBROEK Group until it is withdrawn on the night of 13th - 14th February.

A/177 Battery will provide the Lone Gun at N.34.a.75.05., which will be placed in position on the night of 13th - 14th February.

2\. TACTICAL RE-DISTRIBUTION.

In para 3, for A/180 Battery, read :-

Battery.	Position.	O.P.	ZONE.	Night Lines.
A/177. (5 guns).	N.9.d.48.02.	N.10.d.45.30. (O P 14).	N.30.c.06.75. to	N.30.c.06.55. N.30.a.18.05. N.30.a.33.27. N.30.a.42.59.
		L K 4.	N.24.c.00.25.	N.24.c.70.15.
(1 gun).	N.34.a.75.05.			N.30.a.60.54.

In all subsequent paras, for A/180 Battery. substitute A/177 Battery. except in para 7, Interim

Distribution, where for A/180 Battery, 4 guns, A/177, 5 guns will be substituted.

L. E. S. Ward Lieut. Col. R.F.A.

12-2-17 Commanding SPANBROEK Group, R.F.A.

COPIES TO :-

No.1. A/180.
No.2. B/180.
No.3. D/180.
No.4. B/177.
No.5. D/177.
No.6. A/177.
No. .6. 16th Div. Arty.
No.7. 49th Inf. Bde.
No.8. VIERSTRAAT Group.
No.9. Left Group 36th Div. Arty.
No.10. War Diary.
No.11. File.

SECRET

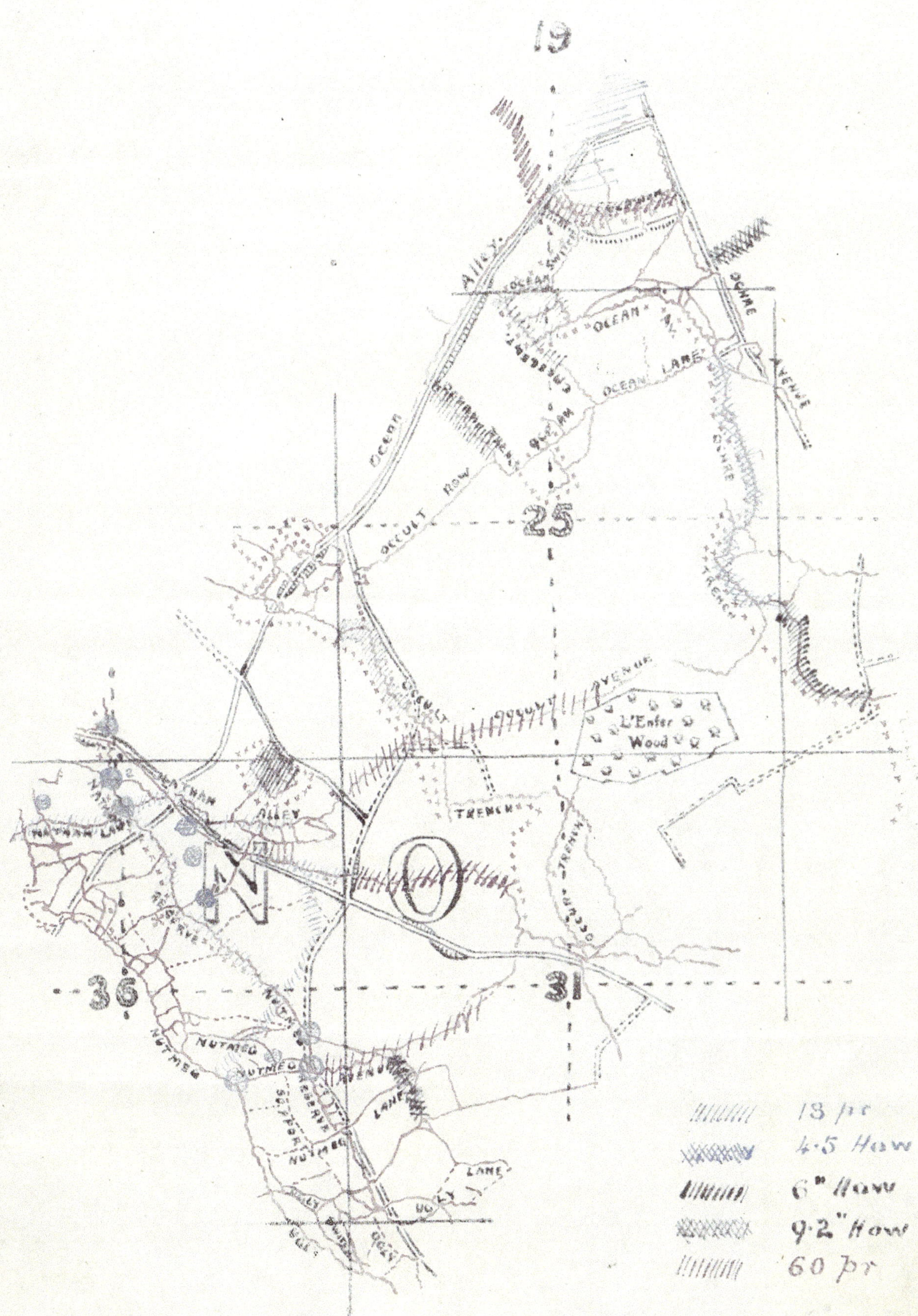

19
25
31
36
OCEAN ALLEY
OCCULT ROW
OCEAN LANE
OCEAN
OCCULT AVENUE
OCCULT TRENCH
TRENCH
DOME AVENUE
DOME TRENCH
L'Enfer Wood
NATHAN ALLEY
NATHAN LANE
RESERVE
NUTMEG
NUTMEG RESERVE
SUPPORT
LANE
OGLE
N
O
18 pr
4·5 How
6" How
9·2" How
60 pr

SECRET. COPY NO. 7

SPANBROEK OPERATION ORDER NO. 8.

by

Major N.A.STEBBING., D.S.O., R.F.A.

Commanding SPANBROEK Group. R.F.A.

::::::::::::::::::::::::::::::::::::

14-2-17.

1. Herewith Table of Tasks in connection with operations to take place at a very early date.

2. Zero day and hour, and further instructions will be issued later.

3. Necessary registrations should commence at once.

4. ACKNOWLEDGE.

D Mackay Lieut. R.F.A.

14-2-17. Adjt. 180th Brigade, R.F.A.

COPIES TO :-

B/180.
D/180.
A/177.
C/177.
D/177.
47th Inf. Bde.
War Diary. ✓
File.

S E C R E T.

TABLE OF BATTERY TASKS.

Ref Map. - WYTSCHAETE & PLOEGSTEERT - 1:10,000.,
Edition 4 A.

Battery.	Time.	Objective.	Ammunition.	Remarks.
A/177.	Zero to Zero plus 3 mins.	Enfilade NATHAN RESERVE from N.36.b.03.78. to N.36.b.24.40.	1698.	Zero to Zero plus 3 mins., all "A", otherwise 25% "A"
	Zero plus 3 till further orders.	Enfilade from N.36.b.20.90. to N.36.b.57.57. One Section concentrate on N 36 b 27.35		
C/177.	Zero to Zero plus 3 mins.	Enfilade NATHAN and NUTMEG RESERVE from N.36.b.24.40. to N.36.d.75.95.	1698.	To pay special attention to N.36.b.27.35. Zero to Zero plus 3 mins. all "A" otherwise 25% "A".
	Zero plus 3 till further orders.	Enfilade from N.36.b.57.57. to O.31.a.00.47. One Section concentrate on N 36 b 27.35		
B/180. (2 guns)	From Zero till further orders	Enfilade NATHAN ALLEY from N.36.b.40.71. to N.36.b.80.70.	1634.	25% "A"
(4 guns)	From Zero plus 3 mins onwards.	Barrage from N.36.b.85.50. to N.36.b.87.17.		
D/177.	From Zero onwards.	Trench Junctions. N.36.b.03.78. N.36.a.96.90. N.36.a.95.93. N.30.c.95.13.	960.	T.M. suspected at N.30.c.95.13.
D/180.	Zero to Zero plus 3 mins.	Trench Mortars :- SYBIL. N.36.b.35.40. SIDNEY N.36.b.33.72. SATAN. N.36.b.35.60. STINKER. N.36.a.77.75.	960.	
	Zero plus 3 onwards.	OCHRE TRENCH from O.26.c. 00.62. to O.25.b.90.15. 3 Hours on OCHRE TRENCH 1 Hour HELLFARM. + O 31 b 42.40		

R A T E S O F F I R E.

(1). **18-pdr. Batteries**

Zero to Zero plus 3.	4 rounds per gun per minute.
Zero plus 3 to Zero plus 40.	3 rounds per gun per minute.
Zero plus 40 onwards.	2 rounds per gun per minute.

(2). **4.5" Howitzer Batteries.**

2 rounds per gun per minute throughout the operations.

----oOo----

SECRET. 180th Brigade R.F.A. No.S.F./26.

Reference SPANBROEK Operation Order No. 8.,

dated 14-2-17.

----------oOo----------

1. Intention.

47th Infantry Brigade will raid the enemy's trenches between N.36.d.20.78. and N.36.a.80.30. on 19th February, 1917.

If the weather conditions are favourable, smoke will be discharged at Zero from the entire front of the 47th and 108th Infantry Brigades.

2. Time.

If the weather is favourable, the raid will take place at Zero hour, 7-15 a.m. 19th inst, or should the weather be unfavourable in the morning, the operation will be carried out, whatever the weather conditions, at Zero hour, 1-15 a.m. on the 20th inst, (night 19th/20th.)

3. Decision as to whether the raid will take place in the morning or in the night time.

(a). At 6-0 p.m. on February 18th, the O.C. Raid will decide whether the conditions are favourable for a morning enterprise.

If a postponement subsequent to this decision is absolutely necessary, O.C. Raid is to inform 47th Inf. Bde. not later than 2½ hours before Zero.

(b). In the event of such a postponement until the night of 19th/20th February, the only further notification that will be sent out to all concerned will be one cancelling the operation in case this is necessary through some unforseen contingency.

(c). Notification as to raid taking place or otherwise will be transmitted to Batteries and Groups on

Right and Left as follows :-

Raid taking place. .... "PROGRAMME"

Raid not taking place .... "ABNORMAL"

4. Signal for Assault.

Infantry will leave our trenches at Zero.

Watches will be synchronized, but the opening of fire by our Artillery will be the Signal for the Assault, for the opening of fire of all Machine Guns and Trench Mortars and for the discharge of smoke.

It is therefore of the utmost importance that all watches should be carefully synchronized, and that the opening of fire should be simultaneous by all Artillery taking part.

5. Synchronization.

Watches will be synchronized from SPANBROEK Group Headquarters by telephone with Batteries at 5-0 a.m. if the operation takes place on the morning of the 19th and at 11-0 p.m. if the operation takes place on the night of 19th/20th.

6. Points of Entry.

Three parties of the 6th Battalion, CONNAUGHT RANGERS enter the enemy's trenches at about the following points :-

N.36.d.20.78.
N.36.b.05.10.
N.36.a.80.30.

7. Liaison.

A Liaison Officer will be detailed by O.C. SPANBROEK Group, to be with O.C. 6th Battalion, CONNAUGHT RANGERS.

8. ARTILLERY PROGRAMME.

(a). Table of Tasks has been issued with SPANBROEK Operation Order No. 8.

(b). Fire will be maintained till O.C. SPANBROEK Group notifies Batteries that the parties have returned.

The code word for stop firing will be :-

"FINISH"

(c). O.C. D/180 Battery will be ready to open fire on the trench mortar emplacements "SYBIL", "SATAN", "SIDNEY" and "STINKER" on receipt of information from the Liaison Officer that the Infantry are withdrawing.

The Liaison Officer will inform the Howitzer Battery direct.

9. Communications.

There will be a direct line from Liaison Officer with O.C. 6th CONNAUGHT RANGERS to Group Headquarters, and to B/180 and D/180. Batteries.

10. A C K N O W L E D G E .

E. H. Walker

2 Lieut. R.F.A.

16-2-17. (f) Adjt. 180 Brigade, R.F.A.

COPIES TO :-

B/180.
D/180.
A/177.
C/177.
D/177.
47th Inf. Bde.
War Diary.
File.

S E C R E T   Copy No. 11

SPANBROEK OPERATION ORDER No. 9.

by

~~Major N.A. STEBBING, D.S.O.~~, R.F.A.,

Ref. Map 1/12,000. Sheet 28. S.W.

16th. D.A. O.O., No.46.   22nd. Feb. 1917.

16th. D.A. No. R.2708/16.

1. C/180 will relieve C/177 in action at N.15.d.2.2.

2. Guns, with Sights and Aiming Posts will be left in situ.

3. Personnel of one Section will be relieved by 2.30. p.m. 23rd. February.
   The remaining Section will be relieved by 2.30. p.m. 24th. February.

4. An Officer of C/177 will remain with C/180 for twenty-four hours after completion of relief.

5. All maps, planchettes, photographs, panoramas, logbooks Defence Schemes, diagram of communications etc., and all information concerning the front will be handed over.

6. On relief, personnel of C/177 will withdraw to their own Wagon Lines.

7. Passing of Command will take place at 2.30. p.m. 24th. February.

8. O.C. C/180 will give a receipt to O.C. C/177 signed by both shewing amount and nature of ammunition taken over and he will send a duplicate to this office as soon as possible.

9. Completion of relief should be reported in code to this Office.

10. ACKNOWLEGE.

D Mackay Lieut., R.F.A.

Adjt., Spanbroek Group.

Copies to :-

1.	A/177	7.	Vierstraat Group.
2.	C/177	8.	49th. Inf. Bde.
3.	B/180	9.	47th. Inf. Bde.
4.	C/180	10.	16th. Div. Arty.
5.	D/180	11.	War Diary.
6.	Spare	12.	File.

SECRET. Copy No. 11

SPANBROEK OPERATION ORDER No. 10.

by

Major W. A. STEBBING, D.S.O., R. F. A.

23.2.17.

Ref. 16th. D.A., No.R.2706/17. - 22nd. Feb.1917.

1. A/180 will be transferred to the SPANBROEK GROUP and take over the zone of A/177, viz. N.30.c.98.76 to N.24.c.85.25.

2. The transfer will take effect from noon 26th. February, 1917.

3. A/180, will take over the Lone Gun of A/177 at N.34.a.75.05. (personnel only being exchanged) at noon 26th. February, 1917.

4. A/180, will hand over one gun complete with sights, spare parts, etc. to A/177 on the night of the 25th. February, 1917.

5. Maps, Planchette boards of view from O.Ps., photographs, panoramas, log-books, defence scheme, diagram of communications, and all information concerning the front of A/177 should be taken over. Planchettes of the Battery Positions will not be exchanged.

6. O.C. A/180, will report when he has registered and laid on his new S.O.S. lines.

7. O.C. A/180, will give a receipt signed by both B.Cs. shewing the amount and nature of ammunition taken over at the Lone Gun Position, and a duplicate will be forwarded to this Office.

8. A/180, will take up all tasks (mutual support concentrations, strafes, selected squares, etc.) originally alloted to C/177 in SPANBROEK DEFENCE SCHEME.

9. The Officer in charge of Group Communications will make the necessary adjustment of lines to connect up A/180 to Group H.Qs., O.Ps., Battalion H.Qs., and Company Headquarters.

10. ACKNOWLEDGE.

Lieut., R.F.A.

Adjt., Spanbroek Group.

Copies to :-

1.	A/180	7.	16th. D.A.
2.	A/177	8.	Vierstraat Group
3.	C/180	9.	49th. Inf. Bde.
4.	C/177	10.	47th. Inf. Bde.
5.	B/180	11.	War Diary.
6.	D/180	12.	File.

W A R   D I A R Y

FOR   MONTH   OF   MARCH, 1917.

VOLUME 14

UNIT :- 180th Brigade R.F.A.

Vol. 14

Instructions regarding War Diaries and Intelligence Summaries are contained in F. S. Regs., Part II. and the Staff Manual respectively. Title Pages will be prepared in manuscript.

WAR DIARY
or
INTELLIGENCE SUMMARY
(Erase heading not required.)

Army Form C. 2118

180th Bde. R.F.A. No. 14.

Place	Date	Hour	Summary of Events and Information	Remarks and references to Appendices
Little KEMMEL	1 Mar		Brigade still in action in the SPANBROEK Sector	
	7/2	7pm	Minor enterprise attempted without success by 2nd Royal Irish Regt.	O.O. No 12.
	4.		Bombardment carried out between SPANBROEKMOLEN and PECKHAM. from 3.8 pm - 4.20 pm - a simulated raid.	16th D.A. O.O. 49
			Night firing carried out on affected parts of Enemy line from 6pm to 6am. - and on enemy lines of Communications	16th D.A.
			Lieut R.A. SAPCOTE struck off the strength on joining T.M. Battery	O.O. 51
	5th		Bombardment of enemy trenches South of Bull Ring. 7.18 am.	O.O. 50.
	5/6th	NIGHT	NIGHT FIRING. on parts of hostile trenches bombarded during the day and lines of communications	16th D.A. O.O. 51
	7th		2Lieut B.G. Lee. posted to B/180. from 2/16 T.M.B attery	
	8th		Hostile raids carried out ~~[illegible]~~ on various parts of the Divisional front. Special reports by O.C. Brigade & details of firing enclosed. 2Lieut A.B. LYTHGOE went to HOSPITAL	
	9.		No 36222 Gnr EMERSON. H.E. wounded (B/180)	
			Lieut C.E. RIDSDALE. joined from the Base & was posted to A/180.	
	10.		2Lieut P.J.W. STROUS. to A Battery. Lieut M.J. HUNTLEY to C/180. 2Lt G.B. LEE transferred to D/180. Lieut J.W. HEWITT transferred to B/180. Lieut C.E. RIDSDALE to 77th Army Bde R.F.A.	

1875 Wt. W593/826 1,000,000 4/15 J.B.C. & A. A.D.S.S./Forms/C. 2118.

Instructions regarding War Diaries and Intelligence Summaries are contained in F. S. Regs., Part II. and the Staff Manual respectively. Title Pages will be prepared in manuscript.

WAR DIARY
or
INTELLIGENCE SUMMARY
(Erase heading not required.)

Army Form C. 2118

180th Bde RFA No 14

Place	Date	Hour	Summary of Events and Information	Remarks and references to Appendices
Little KEMMEL	10.		No. 170447 Gnr. SHEPHERD H D/180. wounded in action	
			a/Major (Temp Lieut) A Mason ceased to command A/180. & was posted to 16th DAC. Temp Capt S BROWN joined A/180 from 16th DAC.	
	14		Lieut W.S. JONES (SR) RFA. joined D/180.	
	16		1 Section per Battery went out of action to Wagon Lines being relieved by Sections of the 173rd Bde	SPANISH OO No 13
	17		Relief of Brigade was completed by 12 midnight and Bde. Office opens at Billet NO 57 at WESTOUTRE	
WESTOUTRE	18		Bde at rest in Wagon Lines.	
	19.		Lieut G. H HINDS returned to the Brigade from the Base.	
			Training begun	
	22		180th Bde began the relief of the 190th Bde RFA in the Dispendaal Sector.	OO No 14.
LACLYTTE	23		Relief completed by 10.45pm.	
	24		Batteries registered. Help rendered to St ELOI Sp during hostile Raid mainly by D/180. Lieut R. ROBINSON joined D/180.	
	26.		Lieut J.B. CLAY RFA. joined Bde posted to D/180.	
			Lieut C.W. COCKRILL posted to C/180 RFA	

1875 Wt. W593/826 1,000,000 4/15 J.B.C. & A. A.D.S.S./Forms/C. 2118.

Instructions regarding War Diaries and Intelligence Summaries are contained in F. S. Regs., Part II. and the Staff Manual respectively. Title Pages will be prepared in manuscript.

WAR DIARY
or
INTELLIGENCE SUMMARY
(Erase heading not required.)

Army Form C. 2118

180th Bde RFA NO 74

Place	Date	Hour	Summary of Events and Information	Remarks and references to Appendices
LACLYTTE	27th		Lt H.S. BURBERY. joined from Y/16 T.M.B. posted to C/180.	
			Lieut A.Q.N. CLARK. posted to Y/16 T.M.B from C/180.	
			1 section of each Battery relieved by 77th Army F.A. Bde	
	28.		Relief completed. Batteries withdrawn to Wagon Lines	180th Bde O.O. No 15.
	29.		Battery Commanders reconnoitred various Magnum gun positions	
	30.		Reconnaissances completed.	

L Mackay Lt RFA
for O.C. 180th Bde R.F.A

1875 Wt. W593/826 1,000,000 4/15 J.B.C. & A. A.D.S.S./Forms/C. 2118.

COPY No. 10

SECRET.

SPANBROEK OPERATION ORDER No. 12.

by

Lieut-Colonel L. E. S. WARD, D. S. O., R. F. A.

1.3.17.

Ref. Map WYTSCHAETE Edition 4 a 1/10,000.

1. A minor enterprise id being carried out by a party of one Officer and 10 other ranks 2nd. ROYAL IRISH Regt. at N.36.a.55.75. on the night 1st. 2nd. March.

2. A table of battery tasks is attached.

3. Zero hour will be 7.0. p.m.

4. Watches will be synchronized at 6.30. p.m. under arrangements to be made by the Adjutant 180th. Bde. R.F.A.

5. After the completion of the bombardment table, batteries will stand by to render further assistance if required.

The signal for this action will be the code word "RESUME" sent from Group Headquarters.

On the receipt of this message batteries will re-open fire on the last tasks shown on the attached table (box barrag at a rate of fire of 2 rounds per gun per minute until further orders.

6. ACKNOWLEDGE.

D Wardlaw Lieut., R.F.A,

Adjt., SPANBROEK GROUP.

1. A/180
2. B/180
3. C/180
4. D/180
5. 49th. Inf. Bde.
6. 16th. D.A.
7. Vierstraat Group
8. 36th. D.A. Left Group.
9. War Diary
10. File. ✓

TABLE OF TASKS (continued)

Btty.	Time	Tasks	Rate of Fire.
D/180 2 guns.	Zero to Zero plus 2.	Enfilade NATHAN LANE from N.36.a.57.70 - N.36.b.05.78	BX 3 rounds per gun per minute
	Zero plus 2 to Zero plus 20.	1 Gun on Trench Junction at N.36.b.05.78. and 1 Gun on trench Junction at N.36.b.18.82.	30 rounds per gun.
4 guns.	Zero to Zero plus 20.	Communication Trench from N.36.a.78.32 - N.36.b.20.58.	36 rounds per gun.
D/177. 4 guns.	Zero to Zero plus 20.	Communication Trench from N.30.c.54.00 - N.36.a.96.93.	36 rounds per gun.
1 gun.	--do--	On SUNKEN ROAD N.30.c.95.08.	36 Rounds.
1 gun.	--do--	On Trench Junction at N.36.a.82.40.	36 rounds.

Ammunition 50% "A" 50% "AX" except where otherwise detailed.

-----------------oOo-----------------

TABLE OF TASKS.

Btty.	Time	Tasks	Rate of Fire
A/180.	Zero to Zero plus 5.	Barrage Hostile Front Line N.30.c.54.00 - N.36.a.58.70	4 rounds per gun per minute.
5 guns	Zero Plus 5½	Lift 50 yards.	
	Zero Plus 6½	Lift 50 yards.	2 rounds per gun
	Zero plus 7½	Lift to Hostile Support Line N.30.c.96.00 - N.36.b.10.70.	per minute.
	Zero plus 8 to Zero plus 15	Barrage Hostile Support Line N.30.c.96.00 - N.36.b.10.70.	2 rounds per gun per minute.
	Zero plus 15 to Zero plus 20	--do-- --do--	3 rounds per gun per minute.
1 gun (Lone gun)	Zero to Zero plus 20.	Enfilade Hostile Communication Trench from N.36.a.72.56 - N.36.a.92.60	40 rounds "A".
C/180	Zero to Zero plus 5.	Barrage Hostile Front Line N.36.a.58.70 - N.36.a.60.46.	4 rounds per gun per minute.
	ZERO plus 5½	Lift 50 yards.	
	Zero plus 6½	Lift 50 yards.	2 rounds per gun per minute
	Zero plus 7½	Lift to Hostile Support Trench From N.36.b.10.70 - N.36.b.25.40.	
	Zero plus 8 to Zero plus 15.	Barrage Hostile Support Line N.36.b.10.70 - N.36.b.25.40	2 rounds per gun per minute
	Zero plus 15 to Zero Plus 20.	-----do-----	3 rounds per gun per minute.
B/180			
2 guns.	Zero to zero plus 5.	Barrage Hostile Front Line N.36.a.60.46.-N.36.a.80.30	4 rounds per gun per minute.
2 guns.	--do--	Barrage Hostile Front Line N.30.c.41.38 - N.30.c.20.54	
2 guns Det,Sect.	eedo--	Enfilade Hostile Front Line from N.30.c.54.00 - N.30.c.26.52.	
	Zero plus 5 to Zero plus 15	As above	2 rounds per gun per minute
	Zero plus 15 to Zero plus 20.	As above	3 rounds per gun per minute.

SECRET
******

Copy No...2......

16th DIVISIONAL ARTILLERY

OPERATION ORDER No. 47.

Ref. 1/10,000 Trench Map
WYTSCHAETE Edn.4.A.

25th Feb. 1917.

1. 16th Divisional Artillery will carry out a bombardment in conjunction with H.A., IX Corps and Medium and Light Trench Mortars on 27th inst.

2. Object, to induce the enemy to man his trenches to inflict loss, and damage material.

3. ZERO hour will be 3.8 p.m.

4. O.C. SPANBROEK Group will arrange with G.O.C., 49th Infantry Brigade for the clearing of any trenches that may be necessary.

5. Watches will be synchronised by comparison at:

   SPANBROEK Group Hdqrs. at 1.0 p.m.
   VIERSTRAAT Group Hdqrs.at 12.30 p.m.
   H.A., IX Corps at 12.0 noon.

6. Bombardment Table is attached.

7. ACKNOWLEDGE.

[signature] Major, R.A.
Brigade Major, 16th Divl.Arty.

Issued at 4.30 p.m.

Copies to:-

1 to 5. SPANBROEK Group.	21. No. 5 Balloon Coy.
6 to 8. VIERSTRAAT Group.	22. No. 53 Sqdn, R.F.C.
9 to 11. 36th Divl.Arty.	23. D.T.M.O.,16th Div.
12 to 14. H.A., IX Corps.	24. 16th Div. Signals.
15. 16th Division.	25. C.R.A.
16. 47th Inf. Bde.	26. Bde Major, 16 D.A.
17. 48th Inf. Bde.	27. Staff Capt.,16 D.A.
18. 49th Inf. Bde.	28. War Diary.
19. 41st Div. Arty.	29.) File.
20. R.A., IX Corps.	30.)

SECRET
******

(0047)

18-pdrs. BOMBARDMENT TABLE February 27th, 1917.

Battery	Time	Task	Rates of Fire Rnds per gun per min.	Ammunition 50% AX	Remarks
VIERSTRAAT Gp.					
3 - 18-pdr.Battes.	Zero to 0 plus 5 mins.	(a) N.30.a.50.50.to N.30.a.30.13.	4	280	Ammunition calculate on 14 guns per Group
- do -	Plus 5 to plus 9 Plus 9 to plus 15	(b) Lifts at 50 yards per minute to line of NAPLES SUPPORT from N.30.a.95.40 to N.30.a.70.00 and stands.	3 2	168 168.	
- do -	Plus 15 to plus 18	(c) Drop to Front Trench as in (a)	4	168	
- do -	Plus 18 to plus 38	PAUSE.			Overhaul & sponge ou
- do -	Plus 38 to plus 43	(d) NAPLES RESERVE from N.30.b.70.72 to N.30.b.20.30.	3	210	
- do -	Plus 43 to plus 1 hour 30 mins.	(e) NAP AVENUE, NAPLES AVENUE (West of NAPLES SUPPORT)	Bursts of fire at irregular intervals of time	300	100 rnds per Battery.
SPANBROEK Gp.					
3 - 18-pdr.Battes.	Zero to 0 plus 5 mins.	(a) N.30.a.30.13 to N.30.c.10.75.	4	280	
- do -	Plus 5 to plus 9 Plus 9 to plus 15	(b) Lifts at 50 yards per minute to line of NARROW SUPPORT from N.30.a.70.00 to N.30.c.35.67 and stands.	3 2	168 168	
- do -	Plus 15 to plus 18	(c) Drop to front trench as in (a)	4	168	
- do -	Plus 18 to plus 38.	PAUSE			Overhaul & sponge ou
- do -	Plus 38 to plus 43.	(d) NAPLES & NARROW RESERVE from N.30.b.20.30 to N.30.d.05.72.	3	210	
2 - 18-pdr.Battes	Plus 43 to plus 1 hour 30 mins.	(e) NAPLES DRIVE East & West of NAPLES RESERVE.	Bursts of fire at irregular intervals of time.	2 300	100 rnds per Batty.
				2588	

SECRET
******

(O.O.47)

HOWITZERS

BOMBARDMENT TABLE February 27th, 1917.

Battery	Time	T a s k	Rates of Fire	Ammunition	Remarks
VIERSTRAAT Gp. 1 - 4.5 How.Batty.	Zero till ammunition allotted is expended.	Trench junctions and dugouts: 1 N.30.a.96.98. (One section) 2 N.30.b.06.75. - do - 3 N.30.a.90.52. - do -	Deliberate	650	
SPANBROEK Gp. 1 - 4.5 How.Batty.	- do -	Trench junctions and dugouts: 4 N.30.a.70.02. (One section) 5 N.30.c.40.80. (Two sections)	- do -	650 1300.	
H.A., IX CORPS 6" Howitzers.	- do -	Trench Junctions and dugouts: 6 0.25.b.88.24. 0.25.a.42.60. 9 7 0.19.c.00.10. N.30.b.20.25. 10 8 N.30.b.05.12. 11 Trench, Track, and Tramline junctions and dugouts N.30.d.01.87. 12 Trench & dugouts N.30.a.71.03.	- do -	500	
9.2 Howitzers.	- do -	13 Dump on Tramline from 0.20.c.25.20 to 0.20.c.18.45. 14 Works 0.26.a.81.65 to 90.55. 15 " PICK HOUSE 0.26.a.41.51.	- do -	150	

TABLE OF TASKS.

Battery.	Index Number of Task	Task.
	(a)	5 guns N.30.a.30.13. - N.30.a.16.00. Lone Gun Enfilades N.30.a.27.06. - N.30.a.17.00.
	(b)	5 guns N.30.a.70.00 - N.30.c.53.89. Lone gun Enfilades N.30.c.40.82 - N.30.c.66.92.
A/180	(c)	as in (a)
	(d)	5 guns N.30.b.20.30. - N.30.b.06.18. Lone Gun Enfilades N.30.b.20.30. - N.30.b.00.10.
	(e)	A/180 does not participate in this task.
	(a)	N.30.a.16.00 - N.30.c.06.88
	(b)	N.30.c.57.90. - N.30.c.40.82.
C/180	(c)	as in (a)
	(d)	N.30.b.06.18. - N.30.d.00.90.
	(e)	Enfilades NAPLES DRIVE from front line to NARROW RESERVE - N.30.a.47.30. - N.30.b.00.10.
	(a)	4 guns N.30.c.06.88 - N.30.c.10.75. Detached Section Enfilades N.30.c.07.92. - N.30.c.10.75.
	(b)	4 guns N.30.c.40.82. - N.30.c.35.67. Detached Section N.30.c.35.68. - N.30.c.40.82.
B/180	(c)	as in (a)
	(d)	4 guns N.30.d.00.90. - N.30.d.05.72. Det.Sect. N.30.d.00.86. - N.30.b.00.10.
	(e)	4 Guns enfilade N.30.b.00.10. - N.30.b.50.03.
D/180		Tasks etc. as shown in D.A. Operation Order.

AMMUNITION 18-pdr Ammunition alloted will be shared equally among the batteries.

S E C R E T.

180th. Bde. R.F.A. No. S.F/33/3

O.C. A/180
B/180
C/180
D/180

Reference Tables of Night Firing issued under this Office No. S.F./33/2 dated 28.2.17.

Herewith 16th. D.A., O.O. No.51.

Please Note

(1) The Howitzers (D/180) detailed in S.F/33/2 are not to take part.

(2) Following corrections ;-

A/180 - task (1) for Night of 4/5th.March should read N.30.d.33.57. not N.30.d.27.58

B/180 - task (2) for Night of 5/6th.March should read N.36.b.90.73 not N.30.b.90.73.

ACKNOWLEDGE.

A Macka[illegible] Lieut., R.F.A.

3.2.17. Adjt., 180th. Brigade R.F.A.

S E C R E T
****

Copy No.....5......

16th DIVISIONAL ARTILLERY
OPERATION ORDER No. 51.

Ref. 1/10,000 WYTSCHAETE & PLOEGSTEERT Maps. Edn.4.A.

3rd March 1917.

1. Night firing will be carried out by 18-pdr. Batteries between 6.0 p.m. and 6.0 a.m. on the nights of the 4th/5th and 5th/6th March in accordance with the attached programme.

2. The rates of fire will be:-

6.0 p.m. to 10.0 p.m.	30	rounds per Battery per hour.
10.0 p.m. to 4.0 a.m.	20	" " " " "
4.0 a.m. to 6.0 a.m.	25	" " " " "

These should be fired in single rounds with occasional section or battery salvoes at irregular intervals spread over the whole period.

3. ACKNOWLEDGE.

Issued at 4 pm

R.A. Spencer
a/ Major, R.A.,
Brigade Major, 16th Divl. Arty.

Copies to:-

1 to 5. SPANBROEK Group.
6 to 8. VIERSTRAAT Group.
9. 36th Divl. Arty.
10. H.A., IX Corps.
11. 16th Division.
12. 47th Inf. Bde.
13. 48th Inf. Bde.
14. 49th Inf. Bde.
15. 41st Div. Arty.
16. R.A., IX Corps.
17. No. 5 Balloon Coy.
18. No. 53 Sqdn., R.F.C.
19. D.T.M.O., 16th Div.
20. 16th Div. Signals.
21. C.R.A., 16th Div.
22. Bde Major, 16th D.A.
23. Staff Capt., 16thD.A.
24. War Diary.
25) 26) File.

SECRET
******

(0.0.51)

TASKS FOR NIGHT 4th/5th MARCH.

VIERSTRAAT Group.

A/177.	Railway from 0.19.c.45.66 to 0.20.c.20.35.
B/177.	Dump & Railway in 0.20.a.25.05 to 0.19.b.90.48.
C/177	Road from 0.19.d.65.98 to 0.20.d.40.42.

SPANBROEK Group.

A/180	(1)	TRAMWAY	N.30.d.00.87 - N.30.d.[33.57].
	(2)	TRAMWAY	N.30.b.50.30 - 0.25.c.00.97.
	(3)	NAPLES DRIVE	N.30.b.40.05 - N.30.d.80.78.
	(4)	RATION DUMP	N.30.b.05.72.
B/180	(1)	NARROW SUPPORT	N.30.c.40.82 - N.30.a.70.00.
	(2)	TRAMWAY	N.30.c.60.70 - N.30.d.00.86.
	(3)	NAPLES DRIVE	N.30.a.70.17 - N.30.b.40.05.
	(4)	BATTN. H.Q. (HOP POINT)	N.30.d.90.65.
C/180	(1)	TRAMWAY	N.30.a.90.70 - N.30.b.34.72.
	(2)	TRAMWAY	0.25.c.02.98 - to SCOTT FARM.
	(3)	MAP AVENUE	N.24.d.74.09 - 0.19.c.40.00.
	(4)	TRENCH	N.30.d.63.70 - 0.25.c.15.55.

TASKS FOR NIGHT 5th/6th MARCH.

VIERSTRAAT Group.

A/177	RAILWAY	N.24.b.80.00 to 0.19.d.35.98.
B/177	ROAD	N.30.d.90.90 to 0.19.d.35.70.
C/177	RAILWAY	0.13.c.50.70 to 0.19.b.40.00.

SPANBROEK Group.

A/180	(1)	TRAMWAY	N.30.d.00.08 - N.36.b.42.66.
	(2)	TRENCH	N.36.a.95.95 - N.36.b.[27].34.
	(3)	RATION DUMP	N.30.b.05.72.
B/180	(1)	TRAMWAY	N.36.b.00.35 - N.36.b.50.56.
	(2)	NATHAN ALLEY	N.36.b.40.72 - N.(36).b.90.73.
	(3)	TRAMWAY	N.36.b.43.66 - to L'ENFER WOOD.
C/180	(1)	TRAMWAY	N.36.b.43.66 - 0.31.a.50.18.
	(2)	NATHAN RESERVE	N.36.b.25.40 - N.36.b.70.00.
	(3)	C. TRENCH	N.36.b.57.60 - 0.31.a.60.50.

S E C R E T
****

16th D.A. No. R.2708/38. 3rd Mar.1917

Reference 16th Div. Arty. O.O. No. 50 dated 3rd March, 1917.

Delete the last three lines of para. 6 and substitute:-

"The H.A., IX Corps will commence the bombardment on "B" day at ZERO minus 3 minutes and not at ZERO as shown "in the table for "B" day."

H.H. [signature] Major, R.A.,
Brigade Major, 16th Div. Arty.

(Copies to recipients of O.O. No. 50 dated 3/3/17.)

S E C R E T
****

Copt No. 3

16th DIVISIONAL ARTILLERY

OPERATION ORDER No.50.

Ref. 1/10,000 WYTSCHAETE and
PLOEGSTEERT Maps, Edn. 4.A.

3rd March 1917.

1. 16th Divisional Artillery will carry out bombardments in conjunction with H.A., IX Corps on the 4th and 5th March.
These days are known as "A" and "B" days respectively.

36th Div. Artillery have arranged to assist on "B" day.

2. Object.

(a) Destruction of enemy trenches and strong points on 16th Division Front.

(b) To inflict loss on the enemy.

(c) To carry out demonstrations of an actual creeping barrage for the benefit of the troops in the line.

(d) To practice the Field Artillery in Barrages and lifts.

3. ZERO hour on March 4th ("A" day) 3.8 p.m.
ZERO hour on March 5th ("B" day) 7.18 a.m.

4. Clearing of trenches

O.C., SPANBROEK Group will arrange with G.O.C., 47th Infantry Brigade for the clearing of any trenches that may be necessary.

5. Synchronization.

On "A" day. Watches will be synchronized by comparison at:-

SPANBROEK Group Hdqrs. at 12.0 noon
VIERSTRAAT " " " 12.30 p.m.
H.A., IX Corps Hdqrs. " 1.0 p.m.

On "B" day. By telephone from 16th Div. Arty Hdqrs. at 4.0 a.m. with:
SPANBROEK Group Headquarters.
VIERSTRAAT " "
36th Div. Arty. Headquarters.
H.A., IX Corps "

6. Bombardment Tables for "A" day have been issued to all concerned with 16th Div. Arty. O.O. No. 47 dated 25th February 1917.
Bombardment Tables for "B" day are attached.

P.T.O.

The H.A., IX Corps will commence the bombardments at ZERO minus 3 minutes and not at ZERO as shown in the Tables.

7. ACKNOWLEDGE.

H.H. Jill.
Major, R.A.,

Issued at noon Brigade Major, 16th Divl.Arty.

Copies to:-

1 to 5 SPANBROEK Group.
6 to 8. VIERSTRAAT Group.
9 to 11. 36th Divl. Arty.
12 to 14. H.A., IX Corps.
15. 16th Division.
16. 47th Inf. Bde.
17. 48th Inf. Bde.
18. 49th Inf. Bde.
19. 41st Div. Arty.
20) R.A., IX Corps.
22. No. 5 Balloon Coy.
22. No. 53 Sqdn., R.F.C.
23. D.T.MO., 16th Divn.
24. 16th Div. Signals.
25. C.R.A.
26. Bde Major, 16 D.A.
27. Staff Capt., 16 D.A.
28. War Diary.
29.) File.
30.)

S E C R E T (0.0.50)
****

BOMBARDMENT TABLE "B" DAY.

18-pdrs.

Battery	Time	T a s k	Rates of Fire	Ammunition 50% AX	Remarks
36th Div. Arty.					
1 - 18-pdr.Batty.	0 to 0 plus 8 mins.	Enfilade NUTMEG AVENUE	2	96	
- do -	- do -	Enfilade NATHAN LANE	2	96	
SPANBROEK Group.					
1 - 18-pdr.Batty.	0 to 0 plus 8 mins.	Enfilade NATHAN ALLEY from N.36.b.39.72 to N.36.b.90.73.	2	96	
B	Plus 8 to plus 1 hr. 20 mins.)	- ditto -	(Bursts of Fire (at irregular (intervals.	200	
1 - 18-pdr.Batty.	0 to 0 plus 8 mins.	(a) Enfilade C.T. from N.36.b.57.60. to 0.31.a.15.48.	2	96	
	0 plus 8 to 0 plus 30 mins.	(b) PAUSE	-		
C	0 plus 30 to 0 plus 50 mins.	(c) NUTMEG RESERVE from N.36.b.60.07 to NUTMEG AVENUE.	2	240	
	0 plus 50 to 0 plus) 1 hr. 1 min.	PAUSE	-		
	0 plus 1 hr.1 min. to) 0 plus 1 hr.6 mins.	(d) Lift at 50 yards a minute to line N.36.b.57.60 - 0.31.a.00.48.	3	90	
	0 plus 1 hr.6 mins.to) 0 plus 1 hr.9 mins.	(e) Lift at 50 yards a minute to line N.36.b.90.73 - 0.31.a.10.70.	3	54	
				968	

SECRET (0.0.50)
******

18-pdrs. (Contd)

BOMBARDMENT TABLE "B" DAY (Contd)

Battery	Time	Task	Rates of Fire	Ammunition 50% AX	Remarks
SPANBROEK Group. Contd.				968	
1 -18-pdr.Batty.	0 to 0 plus 3 mins.	(a) Enfilade NUTMEG RESERVE from N.36.b.24.40 to N.36.b.60.07.	2	36	
	0 plus 3 to 0 plus 8.	(b) Enfilade front trench from N.36.a.78.30 to N.36.b.05.07.	4	120	
	0 plus 8 to 0 plus 30 mins.)	PAUSE	-		
	0 plus 30 to 0 plus 50.	(c) Enfilade NUTMEG RESERVE as in (a)	2	240	
	0 plus 50 to 0 plus 1 hr. 1 min.)	PAUSE	-		
	0 plus 1 hr.1 min.to 0 plus 1 hr.6 mins.)	(d) Lift at 50 yards a minute to line N.36.b.40.72 - 53.72 - 72.62.	3	90	
	0 plus 1 hr.6 mins.to 0 plus 1 hr.9 mins.)	(e) Lift at 50 yards a minute to line N.36.b.72.82 - N.36.b.90.73.	3	54	
VIERSTRAAT Group.					
1 -18-pdr.Batty.	0 to 0 plus 3 mins.	(a) Enfilade NATHAN RESERVE from N.36.b.03.79 to N.36.b.24.40.	2	36	
	0 plus 3 to 0 plus 8 mins.)	(b) Enfilade front trench from N.36.b.05.07 to N.36.d.30.72.	4	120	
	0 plus 8 mins. to 0 plus 30 mins.)	PAUSE	-		
	0 plus 30 to 0 plus 50	(c) Enfilade NATHAN RESERVE as in (a)	2	240	
	0 plus 50 to 0 plus 1 hr. 1 min.)	PAUSE.	-		
	0 plus 1 hr.1 min.to 0 plus 1 hr.6 mins.)	(d) Lift at 50 yards a minute to line N.36.b.15.95. - N.36.b.40.72.	3	90	
	0 plus 1 hr.6 mins.to 0 plus 1 hr.9 mins.)	(e) Lift at 50 yards a minute to line N.36.b.60.97 - N.36.b.72.82.	3	54	
			TOTAL ..	2048.	

SECRET (O.O.50)

BOMBARDMENT TABLE "B" DAY (Contd)

HOWITZERS

Battery	Time	Task	Rates of Fire	Ammn.	Remarks
SPANBROEK Group. 1 -4.5"How.Batty.	Zero until ammunition allotted expended	(1) SYBIL and SATAN (2 guns) (2) T.J. N.36.d.82.62 (1 gun) (3) Trench, tram & road junctions O.31.central (2 guns) (4) O.31.b.42.40.	To be ordered by Battery Commander.	650	
VIERSTRAAT Group. 1 -4.5"How.Batty.	- do -	(5) T.M. emplacement N.30.c.50.55 (2 guns) (6) Trench N.36.a.96.92 to N.36.b.22.82 (4 guns)	- do -	650	
			TOTAL ..	1300	
H.A., IX CORPS 6" Hows.	- do -	(7) Work at N.36.b.70.90 (BONE POINT) (8) Trench & dugouts O.25.c.10.80 to O.25.c.15.4647.	To be ordered by Battery Commander.	500	
9.2" Hows.	- do -	(9) PETIT PUITS (O.26.a.20.20). (10) Work at O.32.a.58.60.	- do -	150	
Heavy T.M. DUCHESS	- do -	(11) Trench Mortar SIDNEY.	- do -	15	

SPANBROEK GROUP
DATE 8th MARCH 1917

8/3266
8/3/17

4 P.M. 7.3.17.
to
4 P.M. 8.3.17.

OUR FIRE

BATTERY	TIME	NO. OF ROUNDS		OBJECTIVE.	REASON FOR FIRING.	REMARKS.
D/180	4.19 P.M.		16 BX.	"SYBIL" AND "SIDNEY."	PUNISHMENT FOR HOSTILE T.M'S.	
	4.35 P.M.		12 BX.	"SYBIL" AND "SIDNEY"	" " " " "	
	10.43 A.M.		20 BX.	N30c 73.78	BY ORDER OF C.B. GROUP	
	2.42 P.M.		30 BX.	"KK."		
	3.39 P.M.		12 BX.	STRAFE "A" ("D" BTY TARGET.)	PUNISHMENT FOR HOSTILE T.M'S.	
	3.45 P.M.		10 BX.	STRAFE "A" " " "	" " " " "	
	3.50 P.M.		36 BX	CONCENTRATION "C"	ORDERED BY "GROUP".	
	4.0 P.M.		36 BX.	" " "C"	" " " "	
C/180.	3.32 P.M.	4 A.	4 AX.	S.O.S. LINES.	PUNISHMENT:	REQUEST OF INFANTRY.
	3.35 P.M.	4 A.	4 AX.	S.O.S. LINES.	" "	
	3.40 P.M.	4 A.	4 AX.	S.O.S. LINES.	" "	
	3.50 P.M.	27 A.	27 AX.	CONCENTRATION "C"	ORDERED BY "GROUP"	
	4.0 P.M.	27 A.	27 AX.	" " " "C"	" " " " "	
A/180	6.40 P.M.		1 AX.	S.O.S. LINES.	TEST FROM "INFANTRY" REGISTRATION.	
	3.20 P.M.	13 A	7 AX.	S.O.S "	ORDERED BY "GROUP"	
	3.50 P.M. / 4.0 P.M.	28 A	63 AX	CONCENTRATION "C". / " " " "C"	" " " " "	
B/180.	2.20 to 4.50 P.M.	120 A.		N30c 11.60.	IN ACCORDANCE WITH "INSTRUCTIONS"	
	3.50 P.M. to 6.35 P.M.	591 A.	197 AX.	N30c 95.28 to N30d 01.63 N36a 10.94 to N36a 12.31 N36a 62.54 - N36a 60.72 N36a 65.91 - N30c 65.22 N30c 35.50 - N30c 10.63	CONCENTRATION "C" S.O.S. LINES LEFT ATTACK ORDERED BY GROUP.	

[illegible signature]
Lt. Col.
SPANBROEK GROUP.

SPANBROEK GROUP

DATE 9 MARCH 1917

4 P.M 8.3.17 to 4 P.M 9.3.17

X3283 9/3/17.

OUR FIRE.

BATTERY	TIME		NO. OF ROUNDS.	OBJECTIVE	REASON FOR FIRING	REMARKS.
D/180.	4.16 P.M.	8/3/17	428 BX.	S.O.S. LINES.	ORDERED BY "GROUP"	
	3.26 P.M.		96 BX	HELP F.F.S.		
	6.3 P.M.		42 BX	HELP F.F.S.		
	12.35 AM.	9/3/17	20 BX	CONCENTRATION "C" "D" BTY. TARGET		
	4.18 AM.		210 BX	S.O.S. LINES.		
	10.37 AM.		30 BX	K 4.	ORDERED BY C.B. GROUP.	
	12.3 P.M.		30 BX	O 27a 40.85.		

[signature] LT. COL. R.F.A.

O.C. SPANBROEK GROUP.

SPANBROEK GROUP.

DATE 9th MARCH 1917

4 P.M. 8.3.17.
to
4 A.M. 9.3.17.

OUR FIRE.

BATTERY.	TIME.	NO. OF ROUNDS.	OBJECTIVE.	REASON FOR FIRING	REMARKS.
B/180 (DET. SECT.)	3.50 P.M.	18 AX.	CONCENTRATION "C".	ORDERED BY GROUP	
	4.0 P.M.	18 AX.	" " " "C".	" " "	
	4.15 P.M. to 6.50 P.M.	297 A	N36a 15.98 to N36a 90.16.	ORDERED BY GROUP.	
	4.29 AM to 4.58 AM	56 A 18 AX.	N36a 53.85 to N30a 48.28.		
B/180.	12.8 AM.	16 AX	N36a 10.99 to N36a 13.31.	" " "	
	4.20 AM to 5.0	97 A. 67 AX	N36a 62.48 to N36a 56.66		
C/180.	4.30 P.M. to 6.30 P.M.	519 A. 237 AX	S.O.S. LINES HOSTILE FRONT LINE FROM PECKHAM TO SPANBROEK MOLEN "HELP F.F.S."	" " "	
	4.20 to 4.50 AM	62 A. 60 AX	S.O.S. LINES.	" " "	
	10.56 AM.	1 A.	N30c 10.72.	"TEST TRENCH" N29.1. ORDERED BY F.M.6.	
A/180.	4.15 P.M. to 6.35 P.M.	458 A. 250 AX	N30a 60.85 to N24c 70.15 S.O.S. LINES HELP F.F.S.	ORDERED BY GROUP.	
	7.59 P.M. to 4.3[illegible] AM	132 A 114 AX	S.O.S. LINES.	REQUEST OF INFANTRY & ORDERED BY GROUP.	

VIERSTRAAT GROUP.
SPANBROEK GROUP.
D.T.M.O.

16th D.A.No. Q/760 dated 9-3-17.

The following telegram has been received from 16th Division, begins;-

"Army Commander wishes his appreciation and congratulation to be conveyed to Group Commanders and all ranks Artillery and Trench Mortar Batteries aaa To these I add my own thanks

GENERAL HICKIE "

G.O.C.R.A. wishes this to be communicated to all ranks coupled with his own thanks.

[signature] Captain, R.A.,
Staff Captain, 16th Divisional Artillery.

SECRET.

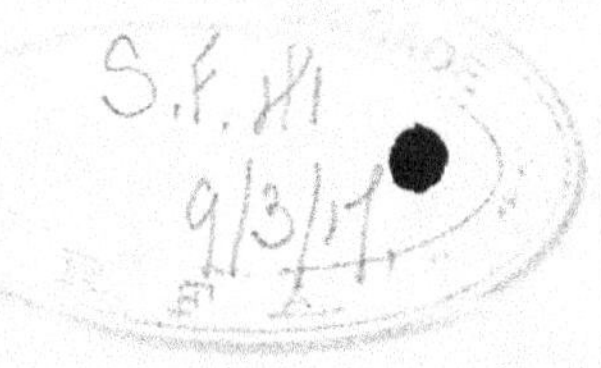

REPORT ON HOSTILE RAID
ON NIGHT 8/9th.MARCH.

Throughout the night the enemy maintained bursts of fire on our front line system.

About 4.10. a.m. 9th. March a heavy hostile barrage developed on the front DURHAM ROAD - PICCADILLY.

At 4.22. a.m. the S.O.S. call was received from Right Battalion H.Q. and repeated. All batteries came into action on their S.O.S. lines at S.O.S. rates, our fire reaching its full development within 4 minutes of the receipt of the S.O.S. messages.

About 15 minutes after the commencement of fire, rates of expenditure were slowed down to one round per gun per minute.

"STOP" firing was given at 4.48 p.m. reports that all was quiet having been received from both Liaison Officers.

Left Group 36th. Divisional Artillery again assisted.

The enemy failed in his objective, leaving prisoners in our hands and dead in front of our trenches.

L P Steward. Lt-Col., R.F.A.

9.3.17. Commdg. SPANBROEK GROUP.

S.F.40 9/3/17

REPORT ON HOSTILE ATTACKS IN THE SPANBROEK SECTOR ON AFTERNOON MARCH 8th. 1917.

Ref. Maps. WYTSCHAETE edition 4 a (our trenches) 1/10,000.
WYTSCHAETE " " " --- 1/10,000.

GENERAL NARRATIVE.

In the early stages of the operation the enemy bombardment appeared to be in the nature of retaliation for previous attacks on our part.

Between 3.30. p.m. and 3.40. p.m. batteries carried out punishment fire according to normal procedure.

At 3.45. p.m. as the hostile fire continued I ordered a concentrated punishment bombardment by the Group (Concentration "C" SPANBROEK DEFENCE SCHEME). Concentration "C" was repeated again at 4.0. p.m.

As the reports from O.Ps and Artillery Liaison Officers evidenced the continuance and increase of hostile fire and observation reports during the morning had established the forward movement of bodies of hostile infantry, I considered that an enemy attack was possibly in contemplation, and therefore, at 4.12. p.m. I ordered all batteries of the Group into action on S.O.S. lines barraging the hostile front trenches at a steady rate of fire and awaited developments.

About 4.40. p.m. reports from all sources indicated that the main scene of operations was from PECKHAM northwards along the front of the 48th. Infantry Brigade. I decided to strengthen my barrage about PECKHAM and north of it and directed a general switching of batteries to this effect. At the same time, I requested the Left Group 36th. Div. Arty. which was already assisting in accordance with the "MUTUAL SUPPORT" arrangements at a slow rate of fire, to take over the front of B/180 as far as N.30.b.52.00 with an additional battery. My request was promptly complied with.

At 5.15. p.m. the code call "HELP F.F.5" was received from the VIERSTRAAT GROUP and complied with.

At 5.32. p.m. on instructions from B.G., R.A. 16th. Division I ordered A/180 to barrage from N.24.d.20.[illegible] to N.24.b.20.21.

At 5.45. p.m. as the situation appeared to be much easier generally I ordered all batteries to stop firing, informing Left Group 36th. Div. Arty. at the same time.

At 5.54. p.m. information was received that the enemy was massing at MAEDELSTEDE FARM. The Group was again brought into action on the "HELP F.F.5" targets - B/180 taking over frontage of C/180 and the Left Group 36th. Div. Arty. taking over the frontage of B/180.

At 5.58. p.m. I ordered A/180 to concentrate all 5 guns on MAEDELSTEDE FARM and fire for three minutes at the rate of 3 rounds per gun per minute. From this onwards all batteries fired at a slow rate of fire (1 round per gun per minute).

At 6.30. p.m. the order "STOP" and resume normal Night Lines was given to all concerned

HOSTILE ARTILLERY FIRE.

The enemy commenced a bombardment of our first line system of defences about 3.30. p.m. March 8th. This bombardment first affected our Right subsector, from DURHAM ROAD to THE BULL RING but gradually extended northwards until the entire front held by the 47th and 48th Infantry Brigades was involved.

The enemy employed Trench Mortars, 77 mm. Guns and 10.5 cm. Howitzers to commence with.

About 4.0. p.m. the intensity of the hostile fire decreased, but at 4.30. p.m. a very heavy barrage and general bombardment was observed on the VIERSTRAAT Sector, while the hostile fire on the SPANBROEK Sector again became intense. The hostile fire continued till about 5.15. p.m. when it became feeble and finally died away.

There is no evidence from Artillery observation Officers that 15 cm. Howitzers were employed by the enemy. I made a personal examination of part of the trenches of our Left subsector, which was the most heavily shelled. THE VIA GELLIA especially offered good data for forming a judgement.
I did not see any damage which might not have been caused by 10.5. cm. Howitzers.

I attach a report by Major A.K. DIGBY, D.S.O. who was observing the hostile fire from his O.P.

OUR FIRE.

All reports indicate that our fire was good and accurate. The Shrapnel barrages appear to have been effective with low bursts as the predominating feature.

COMMUNICATIONS.

S.O.S. lines between companies and batteries were all cut. As these are not buried lines they are particularly vulnerable in such an intense bombardment as was experienced on this occasion. All Group communications worked admirably and I was in close touch throughout the operation with LIAISON OFFICERS at both Battalion Headquarters.

CONCLUSION.

I desire to place on record my high appreciation of the prompt and valuable assistance rendered by the Left G Group 36th, Divisional Artillery.

Further I desire to bring to the favourable notice of the Brigadier General Commanding R.A., 16th. Division the name of 2nd. Lieut. A.L. PERRY, A/180, who as an observing Officer gave valuable, timely and accurate information.

I attach a precis of orders etc. emanating from the Group H.Q. as an indication of the general features of the action. The times shown therein can be considered as substantially correct.

Lt-Col., R.F.A.

9.3.17. Comdg. SPANBROEK GROUP.

PRECIS of ORDERS etc.

emanating from SPANBROEK GROUP HDQRS.

in connection with a hostile raid on 8.3.17.

3.30. p.m. Heavy bombardment (10.5 cm. 77 mm. and T.Ms) on the whole Group front - most intense on the Sector N.24.c - N.30.a. Batteries retaliated and reported to Group Hdqrs.

3.43. p.m. Concentration "C" (NARROW RESERVE - Area N.30.central) ordered for Zero time 3.50. p.m. All Batteries and Detached Section of B/180 in action. 3 minutes at rate of 3 rounds per gun per minute.

3.55. p.m. Batteries ordered to repeat "Concentration C"; at Zero time 4.0. p.m.; rates and duration as before.

4.5. p.m.) 4.10. p.m.) Continuation of heavy bombardment reported from O.Ps and LIAISON OFFICERS. Divisional Artillery informed.

4.12. p.m.) 4.16. p.m.) Batteries including Detached Section B/180 ordered into action on S.O.S. lines at rate of 1½ rounds per gun per minute . Assistance of Left Group 36th. D.A. on their "HELP F.F.8" lines requested and granted.

4.30. p.m. Observer at F.4. (A/180) reported a steady barrage put down along the front from N.18.a. to N.30.c. Similar report received from Observer at K.18(C/180)

4.40. p.m. Lone Gun A/180 ordered into action on its NIGHT LINE - N.30.a.47.70.

4.45. p.m. Observer at F.4. (A/180) reported Green Rockets fired from the whole of PETIT BOIS and WYTSCHAETE WOOD and from WYTSCHAET itself. Following this signal barrage slackened except on the front PECKHAM to PETIT BOIS where it became more intense

4.48. p.m. Left Group 36th. D.A. requested to put on another battery and take over the zone of B/180.

4.50. p.m. B/180 ordered to take over the zone of C/180 and C/180 to switch to cover the Sector SPANBROEK MOLEN. - PECKHAM.

4.51. p.m. D/180 ordered to switch one Howitzer on to PECKHAM - this in addition to the two already firing on that area (normal NIGHT LINES of Nos 5 and 6 guns.)

5.13. p.m. Code Call "HELP F.F.5" from VIERSTRAAT GROUP received and sent to A/180, C/180 and D/180. Rate of fire; 2 rounds per gun per minute. F.4. reported Red Rockets seen just north of our Group Front at 5.12. p.m. and hostile barrage lifted 300 yards.

5.32. p.m. A/180 ordered to switch to front of PETIT BOIS N.24.d.20.80 - N.24.b.20.21.

5.35. p.m.) 5.40. p.m.) Rates of fire slackened to 1 round per gun per minute.

5.45. p.m. Order "STOP" sent to Left Group 36th. D.A. and all batteries.

5.54. p.m. Information from VIERSTRAAT GROUP that enemy was massing at MAEDELSTEDE FARM.

5.55. p.m. A. C. and D/180 ordered into action on their "HELP F.F.S" lines - B/180 taking over C/180's front and Left Group 38th. D.A. taking over B/180's front. Rate of fire one round per gun per minute.

5.58. p.m. A/180 ordered to concentrate all 5 guns on MAEDELSTEDE FARM at the rate of 3 rounds per gun per minute, to be followed by 2 rounds per gun per minute.

6.0. p.m. Detached Section ordered into action on their S.O.S. lines one round per gun per minute - considerable artillery activity on front of Right Company Right Battn. reported.

6.13. p.m.)
6.20. p.m.) Fire slackened; all 18-pdr. batteries reduced to one round per gun per two minutes. D/180 (How) ordered to stop. Enemy fire now reported feeble.

6.30. p.m. Order "STOP" received from VIERSTRAAT GROUP. Sent to all concerned.

<u>N O T E S.</u>

4.40. p.m.)
5.0. p.m.) 77 mm. guns shelled the area DAYLIGHT CORNER and B/180's position without doing any damage. A few rounds fell near C/180's position.

About 5.p.m. Dump was seen to explode near MIDDLE FARM.

5.45. p.m. Gun flashes observed on T.B. 87° and 101° from K.19.

-----------oOo-----------

Report by MAJOR A.K. DIGBY, D.S.O.

Observing Officer at K.18.

Reference your telephone message,

M.A.768.

I was on duty at O.P. during to-day's operations. At about 3.30. p.m. the enemy started bombarding with T.Ms on the Right of our Divisional Front and gradually crept further to the left.

Their chief objective appeared to be S.P.7 and S.P.6 and ULSTER ROAD.

About 3.32. p.m. I called on C/180 for retaliation which was given - but the enemy Straffe, seeming too heavy for one battery to compete with I called up SPANBROEK GROUP and asked for a "Straffe" or concentration. This was given twice - "CONCENTRATION C" being ordered on both occasions.

The second concentration was at about 4.0. p.m. After this the Group ordered the battery to fire on its Night Lines at a rate of 1½ rounds per gun per minute. This went on till about 5 p.m. when the Group ordered a switch by sections to the line PECKHAM SPANBROEKMOLEN at the same rate. "[illegible] F.F.5" 2 rounds per gun per minute was ordered by Group at 5.15. p.m. This was kept up until the end of the operations.

HOSTILE FIRE.

The enemy put up at first a very heavy T.M. barrage on the whole of the Right Battalion Front - special attention being paid to ULSTER ROAD, DURHAM ROAD and S.P.7. 10.5 cm 7.7 cm. shells were also used in this barrage. This barrage decreased after 4.0. p.m. and about 4.30. p.m. the barrage, though not stopped, was lighter.

About 4.30. p.m. the barrage on the VIERSTRAAT GROUP front became very heavy. A good many 7.7 cm shrapnel shells were fired well behind our lines- some falling about the battery positionof B/180 and DAYLIGHT CORNER and some about C/180 position - no harm being done. The enemy's fire kept up till about 6.15. p.m. when it became very feeble.

OUR FIRE.

The barrages appeared to be quite good - most of the time shrapnel bursting low or on graze.

A Dump was seen to explode near MIDDLE FARM. 4 Germans were seen running to support trench opposite to PECKHAM about 5.p.m.

Our T.M. retaliation appeared very good on the front of the Right Battalion - but could not be very well observed in the VIERSTRAAT GROUP front from K.18.

(sd) A.K. Digby., Major.
Commanding. C/180.

S E C R E T.   47th Inf. Bde. No. G. 1609.

Headquarters

16th Division.

REPORT ON HOSTILE OPERATIONS ON THE EVENING of 8th AND THE MORNING OF 9th MARCH, 1917.

1. On the evening of 8th March and the morning of 9th March, 1917, the enemy carried out operations on the front held by my Brigade, which consisted of a series of heavy bombardments combined with several attempts against our trenches by parties from 40 to 130 strong. Another attack against the Brigade on my left closely concerned the Battalion holding the Left Subsection of my front and in consequence will be briefly dealt with in this report.

2. In order to more clearly define the scope of the operations it is necessary to deal with them under two headings:-

Evening 8th March.
Morning 9th March.

3. Operations on the evening of 8th March.

At 3.30 p.m. the enemy opened a heavy bombardment on our front and support lines from DURHAM ROAD to the BULL RING with 77 mms, 10.5 cm and Trench Mortars this extending gradually northwards until the whole Brigade Front was involved. At 4 p.m. there was a perceptible diminution of the hostile fire, but at 4.30 p.m. it again became intense especially so on the left Company front of the Left Battalion (6th Connaught Rangers). At about 5 p.m. a party of the enemy about 50 strong endeavoured to advance against our trenches at about N.24.1. but met by a heavy fire from our Lewis Guns and rifles they returned in disorder to their own line. At the same time a stronger party forced their way into the front of the Brigade on the left. The Left Company Commander of the 6th Connaught Rangers summing up the situation dispatched a party of bombers who in a counter attack forced their way along and 20 yards beyond BROADWAY and materially assisted in the subsequent ejection of the enemy. Meanwhile the O.C. Left Support Company had formed a defensive flank along VIA GELLIA and manned S.P.11 with its emergency garrison.
As the enemy entered from the front of the Brigade on our left they came under a heavy cross fire from our rifles, Vickers and Lewis Guns and had to find their way through our artillery barrage which had been concentrated on this point at the moment that the attack developed and which inflicted considerable casualties on them. At 6.30 p.m. the situation became normal.

4. Morning of 9th

4. Morning of 9th March.

(a) Right Subsection.

Throughout the night of 8/9th March the enemy continuously shelled our front but the suspicions of the O.C. Right Subsection (7th Leinster Regt) being especially aroused by the apparent deliberate hostile attempts to cut wire in front of S.P's 6 & 7, he made dispositions in anticipation of an attempt by the enemy in the neighbourhood of KINGSWAY.
At about 4 a.m. on the morning of March 9th the hostile bombardment reopened on the entire Brigade Front and at 4.25 a.m. a body of the enemy estimated at about 130 attacked our line between the BULL RING and KINGSWAY, met by a heavy fire from our rifles, Lewis Guns and Machine Guns and also by bombs they retreated leaving two unwounded prisoners of the 181st Regt. in our hands and a considerable number of dead and dying in NO MAN'S LAND. At no point in this Subsection did the enemy enter our line except as prisoners.

(b) Left Subsection.

At about 4 a.m. a party of the enemy believed to have been about 50 in number crept down on the North side of the GLORY HOLE under cover of some trees and the bombardment and captured 10 men of the 6th Connaught Rangers, of these 7 formed a Lewis Gun post and 3 a bombing post. They consisted of a young corporal and 9 men of the last draft.
The Lewis Gun is missing.
The enemy were not observed till on their way back to their own line, a Lewis Gun further to the North that should have fired jammed at the critical moment.

5. Artillery.

I cannot speak too highly of the able manner in which the SPANBROEK GROUP dealt with the situation. The response to the S.O.S Signal in every case was prompt and effective and the manner in which the fire was concentrated on the threatened point on the evening of 8th March was most satisfactory.

6. Machine Guns.

(a) 49th Machine Gun Company.

In the case of both operations the guns came into action within a few moments of the S.O.S. Signal being sent up.
On the first occasion 14 guns were in action immediately and the two reserve guns were in position and firing within the short period of 23 minutes.
All guns stood to during the night and thus the entire 16 were able to open fire together on the following morning. 81,000 rounds were fired in all.

(b) 47th Machine Gun

(b) 47th Machine Gun Company.

This Company was not called upon for assistance until the morning although all teams stood to on the evening of 8th March, in some cases under a heavy fire. The officer Commanding in cooperation with the O.C. 7th Leinster Regt. made dispositions during the night to cover S.P's 6 and 7.
On the S.O.S. being sent up all 12 guns in the line opened fire instantaneously and with excellent effect. 32,000 rounds were fired.
Both Machine Gun Companies displayed promptness and and efficiency and the troops in the line testify to the assistance they afforded.

7. Casualties.

I regret to have to report the following casualties:-

	Killed.	Died.	Wounded.	Missing.	Missing believed Killed.	Total.
1st R.Muns.Fus.	-	-	8	-	-	8
6th Conn.Rangers.	8	1	38	10		57
7th Leinster Regt.	@ 9	1	21	-	1	32
47th M.Gun Coy.	-	-	1	-	-	1
49th do.	-	-	4	-	-	4
49th T.M.Battery.	-	-	-	-	1	1
						103.

@ Includes 1 Officer.

8. Damage to Trenches.

(a) Left Subsection.

Front line is passable except for 60 - 70 yards at the GLORY HOLE which are demolished save for a short piece in the centre, at the western end there is a very large crater.

(b) Right Subsection.

Owing to excellent work by 7th Leinster Regt., Front line is now passable as far as BOWLES LANE but the shelters between REDAN AVENUE and KINGSWAY have suffered considerably. ULSTER ROAD has 4 direct hits in it between DEAD MAN'S FARM and KINGSWAY. Damage to S.P.7 is not serious. Main communication trenches are very little damaged and are quite passable.

9. General Remarks.

I would point out that in my opinion the bombardment that the troops in the line underwent was, with the possible exception of the SOMME, the worst this Brigade has ever been subjected to.

The officers

The officers displayed great power of initiative
and the N.C.Os and men keenness for the fray.
The only regrettable incident was the capture of the post
of the men. Owing to the heavy bombardment it is
probable that they did not keep proper lookout and
were rushed before they had time to offer resistance.

E Pereira Brigadier General,

9-3-17. Commanding 47th Infantry Brigade.

S E C R E T. Copy No. 7

SPANBROEK OPERATION ORDER No. 13.

by

Lieut-Colonel L. H. G. WARD D.S.O., R.F.A., Commanding.

13.3.17.

1. The Spanbroek Group will be relieved by the Right Group, 36th. Divisional Artillery.
The relief to be completed by 9.0. a.m. 18th. instant.

2. Reliefs will be carried out as follows ;-

On the night of the 16th/17th one section from each Battery will withdraw to its Wagon Lines as soon as relieved by a section of 36th. Divisional Artillery.
On the night 17th/18th the remaining two sections of each Battery will withdraw to their Wagon Lines as soon as relieved by two remaining sections of each 36th Divisional Artillery Battery.

3. Guns will not be handed over, but aiming posts will be left in position.

4. Ammunition in Gun-pits will be handed over to 36th. Divisional Artillery at 12 noon on 17th. March.
Amounts handed over will be reported to this Office by 12.30. p.m. on the 17th
A certificate detailing the amount of ammunition handed over, and signed by both Battery Commanders or their representatives will be rendered to this office by 4.30.pm.
After noon 17th. March the 36th. Divisional Artillery will be responsible for the supply of ammunition to the Gun-Line of SPANBROEK GROUP.

5. Reliefs will not take place before 7.0. p.m.

6. All registers, defence schemes, map boards, photographs log-books, panorama sketches etc., and all information con-cerning the front will be handed over to incoming batteries in accordance with G.H.Q. Artillery Circular No.2. Other Trench Maps will not be handed over. "B.A.B" Code Books will not be handed over.

7. An Officer, two telephonists, and one linesman will be attached to each Battery of Spanbroek Group from 15th. March until relief is complete.

8. Command will pass on the night of 17th/18th March as soon as the relief has been completed.

9. Completion of reliefs will be reported to Group Hdqrs. by means of the code word "SATISFACTORY".

10. Certificates for all trench stores in duplicate will be made out and handed over at the Gun-Line signed by both Battery Commanders, or their representatives. A duplicate will be rendered to 180th. Bde. Hdqrs. as soon as possible.

11. ACKNOWLEDGE.

for J Miller Lieut., R.F.A.
Adjt., 180th. Brigade R.F.A.

A/180 16th. Div.Arty.
B/180 War Diary
D/180 File.

Reference SPANBROEK O.O. No.13.

Para No. 10 should read

Certificates for all Trench Stores handed over at the Gun-Line will be made out in duplicate and signed by both Battery Commanders or their representatives. A duplicate will be rendered to 180th. Bde. Hdqrs. as soon as possible.

Lieut., R.F.A.

13.3.17. Adjt., SPANBROEK GROUP.

SECRET.   Copy No. ___

180th. Brigade R.F.A. OPERATION ORDER No.14.
by
Lieut-Colonel L. H. S. WARD, D.S.O., R.F.A., Commanding.

Reference 16th. Div. Arty. O.O. No. 56.

Ref. Map. WYTSCHAETE Edition 4 a 1/10,000.

1. The 180th. Brigade R.F.A. 16th. Divisional Artillery will relieve the 190th. Brigade R.F.A. 41st Divisional Arty. on the nights of 22nd/23rd. 23rd/24th March, 1917, in accordance with attached table.
Reliefs to be completed by 12 midnight on the night 23rd/24th. March.

2. One Section from each Battery will relieve the first night and the remainder of the Battery the second night. No movement will take place near battery positions before 7.0. p.m. Batteries will take their own guns into action.

3. All Air Photos, Defence Schemes, Artillery Boards, Log Books O.Ps. etc., will be taken over from 41st Divisional Batteries in accordance with G.H.Q. Artillery circular No.2.

4. Details of Reliefs will be arranged between Group and Battery Commanders concerned.

5. An advanced party of 1 Officer and as many telephonists and linesmen as are considered necessary from Brigade Hdqrs. and from Batteries of 180th. Bde. R.F.A. will be attached to the Group Headquarters and Batteries of 41st Division for 48 hours before relief is completed, and will take two days' rations with them.

6. All ammunition left in Gun-pits by 41st Div. Arty. will be taken over by Batteries of 16th. Division Arty. at 12 noon 23rd. March and receipts given. Amounts taken over will be reported to this Office by wire.

7. Command will pass on night of 23rd/24th March on completion of relief.

8. Completion of reliefs will be reported to Group Artillery Headquarters by wire.

9. ACKNOWLEDGE.

E. A. Walker
Lieut., R.F.A.

20.3.17.   for Adjt., 180th. Brigade R.F.A.

Copies to :-

16th. Divisional Arty.
A/180   C/180
B/180   D/180

SECRET.   Copy No. ●

180th. Brigade R.F.A. OPERATION ORDER No.14.
by
Lieut-Colonel L. E. S. WARD, D.S.O., R.F.A., Commanding.

Reference 16th. Div. Arty. O.O. No. 56.

Ref. Map. WYTSCHAETE Edition 4 a 1/10,000.

1. The 180th. Brigade R.F.A. 16th. Divisional Artillery will relieve the 190th. Brigade R.F.A. 41st Divisional Arty. on the nights of 22nd/23rd. 23rd/24th March, 1917, in accordance with attached table.
Reliefs to be completed by 12 midnight on the night 23rd/24th. March.

2. One Section from each Battery will relieve the first night and the remainder of the Battery the second night. No movement will take place near battery positions before 7.0. p.m. Batteries will take their own guns into action.

3. All Air Photos, Defence Schemes, Artillery Boards, Log Books O.Ps. etc., will be taken over from 41st Divisional Batteries in accordance with G.H.Q. Artillery circular No.2.

4. Details of Reliefs will be arranged between Group and Battery Commanders concerned.

5. An advanced party of 1 Officer and as many telephonists and linesmen as are considered necessary from Brigade Hdqrs. and from Batteries of 180th. Bde. R.F.A. will be attached to the Group Headquarters and Batteries of 41st Division for 48 hours before relief is completed, and will take two days' rations with them.

6. All ammunition left in Gun-pits by 41st Div. Arty. will be taken over by Batteries of 16th. Division Arty. at 12 noon 23rd. March and receipts given. Amounts taken over will be reported to this Office by wire.

7. Command will pass on night of 23rd/24th March on completion of relief.

8. Completion of reliefs will be reported to Group Artillery Headquarters by wire.

9. ACKNOWLEDGE.

E.W. Walker
2Lieut., R.F.A.

20.3.17.   for Adjt., 180th. Brigade R.F.A.

Copies to ;-

16th. Divisional Arty.
A/180   C/180
B/180   D/180

SECRET.

RELIEF TABLE.

NIGHT 22nd/23rd March.

Unit.	Relieves	Position.
A/180 (1 Sect.)	34th. Batty. (1 Sect.)	N.15.b.05.95.
B/180 (1 Sect.)	A/190 (1 Sect.)	N.4.b.4.2.
C/180 (1 Sect.)	C/190 (1 Sect.)	N.16.a.30.80.
D/180 (1 Sect.)	D/190 (1 Sect.)	N.4.c.90.80.

NIGHT 23rd/24th March.

Unit	Relieves.	Position.
A/180 (2 Sects.)	34th. Batty. (2 Sects.)	N.15.b.05.95.
B/180 (1 Sect.) (1 Sect.)	A/190 (1 Sect.) (1 Sect.)	N.4.d.30.95. N.4.d.20.40.
C/180 (2 Sects.)	C/190 (2 Sects.)	N.16.a.30.80.
D/180 (1 Sect.) (1 Sect.)	D/190 (1 Sect.) (1 Sect.)	N.4.c.90.80. N.16.b.45.30.

Hdqrs. 190th. Brigade R.F.A. are at N.7.c.00.90.

SECRET.

RELIEF TABLE.

NIGHT 22nd/23rd March.

Unit.	Relieves	Position.
A/180 (1 Sect.)	34th. Batty. (1 Sect.)	N.15.b.05.95.
B/180 (1 Sect.)	A/190 (1 Sect.)	N.4.b.4.2.
C/180 (1 Sect.)	C/190 (1 Sect.)	N.16.a.30.80.
D/180 (1 Sect.)	D/190 (1 Sect.)	N.4.c.90.80.

NIGHT 23rd/24th March.

Unit	Relieves.	Position.
A/180 (2 Sects.)	34th. Batty. (2 Sects.)	N.15.b.05.95.
B/180 (1 Sect.) (1 Sect.)	A/190 (1 Sect.) (1 Sect.)	N.4.d.30.95. N.4.d.20.40.
C/180 (2 Sects.)	C/190 (2 Sects.)	N.16.a.30.80.
D/180 (1 Sect.) (1 Sect.)	D/190 (1 Sect.) (1 Sect.)	N.4.c.90.80. N.16.b.45.30.

Hdqrs. 190th. Brigade R.F.A. are at N.7.c.00.90.

S E C R E T

(O.O.56)

R E L I E F   T A B L E

NIGHT 22nd/23rd March.			NIGHT 23rd/24th March.		
Unit	Relieves	Position	Unit	Relieves	Position
A/180 (1 Sect)	34th Batty.(1 Sect)	N.15.b.05.95.	A/180 (2 Sects)	34th Batty (2 Sects)	N.15.b.05.95.
B/180 (1 Sect)	A/190 (1 Sect)	N.4.b.4.2.	B/180 (1 Sect.) (1 Sect.)	A/190 (1 Sect) (1 Sect)	N.4.d.30.95. N.4.d.20.40.
C/180 (1 Sect)	C/190 (1 Sect)	N.16.a.30.80.	C/180 (2 Sects)	C/190 (2 Sects)	N.16.a.30.80.
D/180 (1 Sect)	D/190 (1 Sect)	N.4.c.90.80.	D/180 (1 Sect.) (1 Sect.)	D/190 (1 Sect) (1 Sect)	N.4.c.90.80. N.16.b.45.30.

Hdqrs. 190th Brigade, R.F.A. are at N.7.c.00.90.

S E C R E T. Copy No. 5

180th. BDE. OPERATION ORDER No.15.

by

Lieut-Colonel L. E. S. WARD, D.S.O., R.F.A., Commanding.

Ref. 1/10,000 Map WYTSCHAETE & KEMMEL 27.3.17.
28. S.W. 1 & 2. Edn. 4 a.

1. The 180th. Bde. R.F.A. will be relieved in action by the 77th. Army F.A. Bde. in the DIEPENDAAL SECTOR on the nights 27th/28th and 28th/29th March, in accordance with the attached Tables.

2. One Section from each Battery will be relieved the first night and the remainder of the Battery the second night. No movement will take place East of LA CLYTTE - LOCRE Road before 8.0. p.m. Guns will not be handed over, but aiming posts will be left in position.

3. All registers, defence scheme, map boards, air photographs, log-books, panoramas, O.Ps and all information concerning the front will be handed over to incoming units, in accordance with G.H.Q. Artillery Circular No.2. Trench Maps will be handed over. B.A.B. Code Books will not be handed over.

4. Details of relief will be arranged between Group and Battery Commanders concerned.

5. An advanced party of 1 Officer, 2 telephonists, and 1 linesman from Brigade Hdqrs. and from Batteries 77th. Army F.A. Bgde. will be attached to Brigade Hdqrs. and Batteries 180th. Brigade R.F.A., and will take one day's rations with them.

6. Ammunition in Gun-pits will be handed over to Batteries 77th. Army F.A. Brigade and receipts obtained.

7. Command will pass on the night 28th/29th March on completion of releif.

8. Completion of releif will be reported to Group Headquarters by means of the code word "SATISFACTORY".

9. Certificates for all Trench Stores handed over at the Gun-Line will be made out in duplicate and signed by both Battery Commanders or their representatives. A duplicate will be rendered to 180th. Bgde. Hdqrs. as soon as possible.

10. ACKNOWLEDGE.

[signature] Lieut., R.F.A.

Adjt., 180th. Brigade R.F.A.

Copies to ;-

COPY No 1 O.C. A/180 COPY No 3 O.C. C/180
" " 2 B/180 " " 4 D/180
" " 5 FILE ✓

S E C R E T. (O.O.15.)

R E L I E F   T A B L E

NIGHT 27th/28th March

Unit	From	To
A/180 1 Sect.	N.15.b.05.95.	Wagon Lines.
B/180 1 Sect.	N.4. b.40.20.	--do--
C/180 1 Sect.	N.16.a.40.75.	--do--
D/180 1 Sect.	N.4. c.90.80.	--do--
A/77 1 Sect.	Wagon Lines.	N.15.b.05.95.
B/77 1 Sect.	--do--	N.4. b.40.20.
C/77 1 Sect.	--do--	N.16.a.40.75.
D/77 1 Sect.	--do--	N.4. c.90.80.

NIGHT 28th/29th March.

Unit	From	To
A/180 2 Sect.	N.15.b.05.95.	Wagon Lines.
B/180 1 Sect. 1 Sect.	N.4. b.40.20. N.4. d.23.43.	--do-- --do--
C/180 2 Sect.	N.16.a.40.75.	--do--
D/180 1 Sect. 1 Sect.	N.4. c.90.80. N.16.b.45.30.	--do-- --do--
A/77 2 Sect.	Wagon Lines.	N.15.b.05.95.
B/77 1 Sect. 1 Sect.	--do-- --do--	N.4. b.40.20. N.4. d.23.43.
C/77 2 Sect.	--do--	N.16.a.40.75.
D/77 1 Sect. 1 Sect.	--do-- --do--	N.4. c.90.80. N.16.b.45.30.
Hdqrs.180th. Bde.	N.7.c.35.55.	N.9.c.88.32.
Hdqrs. 77th Army F.A. Bde.	N.9.c.88.32.	N.7.c.35.55.

WAR DIARY FOR MONTH OF APRIL, 1917.

VOLUME:- 15

UNIT:- 180th Brigade R.G.A.

Vol/15

Instructions regarding War Diaries and Intelligence Summaries are contained in F. S. Regs., Part II. and the Staff Manual respectively. Title Pages will be prepared in manuscript.

WAR DIARY No 15.
or
~~INTELLIGENCE~~ SUMMARY
(Erase heading not required.)

180 Bde. RFA.

Army Form C. 2118

Place	Date	Hour	Summary of Events and Information	Remarks and references to Appendices
WESTOUTRE	1/4/17		Batteries still in wagon lines near WESTOUTRE	
"	2/4/17		Batteries went into position, but not into action, covering VIERSTRAAT sector.	
			2/Lt R.A. Smith, B/180 Bde RFA. admitted to hospital.	
"	3/4/17		Heavy snowstorm prevented batteries registering for O.O. No 16.	
"	4/4/17		2/Lt G.H. Hinds, A/180 returned to duty from hospital.	
"	5/4/17	8.45pm	Raid carried out by 6th Royal Irish Regiment at MAEDELSTEDE FARM. 180th Bde RFA co-operated in the artillery support. Successful. 21 prisoners taken	O.O. N° 16
"	6/4/17		Brigade marched to GODEWAERSVELDE from wagon lines. Billeted for the night at GODEWAERSVELDE. General March orders attached.	~~Bde Order No 180~~ O.O. No 17
"	7.4.17		Brigade marched to WARDRECQUES. Billet for the night at WARDRECQUES	Bde Order No 180
	8.4.17		Brigade marched to AFFRINGUES and NIELLES-LEZ-BLEQUIN area. Bde H.Q. at NIELLES-LEZ BLEQUIN	Bde Order No 185
NIELLES-LEZ-BLEQUIN	9.4.17		Brigade commenced training. Programme attached.	
"	10.4.17		~~Brigade march~~ Major P.J.B. Hedas RFA joined the Brigade and took over command of A/180. Capt S. Brown A/180 posted to 16th D.A.C. 2/Lt R.A. Smith, B/180, evacuated to England.	
"	21.4.17		Brigade marched to WARDRECQUES. and billeted there for the night.	Brigade Order No 260
	22.4.17		Brigade marched to GODEWAERSVELDE and billeted there for the night	Brigade Order No 268

1875 Wt. W593/826 1,000,000 4/15 J.B.C. & A. A.D.S.S./Forms/C. 2118.

Instructions regarding War Diaries and Intelligence Summaries are contained in F. S. Regs., Part II. and the Staff Manual respectively. Title Pages will be prepared in manuscript.

WAR DIARY No 15
or
~~INTELLIGENCE SUMMARY~~
(Erase heading not required.)

180th Bde RFA

Army Form C. 2118

Place	Date	Hour	Summary of Events and Information	Remarks and references to Appendices
GODEWAERS-VELDE	23.4.17		Gas appeared at GODEWAERSVELDE about 6.30 am Origin not known. Many men slightly sick. Brigade marched to wagon lines on Mont VIDAIGNE. Bde H.Q. at LOCRE.	
LOCRE	24.4.17		Following to hospital gassed :- 31425 Sgt CHURCH. H., 1844 FARR. SGT. PHILLIPS W.G. 42964 S/S COLES F., 36166 DR. ATTAWAY J.G., 79929 DR SEAVERS J.W.	
"	25.4.17		A/180 and D/180 went into reinforcing positions covering VIERSTRAAT SECTOR. Brigade is supplying daily 200 men for constructing M.O. positions.	
"	28.4.17		2/Lt E.H. Walker, HQ, 180 Bde, admitted to hospital.	
"	29.4.17		Brigade began preparation of new wagon lines at Mont VIDAIGNE.	
"	30.4.17		Brigade began relief of the 88th Bde RFA in the DIEPENDAAL Sector, tonight A & B relieving a section each, and C & D two sections.	
"	"		2/Lt J.R.D. MARTIN, B/180 returned to duty from hospital.	
"	"		2/Lt B.H. LANE RFA, joined the Brigade and was posted to C/180.	

L. E. S. Ward
Lt Col. RFA
Commanding 180th Bde RFA

1875 Wt. W593/826 1,000,000 4/15 J.B.C. & A. A.D.S.S./Forms/C. 2118.

S E C R E T
-:-:-:-:-:-

Copy No. 10

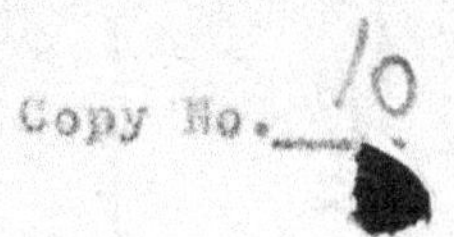

180th. BRIGADE OPERATION ORDER No.A.1.

by

Major N. A. STEBBING, D.S.O., R.F.A., Comdg.

Ref. Map WYTSCHAETE, 1/10,000 Trench Map.

1. The Batteries of 180th. Brigade R.F.A. will relieve their opposite numbers of the 88th. Brigade R.F.A. between the hours of 4.0. p.m. and 8.0. p.m. 19th. June, by Sections, batteries of the 88th. Brigade R.F.A. similarly relieving batteries of the 180th. Brigade R.F.A. (personnel only).
A/88th. Battery will remain in action and come under the orders of the 180th. Brigade R.F.A.

2. All guns and gunestores, but not Battery H.Q. Stores and instruments will be exchanged under arrangements to be made bewteen Battery Commanders.

3. All guns of both Brigades will be in action during the reliefs

4. In cases where Batteries of the 180th. Brigade R.F.A. take over less than 6 guns or howitzers, they will take over guns or howitzers to complete from their present positions in action.

5. At 8.0. p.m. 19th. June, 180th. Brigade will take over the defence of the front of the present Left Group 19th. Divisional Artillery with S.O.S. lines 600 yards beyond our Infantry Front line. The 88th. Brigade R.F.A. less A/88 Battery will then withdraw to their Wagon Lines with 180th. Brigade Guns.

6. Battery Zones for S.O.S. purposes will be as follows ;-

A/88 Battery	O.17.c.50.30.	-	O.17.c.46.90.
B/180 "	O.17.c.46.90.	-	O.17.a.42.50.
C/180 "	O.17.a.42.50.	-	O.11.c.38.10.
D/180 "	O.17.c.50.30.	-	O.11.c.38.10.

7. The 177th. Brigade R.F.A. are taking over the defence of the Right Group Front and are detailing a Senior Liaison Officer to take over Liaison duty with the 57th. Infantry Brigade at 8.0. p.m.

8. B/180 will detail a Liaison Officer to take over at the Left Battalion H.Q. near DENNIS FARM at 7.0. p.m.
The present Liaison Officers, Senior and Junior, will not leave until the Brigade or Battalion Commanders move out in relief.

9. No movement of horses or vehicles East of the KEMMEL - VIERSTRAAT - BRASSERIE Road will take place befoer 9.0. p.m. or after 4.0. a.m.

SECRET. Copy No. 6

180th. BRIGADE OPERATION ORDER No. 19.

Ref. 1/10,000 Trench Map.
Edn. 5 a. 1/20,000 Sheet 28.

---

1. 180th. Brigade R.F.A. will relieve the 88th. Brigade R.F.A. in the line on the nights 30th APril/1st. May and 1st/2nd May in accordance with the attached relief table.
   49th. Infantry Brigade is relieving 56th. Infantry Brigade in the DIEPENDAAL Sector on the night of May 1st/2nd.

2. Ammunition will be taken over from 88th. Brigade R.F.A. in the new positions.
   Ammunition of the 180th. Brigade R.F.A. now in the line will be withdrawn. Boxed ammunition will be withdrawn by D.A.C.
   180th. Brigade R.F.A. will account to the 16th. Divisional Artillery Hdqrs., for Ammunition from Noon May 1st.
   A statement of all ammunition taken over, countersigned by outgoing Battery Commanders, showing natures, will be forwarded to this office.

3. Guns will not be exchanged.

4. 180th. Brigade R.F.A. will take over all Defence Schemes, Schemes for work on positions etc., M.O. documents, Battery Boards, Local Maps, photographs, panoramas, and all information concerning the front.

5. Instructions as to work on M.O. positions will be issued separately.

6. Command of DIEPENDAAL Group will pass to O.C. 180th. Bde. R.F.A. on completion of reliefs.

7. It is desirable that reliefs shall be carried out in such a way that ingoing Batteries can register their night lines before assuming the responsibility for the defence of the line. With this object verbal instructions have been issued to Battery Commanders to effect a daylight relief if weather and visibility conditions justify it. The final decision on this point will be given by the Lieut-Colonel Commanding who accepts all responsibility.

8. Fatigue parties for M.O. (16th. Division) positions are meanwhile cancelled.

9. Orders about Wagon Lines will be issued later.

10. ACKNOWLEDGE.

[signature] Lieut., R.F.A.

29.4.17. Adjt., 180th. Brigade R.F.A.

Copies to ;-
A/180 C/180
B/180 D/180
16th. D.A. War Diary.

O.O. No.19.

RELIEF TABLE.

16th. D.A.	To Relieve	Position.	Apl. 30/May 1st.	May 1st/2nd.
A/180	A/88	(6 guns (N.16.a.4.8.	2 Guns	4 Guns.
B/180	B/88	(6 guns (N.9.d.0.0.	2 guns	4 guns.
C/180	C/88	(4 guns (N.4.b.4.2.	2 guns	2 guns.
		(2 guns (N.4.d.2.4.	2 guns.	----
D/180	D/88	(4 guns (N.4.c.9.8.	2 guns	2 guns
		(2 guns (N.16.b.4.3.	2 guns	----
Hdqrs. 180th. Bde.	Hdqrs. 88th. Bde	LA CLYTTE.		Under arrangements with Hdqrs. 88th. Bde. R.F.A.

SECRET. Copy No. 7

180th. Brigade, OPERATION ORDER No.16.

by

Lieut-Colonel L. E. S. WARD, D.S.O., R.F.A., Commanding.

Ref. Maps Sheet 28 S.W. Edn. 4. 1/20,000.
WYTSCHAETE Edn. 4. 1/10,000.

1. A raid will be carried out on the enemy's front and support trenches in N.24.c. & d. viz. N.24.c.85.35. to N.24.d.20.65. and N.24.d.05.32 to N.24.d.30.48 on a date to be notified later.

2. The raid will be supported by the 16th. Divisional Artillery assisted by : IX Corps Heavy Artillery.
SPANBROEK GROUP, 36th. Divl. Arty.
DIEPENDAAL GROUP, (77th. Army F.A. Brigade)
87th. Brigade R.F.A. 19th. Divl. Arty.

3. The 180th. Brigade R.F.A. will move into the following positions on the night 2nd/3rd April.

A/180 N.9.b.40.67
B/180 N.10.c.90.05.
C/180 N.16.a.50.27.
D/180 N.9.b.37.27.

The Brigade will be withdrawn on completion of the operation.

4. There will be preliminary bombardments on the two days previous to the raid and also on the day of the raid.
These days are known as X, Y, & Z days respectively, Z day being the day on which the raid will take place.
Zero time for the preliminary bombardments will be at 5.30.pm on X, Y, & Z days.
180th. Bde. R.F.A. has no tasks in the preliminary bombardments.

5. Barrage tables for the raid are attached.

6. Batteries will register on the days 3rd and 4th April. No more rounds than are absolutely necessary should be fired in the area to be raided, in order not to attract the enemy's attention.

7. During Y & Z days accommodation for Officers and other ranks remaining with the guns at night is allotted as follows ;-
A & D batteries Farm at N.9.a.50.60.
B & C " " " N.9.a.70.00.

8. Zero hour and instructions for comparison and synchronisation of watches will be issued later.

9. ACKNOWLEDGE.

Lieut., R.F.A.

31.3.17. Adjt., 180th. Brigade R.F.A.

Copies to ;-

16th. D.A.
O.C. A/180
B/180
C/180
D/180
File.

War Diary

BARRAGE TABLE

Btty.	Time	Objective		Rate of fire	Amm.
A/180					
2 Guns	0 to 0 plus 1	50 yds short of front line trench from N.24.c.99.57. to N.24.d.20.63.	(B)	4 rnds per gun per min.	96
4 Guns	0 to 0 plus 1	Front Line Trench from N.24.c.99.57 - N.24.d.20.63			
6 Guns	0 plus 1 to 0 plus 4	Front Line trench from N.24.c.99.57 - N.24.d.20.63			
6 Guns	0 plus 4 to 0 plus 6	Support Trench from N.24.d.30.47 - N.24.d.00.38		3 rnds per gun per min.	36
6 Guns	0 plus 6 onwards	Trench from N.24.d.67.28 - N.24.d.54.48		1½ rnds per gun per min.	1035
B/180					
2 Guns	0 to 0 plus 1	50 yds short of front line trench from N.24.c.83.38. to N.24.c.99.57.	(C)	4 rnds per gun per min.	96
4 Guns	0 to 0 plus 1	Front Line trench N.24.c.83.38 - N.24.c.99.57			
6 Guns	0 plus 1 to plus 4	----do----			
6 Guns	0 plus 4 to 0 plus 6	Support trench from N.24.d.00.38 - N.24.c.99.19		3 rnds per gun per min	36
6 Guns	0 plus 6 onwards	Trench from N.24.d.36.28. to N.24.d.13.07		1½ rnds per gun per min.	1035
C/180					
2 Guns	0 to 0 plus 1	50 yds short of front line trenchffrom N.24.c.62.05. to N.24.c.88.14.	(E)	4 rnds per gun per min.	96
4 Guns	0 to 0 plus 1	Front Line trench from N.24.c.62.05 - N.24.c.88.14			
6 Guns	0 plus 1 to 0 plus 4	---do---			
6 Guns	0 plus 4 to 0 plus 6	Support trench from N.30.a.97.99 - N.30.a.72.93		3 rnds per gun per min.	36
6 Guns	0 plus 6 onwards	Trench from N.30.a.91.95. to N.30.a.65.82.		1½ rnds per gun per min.	1035.

B A R R A G E   T A B L E   (continued)

Btty	Time	Objective	Rate of fire	Ammn.
D/180				
1 Gun	0 to 0 plus 5	Trench junct. N.24.b.55.01	2 rnds per gun per min.	60
1 Gun		" " N.24.d.52.68		
1 Gun		" " N.24.d.53.48		
1 Gun		" " N.24.d.30.99		
1 Gun		" " N.24.d.47.99		
1 Gun		" " N.24.b.55.11.		
	0 plus 5 onwards	as above	1 rnd per gun per min.	330

S E C R E T.

180th. Bde. R.F.A. No. S.F.64.

Reference 180th. Bde. O.O. No.16. dated 31.3.17.

1. "Z" day will be the 5th. April, 1917. "X" and "Y" days will be 3rd and 4th April, respectively.

2. The Artillery Liaison Officer with O.C. Enterprise will be Capt. D.M. McALLISTER, D/177th. Brigade R.F.A.

3. Watches will be synchronised on 5th. April at VIERSTRAAT Group Headquarters at 11.0. a.m. and 20. p.m.
An Officer from each Battery of the 180th. Brigade R.F.A. will be at VIERSTRAAT Group Headqrs. with two watches at the above times.

4. Lieut-Colonel L. H. S. WARD, D.S.O., R.F.A., will be in command of VIERSTRAAT Group and of 180th. Bde. R.F.A. for the operation.

5. The signal that all parties are back in our trenches and for fire to slacken will be a Gold and Silver Rain Rocket.
Red and Green Rockets will also be fired previously to the above Rockets as a signal for the raiders to withdraw.

6. The Zero hour for the raid will be 8.45. p.m. April 5th.

7. A copy of the plan of 18-pdr. barrages is attached. The letters (B), (C), (E) in column 3 of Barrage Table refer to this plan.

8. ACKNOWLEDGE.

D Macay Lieut., R.F.A.

1.4.17. Adjt., 180th. Brigade R.F.A.

Copies to ;-

16th. D.A.
O.C. A/180
B/180
C/180
D/180
War Diary. ✓
File.

O.O. 59.

Secret.

18 Pdr. Barrage's

18 Pdr. Tasks

177 Bde. A, H, J.
180 Bde. B, C, E.
77 Bde. K, L.
87 Bde. F, M, O.
36 D.A. D, G, N.

GREEN CREEPING BARRAGES.
BLUE LEFT FLANK BARRAGES
RED FEINTS AND FLANKING FIRE

BROWN ENFILADE STANDING BARRAGE.

1/5,000 28 S.W. 2.

GENERAL MARCH ORDERS

by

Lieut-Colonel L. E. S. WARD, D.S.O., R.F.A., Comdg.

4.4.17.

1. It is notified for information that the Brigade will march to the Training Area near NIELLES and AFFRINGUES. General Route EECKE - HAZEBROUCK - WARDECQUES.

2. The Brigade will move with full ammunition echelons.

3. All Corps Camp Stores, such as Soyer Stoves, Chaff - Cutters, Water Troughs and Pumps will be left in present Wagon Lines. Receipts will be obtained from the incoming batteries of the 19th. Division.

4. Wagon Lines will be left in a properly clean condition. Huts, stables, stores and harness-sheds will be cleaned and swept . Latrine buckets will be emptied. All old clothing, sacking, and odds and ends will be put in the incinerator before departure. Certificates of cleanliness will be obtained on marching out , from batteries taking over.

5. A rear (cyclist) party consisting of about 22 O.R. under 2/Lieut. A.L. PERRY will remain after batteries have marched out. Cyclists will report to 2/Lieut. PERRY at 11.0. a.m. at A/180 Wagon Line. 2/Lt. PERRY with this party will visit each Wagon Line for a final clear up. On completion of this duty the party will proceed direct to EECKE, joining their Batteries on arrival.

6. Supplies for the march will be drawn as follows ;-

ON	AT	RY.
April 6th.	HAEGEDORNE	Train Transport.
April 7th.	ST. OMER	----do----

A/180 will draw supplies for Brigade Hd.Qrs.

7. A billeting party of one N.C.O. per Battery will parade at Brigade H.Q. Office WESTOUTRE at 11.0. a.m. on the 5th. to proceed to EECKE.
The battery billeting parties for the 7th and 8th April will consist of one Officer and one N.C.O. per battery.
Details will be issued daily.

8. The attention of all Officers is directed to necessity for maintaining strict march discipline.
As it is some time since the Brigade moved by march route special attention is directed to the following ;-
(a) Trotting and joggling to make up distance must be sternly repressed.
(b) No ranks must march outside the line of near wheels nor must men stand outside their line at halts.
(c) At all halts ride and led horses must be turned head to the near side of the column.
(d) Section Commanders must ride in rear of their Sections for the purpose of supervision.

9. All men for whom no transport is available (about 120 in the Brigade) will form a Brigade dismounted party. This party will be in charge of an Officer (dismounted) detailed by O.C. D/180. O.C. C/180 will also detail an Officer (dismounted) for duty with this party. Battery parties (in charge of an N.C.O.) will report to the Officer of D/180 at D/180 Wagon Line as they march out. This dismounted party will proceed direct to EECKE by the shortest raod route.

10. It is probable that one motor lorry per battery will be available for transport purposes.
Further instructions concerning this will be issued later.

11. One man per battery will report to the Regimental Sergt. Major nightly on arriving at the billeting area for police duty.

12. March orders in detail will be issued during the march.

Lieut., R.F.A.

Adjt., 180th. Brigade R.F.A.

Copy No.____

180th. BRIGADE OPERATION ORDER No. 17.

by

Lieut-Colonel L. E. S. WARD, D.S.O., R.F.A., Commanding.

5.4.17.

Ref. Map HAZEBROUCK 5 a, 1/10,000.

1. On April 6th. the Brigade will march from present Wagon-Lines to EECKE, a distance of about 11½ miles.
Route to be taken, WESTOUTRE - HEKSKEN - Cross-roads S of R in RENINGHELST - BOESCHEPE - GODEWAERSVELDE - EECKE.
After leaving GODEWAERSVELDE the road running south by the railway will be taken.

2. Batteries will march so as to pass WESTOUTRE Church at the following times ;-

D/180	Battery	at	10.45. a.m.
C/180	"	at	11.0. a.m.
B/180	"	at	11.15. a.m.
A/180	"	at	11.30. a.m.

Brigade H.Q. will join D/180 Battery at BOESCHEPE.
The above intervals will be maintained when on the march.

3. Brigade H.Q., D/180 and C/180 will water and feed at GODEWAERSVELDE.
B/180 and A/180 will water and feed at BOESCHEPE or any convenient point in its neighbourhood. Halts for water and feed will be for 45 minutes.

4. After passing WESTOUTRE, batteries will observe the regu-lation halts of 10 minutes at the end of every hour of march.

5. Watches will be synchronised under arrangements to be made by the Adjutant.

6. Reports and messages for Brigade Commander will be sent to the head of the column.

D Mackay Lieut., R.F.A.

Adjt., 180th. Brigade R.F.A.

Copies to ;-

O.C. A/180
B/180
C/180
D/180.

SECRET
******

Copy No..12.....

16th DIVISIONAL ARTILLERY
OPERATION ORDER No. 62.

Ref. Sheet. HAZEBROUCK 5A
1/100,000

3rd April, 1917.

1. 87th and 180th Brigades, R.F.A. will withdraw to their respective Wagon Lines on the night of 5th/6th April on receipt of the message "POSE".
   87th Brigade, R.F.A. will then revert under the command of 19th Divisional Artillery.

2. All empty cartridge cases will be stacked in the gun positions ready for removal by the 16th D.A.M.
   Orders for the removal of the empty cases will be issued separately.
   All unexpended ammunition will be removed from the positions by the Batteries concerned.

3. 180th Brigade, R.F.A. will march to the Training Area under orders to be issued by O.C., Brigade, in three stages as follows:-

	Date	From	To	Route
1st Stage	April 6th	Wagon Line	EECKE	Via WESTOUTRE & GODEWAERSVELDE. To be clear of Wagon Lines by 12.0 Noon.
2nd Stage	April 7th	EECKE	WARDRECQUES	Via HAZEBROUCK & SERCUS. Not to enter HAZEBROUCK before 11.0 a.m.
3rd Stage	April 8th	WARDRECQUES	NIELLES & AFFRINGUES	Via HELFAUT.

4. 180th Brigade, R.F.A. will be completed with ammunition before marching out of 16th Divisional Area.

5. O.C., 180th Brigade, R.F.A. will detail an Officer to report to "Q" IXth Corps for orders regarding billets.

6. Supplies for 180th Brigade, R.F.A. will be drawn:-

ON	AT	BY
April 6th	HAEGEDOORNE	Train Transport
April 7th	ST. OMER	- do -

7. Billets at WARDRECQUES, NIELLES and AFFRINGUES will be obtained on application at the MAIRIE of those places.

8. ACKNOWLEDGE.

H.H. Joll
Major, R.A.,
Brigade Major, 16th Divl. Arty.

Issued at..10.0.a.m

Copies to:-

1.177th Bde,R.F.A.	7.16th D.A.C.	13.A.D.M.S.,16th Div.
2.180th Bde,R.F.A.	8.16th Div."G"	14.A.D.V.S.,16th Div.
3. 87th Bde,R.F.A.	9.16th Div."Q"	15.R.A.,IX Corps.
4.SPANBROEK Group.	10.16th Div.Train	16.War Diary.
5.36th Div.Arty.	11.16th Div.Sigs.	17.Staff Capt.,16thD.A.
6.19th Div. Arty.	12.16th Div.Posts.	18.19.20. File.

180th. Brigade R.F.A. Order No. 180.

Ref. Map. HAZEBROUCK 1/100000.

1. The Brigade will continue its March tomorrow 7th. April to WARDRECQUES - a distance of about 18 miles.

2. Route to be taken :-
From GODEWAERSVELDE - Road running S.W. - Two railway crossings - EECKE - Cross Roads near ST.SYLVESTRE CAPPEL - HAZEBROUCK (avoiding the town by taking the turning to the right about half a mile from the Station) - SERCUS - BLARINGHEM - River and Railway Crossing - WARDRECQUES.

3. Batteries will march so as to pass first Railway Crossing South of GODEWAERSVELDE at the following times ;-

C/180	9.15. a.m.
B/180	9.30. a.m.
A/180	9.45. a.m.
D/180	10.0. a.m.

Headquarters will march with C/180 Battery.
For the purposes of synchronisation an orderly from H.Q. will take round a watch in the morning.

4. A halt will be made for water and feed in the neighbourhood of HAZEBROUCK. Reconnaissance for water is being made and further instructions will be issued to Battery Commanders.

5. The Orderly Officer and Interpreters are proceeding to WARDRECQUES this afternoon .
A billeting party of one Officer and one N.C.O. from each Battery will leave from GODEWAERSVELDE Church at 7.0.a.m. tomorrow 7th. inst. and will report to 2/Lt. E.H.WALKER on arrival at the Church WARDRECQUES.

6. The marching party will parade opposite the Church GODEWAERSVELDE at 9.30. a.m. Os.C. A/180 and B/180 R.F.A. will detail Officers to take charge of this party.

7. The cyclist party will also parade opposite the Church at 9.30. a.m. and proceed direct to WARDRECQUES. They should report on arrival to 2/Lt. E.H.WALKER. The Officer in charge of this party will be detailed by O.C. D/180 R.F.A.

8. After time of passing starting point batteries will observe regulation halts of 10 minutes every hour.

9. Reports and messages for the Brigade Commander will be sent to the head of the column.

D Macra Lieut., R.F.A.

6.4.17. Adjt., 180th. Brigade R.F.A.

180th. BRIGADE ORDER No. 185.

by

Lt-Colonel. L. E. S. WARD, D.S.O., R.F.A., Commanding.

Ref. Map. 1/100,000 HAZEBROUCK.

1. The Brigade will march to AFFRINCUES and NIELLES tomorrow 8th. April, a distance of about 15 miles.

2. Route to be taken ;-
Road running West from WARDRECQUES - Main Road to CAMPAGNE - Road running S.W. to LEBIBEROU - HEURINGHEM - BILQUES - HELFAUT - Cross Roads about 500 yards W. of Helfaut - NON CORNET - WIZERNES - HALLINES - AUSTRA - SETQUES - LUMBRES - leaving Main Road at BAYENGHEM - AFFRINGUES and NIELLES.

3. Batteries will march so as to pass the road - turning at CAMPAGNE at the following times ;-

B/180	9.30. a.m.
A/180	9.45. a.m.
D/180	10.0. a.m.
C/180	10.15. a.m.

Headquarters will march with B/180.

4. For the purposes of synchronisation an orderly from H.Q. will take round a watch in the morning.

5. B/180 and A/180 will water and feed at AUSTRA : C/180 and D/180 at HALLINES.

6. The Orderly Officer and Interpreters are proceeding to the Training Area tonight.
A billeting party of One Officer and one N.C.O. from each Battery will leave Church WARDRECQUES at 7.30. a.m. tomorrow 8th. instant and will report to 2/Lt. E.H. WALKER on arrival at Church NIELLES.

7. The marching party will parade opposite the Church at WARDRECQUES at 10. a.m. Os.C. C/180 and D/180 will detail officers to take charge of this party.

8. The cyclist party will also parade opposite the Church at 10. a.m. and proceed direct to NIELLES. They should report on arrival to 2/Lt.E.H. WALKER. The officer in charge of this party will be detailed by O.C. B/180.

9. After time of passing starting point batteries will observe regulation halts of 10 minutes every hour.

10. No one except the Driver is allowed to be carried on G.S. Wagons.

11. Attention is drawn to para 8 (b) of GENERAL MARCH ORDERS. This order must be strictly complied with.

12. Reports and messages for the Brigade Commander will be sent to the head of the column.

[signature] Lieut., R.F.A.

7.4.17. Adjt., 180th. Brigade R.F.A.

PROGRAMME OF TRAINING.

	6. a.m.	7. a.m. to 7.20.	8.45 am. to 9.45.	10 - 11.am	11.45. a.m.
1st. day forenoon	Stables Water & Feed	Physical Exercises Gunners & Drivers	Drivers Exercising horses. Gunners marching & saluting drill.	Drivers Marching & saluting drill. Gunners Rifle drill and Guard duties.	Stables.
	Signallers - Visual Signalling.				

	1.45. p.m. to 2.45.	3.p.m. to 4.15. p.m.	4.30. p.m. to 5.30.	5.40. p.m. - 6.p.m.
1st. day. afternoon.	Drivers Marching & Saluting Drill. Gunners Section Gun Drill.	Drivers Harness Cleaning Gunners Laying & Fuze setting	Stables Water & Feed	Lectures Gunners : Gunnery Drivers : Points of the Horse. (Catechism)
	Signallers - Visual Signalling.			

	6. a.m.	7. a.m. to 7.20.	8.45. a.m. to 9.45.	10. - 11.am.	11.15.am.
2nd. day. forenoon.	Stables Water & Feed.	Physical Exercises Gunners & Drivers	Drivers Rides. Gunners Section Gun Drill.	Drivers ~~Physical Exercises~~ Skeleton Driving Drill Gunners Marching & Saluting Drill.	Stables.
	Signallers - Visual Signalling.				

	1.45. p.m. to 2.45.	3.0. p.m. to 4.15.	4.30. p.m. to 5.30.	5.40. p.m. - 6.0. p.m
2nd. day afternoon.	Drivers Rides. Gunners Section Gun Drill.	Drivers Harness Cleaning. Gunners Rides.	Stables.	Lecture to N.C.Os. Duties in charge of Guards and Picquets.
	Signallers - Buzzer.			9.0. p.m. Lecture to Officers "Moving Warfare" by O.C. Brigade.

PROGRAMME OF TRAINING. (contd)

	6.0. a.m.	7.- 7.20.	8.45. a.m to 9.45.	10. - 11. a.m.	11.15.am
3rd. day forenoon.	Stables Water & Feed.	Gunners & Drivers Marching & Saluting Drill.	Drivers Driving Drill. Gunners Laying & Fuze Setting	Drivers Driving Drill. Gunners Section Gun Drill.	Stables.

Signallers - Visual Station Work.

	1.45. pm. to 2.45.	3.0. pm to 4.15. p.m.	4.30. pm. to 5.30.	5.40.pm. - 6.0
3rd. day. afternoon.	Drivers Lecture with illustrations harness fitting & duties on the march. Gunners Battery Gun-Drill.	Drivers Harness Cleaning. N.C.Os redrilling.	Stables. Gunners Rifle Drill.	Lectures Gunners Casualties to equipment in action. Drivers Horse & Stable management.

Signallers - Visual Station Work.

8.30. p.m. to 9.30. p.m. Signallers (Lamp).

	6.0. a.m.	7.-7.20.am	8.45. a.m. to 9.45.	10. a.m. to 11.am.	11.15 am
4th. day. forenoon.	Stables.	Gunners Rifle Drill. Drivers Physical Exercises.	Drivers Driving Drill. Gunners Section Gun Drill.	Drivers Driving Drill. Gunners Battery Gun Drill.	Stables

Signallers - Visual Signalling.

	1.45. pm. to 2.45.	3.0. pm. to 4.15.	4.30. p.m. to 5.30.	9.0. p.m.
4th. day afternoon.	Drivers Marching & Saluting Drill. N.C.Os and Gunners Rides.	Drivers Harness Cleaning. N.C.Os redrilling.	Stables.	Lecture to Officers. "Horse & Stable management" by Major H.A.STEBBING D.S.O

Signallers, Lectures & illustrations. Linesmens' duties, use and care of equipment.

PROGRAMME OF TRAINING. (contd)

	6.0. a.m.	7 - 7.20.	8.45. a.m. to 9.45.	10 - 11 am.	11.15.am.
5th. day. forenoon.	Stables.	----------	Drill Order Battery Mounted Drills		Stables.

5th. day	1.45. p.m. to 2.45.	3.0. p.m. to 4.15.	4.30. p.m. to 5.30.	5.40. p.m. to 6.0.
afternoon.	Drivers Skeleton Driving Drill. Gunners Section Gun Drill.	Drivers Harness Cleaning. Gunners Battery Gun Drill.	Stables.	----------
	Signallers - Visual Station Work.			

	6. a.m.	7 - 7.20.	8.45. a.m. to 9.45.	10 - 11 am.	11.15.am.
6th. day forenoon.	Stables.	Gunners & Drivers Physical Exercises.	Drivers Driving. Gunners Laying & Fuze Setting.	Drivers Drill. Gunners Battery Gun Drill.	Stables.

	1.45 p.m. to 2.45.	3.0. p.m. to 4.15.	4.30. p.m. to 5.30.	5.40. p.m. - 6.0.
6th. day. afternoon.	Drivers Marching & Saluting Drill. N.C.Os & Gunners Rides.	Drivers Harness Cleaning. Gunners Rifle Drill & Guard duties.	Stables	Lectures, Gunners - Gunnery Drivers - March Discipline and replacement of animal casualties

PROGRAMME OF TRAINING. (contd.)

	6. a.m.	7-7.20.	8.45. a.m. to 9.45.	10.- 11.am.	11.15.
7th. day. forenoon.	Field Service Marching Order Battery Tactical Exercises				

	1.45. p.m. to 2.45.	3.0. p.m. to 4.15.	4.30. p.m. to 5.30.	5.40. p.m. - 6.0.p.m.
7th. day. afternoon.			Stables.	9.0. p.m. Lecture to Officers. Gunnery, ("Lines of fire etc.") by Major A.K. DIGBY,D.SO.

	6. a.m. to 7.20.	8.45. a.m. to 9.45.	10 - 11 a.m.	11.15.a.m.
8th. day. forenoon.	Gunners & Drivers Marching & Saluting Drill.	Drivers Skeleton Driving Drill. Gunners Battery Gun Drill.	Preparation for Inspection.	

	1.45. p.m. to 2.45.	3.0. p.m. to 4.15.	4.30. p.m. to 5.30.	5.40.p.m. - 6.0.
8th. day afternoon.	Drivers Skeleton Order Inspection. All ranks F.S. Marching Order, dismounted.			9.0. p.m. Lecture to Officers by Veterinary Officer.

PROGRAMME OF TRAINING. (Contd.)

		5.40. p.m. to 6.0.
9th. day.	Brigade Tactical Day.	Lectures -Gunners Gunnery (Catechism) Drivers Driving Dril (Catechism)
10th. day.	Tactical day with Infantry.	9. p.m. Lecture to Officers "Communications" by Major R.A. SPENCER.

	6. a.m.	7 - 7.20.	8.45. a.m. to 9.45.	10. a.m. to 11.	11.15.am.
11th. day. forenoon.	Stables.	Gunners & Drivers Physical exercises.	Drivers Lecture Stable duties Gunners Battery Gun Drill.	Drivers Cleaning up Gunners Lecture Gunnery.	

	1.45. pm. to 2.45.	3.0. p.m. to 4.15.	4.30. p.m. to 5.30.	5.40. pm. - 6.0.
11th. day. afternoon.	Gunners Layers Test. Drivers Skeleton Driving Drill.	Gunners Layers Test Drivers Harness Cleaning.		

12th. day. HOLIDAY FOR BRIGADE HORSE SHOW.

NOTES.

Training of specialists, i.e. battery staff, range finders etc. will be specially arranged by Battery Commanders.

All Billets will be inspected daily by Officers before 9.0. a.m. to ensure cleanliness and orderliness.

Inspections of the men for cleanliness and turn-out will take place at all parades.

180th. Brigade Order No. 260.

by

Lieut-Colonel L. E. S. WARD, D.S.O., R.F.A., Commanding.

Reference Map. 1/100,000 HAZEBROUCK, 5 a.

1. The Brigade will march to WARDRECQUES, tomorrow 21st. April, 1917.

2. Route to be taken. NIELLE - AFFRINGUES - LUMBRES SETQUES - AUSTRA - HALLINES - WIZERNES - NOIR CORNET BILQUES - HEURINGHEM - Le BIBEROU - Road crossing South of the P. in CAMPAGNE - WARDRECQUES.

3. Batteries will march as follows ;-
D/180 will march so as to pass the Colonel's Billet at 8.15. a.m. A/180 will pass the same point 8.30. a.m. B/180 will march to reach the main road between NIELLES and AFFRINGUES at the road junction S.E. of the B in R de BLEQUIN by 9.15. a.m. C/180 will march so as to clear AFFRINGUES at 9.45. a.m. Headquarters will march with D/180 and will join the column about 8.30. a.m.

4. For purposes of synchronisation an orderly from each Battery will call at Headquarters at 7. a.m.

5. D/180 and A/180 will water and feed at WIZERNES, B/180 and C/180 at HALLINES.

6. A Billeting Party of One Officer and One N.C.O. from each Battery will leave Brigade Headquarters, NIELLES, for WARDRECQUES, at 7.30. a.m. tomorrow 21st. instant, to accomp--any 2/Lt. E.H. WALKER and the Interpreters.

7. The marching party will parade at Road crossing due east of S in AFFRINGUES at 9.45. a.m. A/180 and B/180 will detail Officers to take charge of this party. Each Battery Party will have a N.C.O. in charge.

8. The cyclist party will parade at the same place as the marching party at 9.45. a.m. C/180 and D/180 will detail one Officer each to take charge of this party.

9. After time of passing starting point, Batteries will observe regulation halts of 10 minutes every hour.

10. No one except the Driver is allowed to be carried on G.S. Wagon.

(continued)

11. Leaders will be provided for the BAGGAGE Wagons.

12. Attention is drawn to GENERAL MARCH ORDERS issued for the recent Brigade Route March.

13. Reports and messages for the Brigade Commander will be sent to the Head of the Column.

J. Miller 2/ Lieut., R.F.A.

20.4.17. for Adjt., 180th. Brigade R.F.A.

180th. BRIGADE ORDER No. 268.

by

Lieut-Colonel L. E. S. WARD, D.S.O., R.F.A., Commanding.

Reference Map 1/100,000 HAZEBROUCK 5 a.

1. The Brigade will march to GODEWAERSVELDE tomorrow, 22nd. April, 1917.

2. Route to be taken, - EBBLINGHEM - STAPLE - HONDEGHEM Station - Cross Roads at LE BREARDE - ST SYLVESTRE CAPPEL - EECKE - GODEWAERSVELDE.

3. Batteries will march as follows ;-
STARTING POINT :- Railway Crossing at WARDREUQUES Station.

A/180	will pass starting point	at	8.30. a.m.
B/180	--do--	at	8.45. a.m.
C/180	--do--	at	9.0 . a.m.
D/180	--do--	at	9.15. a.m.

Headquarters will march with D/180 at 9.15. a.m.

4. For purposes of synchronisation an orderly from each Battery will call at Brigade Headquarters at 7.15. a.m.

5. Water and Feed for all Batteries will take place in the area between HONDEGHEM and LE BREARDE.

6. A Billeting Party of One Officer and One N.C.O. from each Battery will leave Bde. Hdqrs. WARDRECQUES, by Motor Bus, at 7.0. a.m. tomorrow, 22nd. instant, to accompany 2/Lt.E.H.WALKER and the Interpreters.

7. The marching and cyclist parties will parade opposite Brigade Hdqrs. at 9.15. a.m. A/180 will detail an Officer to take charge of the cyclist party and C/180 will detail an Officer to take charge of the marching party.

8. After time of passing starting point, Batteries will observe regulation halts of 10 minutes every hour.

9. An Advance Party of One Officer and two O.R. per battery will proceed by Motor Bus, (same Bus as in para 6) at 7.0. a.m. tomorrow morning, to Wagon Lines in the 16th. Divisional Area.
An Officer's servant may be one of the O.R.
Wagon Lines are allotted as follows ;-

A/180	M.23.a.5.0.
B/180	M.21.c.3.6.
C/180	M.21.c.3.6.
D/180	M.26.b.3.3.

Two days' rations should be taken.

10. Reports and messages for the Brigade Commander will be sent to the Head of the Column.

[signature] Lieut., R.F.A.

21;4.17. Adjt., 180th. Brigade R.F.A.

W A R   D I A R Y :

-----------oOo----------

VOLUME:- 16

FOR MONTH OF MAY, 1917.

UNIT:- 180th Brigade R.G.A.

Vol 16

Instructions regarding War Diaries and Intelligence Summaries are contained in F. S. Regs., Part II. and the Staff Manual respectively. Title pages will be prepared in manuscript.

WAR DIARY
or
~~INTELLIGENCE SUMMARY.~~
(Erase heading not required.)

No16

Army Form C. 2118.

180th Bde RFA

Place	Date	Hour	Summary of Events and Information	Remarks and references to Appendices
LOCRE	30·4·17		Brigade began relief of the 88th Bde RFA in the DIEPENDAAL SECTOR tonight, A and B batteries relieving a section each and C + D two sections. 2ND LT J.R.D. MARTIN, B/180 returned from hospital. 2ND LT B.H. LANE joined the Brigade and was posted to C/180. Nos 36139 DR PARSONS C.R. C/180 and No 36170 DR FOWLER P.R. C/180 both wounded by a Lewis Gun which was being tested by Armourer Staff Sgt. BEARD. A live round had been inadvertently loaded into the magazine. DR PARSONS died from wounds received, at 10.15 PM 30.4.17. Court of Inquiry ordered for May 1st 1917	
LOCRE	1·5·17	10.am	Court of Inquiry as to fatal accident to DR PARSONS held at D.H.Q at 10 am. Relief of 88th Bde RFA completed in the DIEPENDAAL Sector. Batteries moved into old wagon lines on CANADA CORNER — RENINGHELST Road.	O.O. 19.
LA CLYTTE	2·5·17		2/LT A.L. PERRY, A/180 took charge of MAGNUM OPUS Positions and working parties of 19th Div^l. ~~Area~~. 20 men per battery detailed.	
" "	4·5·17		2/Lt H.B. LITTLE. RFA, joined the Brigade and was posted to A/180.	
" "	5·5·17		No L10317 Bdr WATSON J.F. HQ/180 wounded in thigh. LA CLYTTE and neighbourhood heavily shelled. Bde. H.Q. horses removed to B/180 wagon line	
" "	6·5·17		LA CLYTTE again heavily shelled. Infantry Bde. H.Q join Artillery and	

2353 Wt. W2544/1454 700,000 5/15 D. D. & L. A.D.S.S. Forms/C. 2118.

Instructions regarding War Diaries and Intelligence Summaries are contained in F. S. Regs., Part II. and the Staff Manual respectively. Title pages will be prepared in manuscript.

WAR DIARY or INTELLIGENCE SUMMARY. NO 16 (continued).

(Erase heading not required.)

Army Form C. 2118.

180th Bde RFA.

Place	Date	Hour	Summary of Events and Information	Remarks and references to Appendices
			vacate their Signal Office. The Group bombarded OOSTTAVERNE WOOD heavily several times in reply. Resources of Corps H.A. were turned on to opposing brigade head quarters.	
	7.5.17		2/Lt A.B. LYTHGOE returned from hospital and was posted to B/180.	
			Infantry Bde and Artillery Bde move to Headquarters at SCHERPENBERG.	
			Whole Second Army bombarded the rear areas (Hqrs &c) of the enemy opposite for 5 minutes at 8.45 pm and at 11.0 pm. — Object to stop shelling of our rear areas.	
SCHERPENBERG	9.5.17	6.25 and 6.35am	Group engaged objectives in OOSTTAVERNE WOOD for 3 minutes each time (4 rds per gun per min) to attempt to stop hostile shelling of RIDGE WOOD at 6.30 am as he had done for several mornings.	SF 114
			B/180 heavily shelled from 5.10 am till about mid day. One gun B/180 knocked out. 120553 Bdr WHITLOCK, S.H. B/180, 63855 Gr. DONALDSON, T. B/180, 124049 Gr WOODGATE W.J. wounded.	
"	9.5.17	9.15pm	Heavy hostile barrage on front line of left sub sector. Artillery opened at S.O.S. rate on seeing S.O.S. rocket. No hostile infantry attack. All quiet about 10 pm. Batteries fired about 500 rounds each.	
LA CLYTTE	10.5.17		HQ office moved to LA CLYTTE and opened at 10 am. A/180 heavily shelled	
			87th Bde RFA began the relief of this brigade, one section per battery being relieved.	
" "	11.5.17		Brigade Wagon Lines moved to M 21 central (under canvas)	

2353 Wt. W2544/1454 700,000 5/15 D. D. & L. A.D.S.S./Forms/C. 2118.

Instructions regarding War Diaries and Intelligence Summaries are contained in F. S. Regs., Part II. and the Staff Manual respectively. Title pages will be prepared in manuscript.

Army Form C. 2118.

WAR DIARY *or* INTELLIGENCE SUMMARY. NO 16 (Contd)

(*Erase heading not required.*)

180th Bde RFA

Place	Date	Hour	Summary of Events and Information	Remarks and references to Appendices
~~12-5-17~~ LA CLYTTE	12.5.17	10.30pm	Relief completed.	OO 21
			H.Q. at LOCRESTRAAT FARM M22d 2 6½	
LOCRESTRAAT FARM	13.5.17		2 officers and 50 men per battery employed on MAGNUM OPUS positions under Major P.J.B. HEELAS, A/180. A/180 and one section D/180 remain in action for SOS purposes	
"			under VIERSTRAAT Group.	
"	14.5.17		Work continued as above.	
"	15.5.17		Batteries busy with MAGNUM OPUS positions and new wagon lines.	
"	18.5.17		Batteries moved into position in their MAGNUM OPUS POSITIONS	OO 22.
			Brigade H.Q. remained at LOCRESTRAAT FARM	
"	19.5.17		Registration of zero point, datum point, and SOS lines for helping VIERSTRAAT Group	
"	20.5.17		Wire cutting tasks commenced according to programme	~~[illegible]~~
"	21.5.17		Wire cutting, and bombardment of enemy defence system by 4.5 Hows, continued. Work on positions continued.	
"	22.5.17		Wire cutting, etc, continued. 2ND LT W.J. WILLIAMS, D/180 struck off the strength (2ND ARMY NO A/1727 d/21 + 22.5.1917)	
"	23.5.17		Wire cutting continued and nearly completed according to programme. "Instructions for Offensive action" issued to batteries.	

2353 Wt. W2544/1454 700,000 5/15 D. D. & L. A.D.S.S. Forms/C. 2118.

Instructions regarding War Diaries and Intelligence Summaries are contained in F. S. Regs., Part II. and the Staff Manual respectively. Title pages will be prepared in manuscript.

WAR DIARY or INTELLIGENCE SUMMARY. No16 (continued)

(Erase heading not required.)

180th Bde RFA

Army Form C. 2118.

Place	Date	Hour	Summary of Events and Information	Remarks and references to Appendices
LOCRESTRAAT FARM	24.5.17 27.5.17		Wire cutting and bombardment of enemy's defence system continued. Enemy bombarded LOCRE–BAILLEUL Road and CROIX DE POPERINGHE during the night. DRANOUTRE shelled.	
			The following, of A/180, slightly gassed:– 170279 GR STEWART A.; 39389 DR PEMBERTHY A. 14187 GR DEAN L.J.; 134881 GR STODDART T; 40021 BDR FURHMAN F, 43013 GR RICHARDSON F, 123393 GR ELEMENT G; 39224 GR JACKSON D 39760 DR PORTER D; 52442 GR QUEEN J; 72003 SGT HIBBS H. 31425 SGT CHURCH H. 38691 WHEELER TEMPLAR H. 39239 GR CLARKE A.	
ROSSIGNOL WOOD	28.5.17		Bde H.Q. moved into Battle H.Q. at ROSSIGNOL WOOD N22a78, vide ROSS Group OO. No1	
			36234 FTR. CPL. ABRATHAT E.T. A/180 WOUNDED (SHRAPNEL)	
"			92861 GR STEEL, W. A/180 slightly gassed. WIRE CUTTING continued. Night firing begun	
"	29.5.17		a/Capt. STEVEN O. A/180 wounded. (Gun shot wound) Remaining at duty. WIRE CUTTING, BOMBARDMENTS, and NIGHT FIRING continued.	
"	31.5.17		D/180 came under No3 RIGHT SUB-GROUP for tactical purposes. vide ROSS Gp OO No2. 104684 GR YEARDLEY A/180 wounded. (Gun shot wound in foot)	

L. S. Ward
LIEUT.-COL. R.F.A.
COMDG. 180TH. BRIGADE, R.F.A.

2353 Wt. W2544/1454 700,000 5/15 D. D. & L. A.D.S.S./Forms/C. 2118.

S E C R E T.

180th. Bde. R.F.A. No.S.F.114.

O.C. A/180 O.C. C/180
B/180 D/180

Ref. Map. WYTSCHAETE, 28 S.W. Edition 5 a 1/10,000.

1. For several mornings the enemy has shelled RIDGE WOOD at 6.30. a.m.

2. To prevent this recurring the following programme will be carried out by the Group tomorrow morning, 9.5.17.

6.25. a.m. to 6.28. a.m.

3 rounds per gun per minute.

A/180 Dug-outs and Trench about O.15.c.2.9.

B/180 Trench Tramway from O.20.b.42.93. to O.15.c.42.65.

C/180 Railway from O.14.d.70.00. to O.21.a.12.83.

& Track from O.21.a.15.85. to O.15.c.02.15.

D/180 Dugouts about O.15.c.1.6. and O.15.c.7.5.

6.35. a.m. to 6.38. a.m. Ditto.

3. Should the enemy retaliate, another three minutes' fire at three rounds per gun per minute, on the same objectives may be ordered by the Group. This order will be given in the following form ;-
"Reference S.F.114, para 3, Carry on, at (zero time)"

4. Watches will be synchronised with Group Headquarters by telephone at 5.45. a.m.

5. ACKNOWLEDGE.

D Mackey Lieut., R.F.A.

8.5.17. Adjt., 180th. Brigade R.F.A.

S E C R E T.   Copy No.___

180th. BRIGADE OPERATION ORDER No. 21.

by

Lieut-Colonel L. E. S. WARD, D.S.O., R.F.A., Commanding.

Ref. Maps: WYTSCHAETE, Edn. 5 a, 1/10,000, &
Sheet 28 S.W. 1 & 2, Edn. 5 a, 1/20,000.

1. The 87th. Bde. R.F.A. 19th. Divisional Artillery will relieve the 180th. Brigade in the DIEPENDAAL Sector on the nights 11/12, 12/13th. May.

2. Batteries of the 87th. Brigade will relieve their opposite numbers of the 180th. Brigade. Guns will not be exchnaged.

(a) A/87 will go into action at K.84. N.10.a.65.10.
2 Guns on the 11th/12th,May
4 Guns " " 12th/13th, "

(b) A/180 will remain in K.81 and will work on K.83.
A/180 will be responsible for its' present zone till A/87 has registered in K.84.

(c) B/87 will relieve B/180 at K.57, N.9.d.0.0.
2 Guns on the 11th/12th, May
4 Guns " " 12th/13th, May.
B/180 will withdraw guns to Wagon Lines.
Working parties of this Battery will be billeted at PALLAS FARM.

(d) C/87 will relieve C/180 at K.95 N.4.b.40.20.(4) &
N.4.d.25.45.(2)
2 Guns from Battery Position N.4.b.40.20. on 11th/12th, May and remaining 4 guns on 12/13,May.

C/180 will withdraw guns to Wagon Lines.
Working parties will be billeted at K.46, and work at K.50.

(e) D/87 will relieve D/180 at K.102, N.4.c.95.75.(4) &
N.16.b.40.30(2).
2 Guns from N.4.c.95.75 on the 11th/12th, May, and remaining 4 Guns on the 12th/13th, May.

D/180 will withdraw Guns to Wagon Lines.
D/180 will relieve the Section of D/177 at K.44, (N.16.c.1.7.) on the night of 13th/14th, May.
D/180 will leave their wireless station in present position and take over the set at K.44.

3. A/180 and the Section of D/180 will be at the disposal of O.C. VIERSTRAAT Group, in the case of S.O.S.
Guns will be registered but otherwise will not fire except in a case of S.O.S.

4. All ammunition expended by A/180 and the Section of D/180 will be reported to O.C. VIERSTRAAT Group.

5. Ammunition will be handed over in the positions vacated by the 180th. Brigade, R.F.A.
Any boxed ammunition will be left in the position and a report of the quantity forwarded to this office.
Ammunition will be handed over to the incoming Units at 12 noon 12th. May, and receipts showing nature will be forwarded to Group Headquarters by 2. p.m. 12th. May, 1917.

6. Planchettes, Local maps, Defence Schemes, Photographs, M.O. Documents and all information concerning the front will be handed over according to G.H.Q. Artillery Circular No.2.

7. Command will pass on completion of relief.

8. From the 13th. instant onward, each Battery of the 180th. Brigade R.F.A. will find a working party of 2 Officers and 50 Other Ranks, of these 20 Other Ranks will be retained by the Batteries for work on their own positions, the remaining 30 will be employed under central supervision.

9. Major P.J.B. HEELAS, A/180 R.F.A. will superintend all work on MAGNUM OPUS Positions and will be assisted by 2/Lt. T.C. HIPWELL.

10. All empty cartridges will be removed from positions.

11. Certificates of cleanliness for Gun-Line and Wagon-Line will be obtained from incoming Unit.

12. All Area Stores will be left in present Wagon-Line and will be handed over.

13. 180th. Brigade R.F.A. will be in their new Wagon-Lines at M.21.central by night 11th/12th. May.

14. ACKNOWLEDGE.

[signature]
Lieut., R.F.A.

10.5.17. Adjt., 180th. Brigade R.F.A.

Copies to ;- A/180
B/180
C/180
D/180
87th. Bde.R.F.A.
177th. Bde. R.F.A.
16th. Div. Arty.
War Diary.
File.

S E C R E T.

~~Wire cutting~~

180th. BRIGADE OPERATION ORDER No.22.

by

Lieut-Colonel L. E. S. WARD, D.S.O., R.F.A., Commanding.

---

1. Batteries will move into their M.O. Positions during the night 18th/19th. May.

2. Registration will be carried out during the 19th. May. A programme of wire cutting is attached.

3. S.O.S. points will be registered under orders to be issued by O.C. VIERSTRAAT Group.

4. 100 rounds per gun 18-pdr. and 60 rounds per 4,5" Howitzer will be taken up to the Battery Positions when Batteries move into position.
   The ammunition at present dumped at the Positions is on no account to be used.

5. All previous orders concerning fatigue parties under Major HEELAS are cancelled. The personnel of Batteries is in fut-ure at the disposal of Battery Commanders for work on their M.O. Positions, which should be proceeded with at the highest pressure.

6. Communications are not at present fully established.
   For the purposes of registration, GOETHALS FARM is avail-able and will have communication with Battery Positions.
   For the purposes of wire cutting according to the attached programme, efforts are being made to connect GOETHALS FARM with O.P. E.1, (VIERSTRAAT) from whence Batteries must lay out their own lines to the points selected for observation in the POPPY LANE area, which gives the best view of the hostile wire to be cut.
   Failing this, Batteries must lay out lines from GOETHALS FARM.

7. Battery Positions are being placed in communication with H.Q. VIERSTRAAT Group.

8. No movement to take place East of the LOCRE - LA CLYTTE Road before 9.0. p.m.

9. Batteries will report by orderly to Brigade H.Q., when guns are in position - stating the number.

10. A fatigue party of 1 N.C.O. and 6 men will report for attachment to Lt.O'SULLIVAN, R.E. at CANADA CORNER tomorrow morning at 8.0. a.m. This party (which will be relieved by C/180 at the end of one week) will be detailed by B/180. Tentage will be supplied by Battery Wagon Line. This party will be rationed by the Battery.

11. ACKNOWLEDGE.

L E S Ward Lt-Col., R.F.A.

18.5.17. Comdg., 180th. Brigade R.F.A.

War Diary

S E C R E T. Copy No.

ROSS GROUP OPERATION ORDER No.1.

by

Lieut-Colonel L. E. S. WARD, D.S.O., R.F.A., Commdg.

Ref. Map. WYTSCHAETE 1/10,000, Edn. 5 a.
28 S.W. 1/20,000, Edn. 5 a.

1.
Composition.

The ROSS Group is composed as follows ;-

113th. Brigade R.F.A. - 3 Batteries 18-pdr.
1.Battery 4.5" Hows.

180th. Brigade R.F.A. - 3 Batteries 18-pdr.
1 Battery 4.5" Hows.

The Group will assume the defence of the 16th. Div--isional front from 12 noon 28th. May, 1917.

Group Headquarters are at ROSS DUG OUTS N.22.a.70.60.

2.
Infantry
Distribution.

The Divisional front extends from N.24.c.18.25. to N.18.a.70.80. This front is held by one Infantry Bde. with two battalions in front line.
Right Battalion H.Q. are at HARLEY HOUSE, N.23.b.40.70.
Left Battalion H.Q. are at YORK HOUSE, N.16.c.90.30.
Brigade H.Q. are at FAIRY HOUSE M.18.d.40.10.

3.
Artillery
Distribution.

(a) The 180th. Brigade R.F.A. will cover the Right Subsector - zone on hostile front line from N.24.c.87.16. to N.24.a.60.86.

B/180 Battery will cover from N.24.c.87.16. to N.24.d.28.79.

C/180 Battery will cover from N.24.d.28.79. to N.24.b.00.32.

A/180 Battery will cover from N.24.b.00.32. to N.24.a.60.86.

D/180 Battery will cover the whole front from N.24.c.87.16. to N.24.a.60.86.

(b) The 113th. Brigade R.F.A. will cover the Left Subsector zone on hostile front line from N.24.a.60.86. to N.18.b.20.55.

A/113 Battery will cover from N.24.a.60.86 to N.18.d.18.20.
C/113 Battery will cover from N.18.d.18.20.to N.18.d.22.92
B/113 Battery will cover from N.18.d.22.92.to N.18.b.20.55.

D/113 Battery will cover the whole zone from N.24.a.60.86. to N.18.b.20.55.

4.
S.O.S.
Barrages.

S.O.S. points on the hostile front line will be registered by batteries as follows ;-

A/180.	N.24.a.92.48. N.24.a.86.59 N.24.a.80.65. N.24.a.80.74. N.24.a.80.80. N.24.a.80.85.	B/180.	N.24.c.86.18. N.24.c.82.38. N.24.c.82.52. N.24.d.00.56. N.24.d.20.60. N.24.d.29.73.
C/180.	N.24.d.28.85. N.24.d.30.94. N.24.b.27.08. N.24.b.19.22. N.24.b.10.29. N.24.b.00.32.	D/180.	N.24.d.06.28. N.24.d.53.68. N.24.b.59.00. N.24.b.28.55. N.24.b.61.57. N.18.d.62.04.
A/113.	N.18.c.76.00. N.18.c.85.08. N.18.c.95.06. N.18.d.05.13. N.18.d.12.14. N.18.d.18.20.	B/113.	N.18.b.10.00. N.18.b.13.09. N.18.b.16.20. N.18.b.20.38. N.18.b.22.46. N.18.b.20.53.
C/113.	N.18.d.18.31. N.18.d.22.40. N.18.d.22.53. N.18.d.17.67. N.18.d.22.75. N.18.d.22.85.	D/113.	N.18.d.49.05. N.18.d.87.22. N.18.d.42.44. N.18.d.50.67. N.18.b.38.06. N.18.b.59.17.

The points on hostile defences registered by 18-pdrs. batteries are those at which the creeping S.O.S. barrage becomes stationary on the hostile front line.

5.
S.O.S.
Instructions

(a) The call for S.O.S. (which is a priority call) should be in the form "S.O.S. N.18.5."

(b) Batteries responsible for the front attacked will open fire on their S.O.S. lines.

The normal distance of the initial shrapnel barrage from our trenches in this sector will be 150 yards.

(c) Rates of fire.

	Rounds per gun per min.
18-pdr.	
for first two minutes	4.
for next three "	3.
after first five "	1. or as the situation demands.
4.5" How.	Half the above rates.

(d) After two minutes the barrage will lift at 50 yards a minute until it reaches the enemy's wire, where it will remain stationary and H.E. may be substituted wholly or partly for shrapnel.

6. Rocket Picquets.

Rocket Picquets will be established as follows ;-
180th. Brigade R.F.A. at GOETHALS FARM
113th. Brigade R.F.A. at DESTINET Farm.

Rocket Picquets will consist of 1 Sergeant, 3 O.Rs. and one telephonist at each station. These will be found nightly by batteries on a roster to be issued by Adjutant 180th. Brigade.

Detailed instructions for Rocket Picquets are being issued by the Intelligence Officer, 180th. Brigade.

7. O.Ps.

For the purpose of holding the line O.Ps are allotted as follows ;-

113th. Brigade R.F.A. DESINET FARM
H. Right
H Left.

NOTE. These O.Ps are in constant use by 177th. Brigade RFA. Mutual arrangements must be made by Battery Commanders to avoid clashing with each other and gongesting O.Ps.

180th. Brigade R.F.A. GOETHALS FARM.
K.16.
K.4.

B/180 and C/180 will arrnge that K.16. is permanently manned by an Officer and comlement of signallers during the hours of daylight, i.e. from 4 a.,. to 9.30. p.m.

Batteries will take it in turn to man this O.P. commencing with B/180 at noon 28th. May.

A similar procedure will be adopted at GOETHALS FARM by A/180 and D/180 Batteries.

The following O.Ps are at the disposal of all Batteries forming the ROSS Group;-

LK. 1. LK. IV.
LK.II. K. 4.

8. Mutual Support.

Support given to SPANBROEK Group.

B/180 barrages from N.30.a.47.58. to N.24.c.50.35.
D/113, One 4.5" How.N.30.a.95.50.
One 4.5" How.N.30.a.95.98

Code Call : HELP F.F.8. X F H 4 6.

Support given to DIEPENDAAL Group.

C/113 barrages from N.18.b.18.58. to N.18.b.80.90.
A/113 barrages from N.18.b.80.90. to O. 7.c.31.24
D/180 One 4,5" How. N.18.b.52.68.
N.18.b.84.88.
O.13.a.21.97.
O.13.a.42.82.

Code Call : HELP RABETT.

Support given by SPANBROEK Group.

One 18-pdr. barrages from N.24.c.50.35. to N.24.b.00.60.
One 4.5" How " " N.24.d.52.48.
One 4.5" How. " " N.24.b.73.01.

Code Call HELP ROSS.

Support given by DIEPENDAAL Group.

One 18-pdr. barrages from N.18.b.20.55. to N.18.d.20.83.
One 18-pdr. " " N.18.d.20.83. to N.18.d.17.23.
One 4.5" How. N.18.b.25.22. One 4.5" How. N.18.b.35.10.
One 4.5" How. O.13.c.30.85. One 4.5" How N.18.d.47.63.

Code Call : HELP ROSS.

9.
Gas Attack.
(a) In case of a Gas attack unaccompanied by an Infantry attack the signal will be "Gas attack trench ......".

In this case no S.O.S. Signal is to be sent and Rockets are not to be used.

10. (b) On receipt of this message the 4.5" Howitzer will concentrate on the trench named, provided it is not dangerously close to our own trenches, and also in trenches in which enemy Infantry might be concentrating.

Rate of fire one round per howitzer per two minutes.

A light barrage will be placed on the enemy's wire by 18-pdr. Batteries.

Rate of fire one round per gun per minute.

Should however, an Infantry attack subsequently develop the ordinary S.O.S. procedure will be carried out.

10.
Communications. Batteries are connected with all O.Ps, other batteries, and Group H.Q. through the main exchange FD. 67.

No communications exist with the Infantry forward of the Battalion H.Q.

No battery S.O.S. telephone lines now exist.

11.
Liaison. The 180th. Brigade will find a Liaison Officer with the Right Battalion.

The 113th. Brigade will find a Liaiso n Officer with the Left Battalion.

Detailed instructions for Liaison Officers will be issued by the Adjutant, 180th. Brigade R.F.A.

12.
Retaliation. Company Commanders requiring punishment for hostile shelling will communicate with their Battalion H.Q.

Battalion Commanders will c ll direct on the Group for punishment naming the trenches in our system being shelled.

13.
177.Bde.RFA. In the event of S.O.S. the 177th. Brigade will assist by strengthening the barrage as follows ;-

A/177 from	N.24.c.85.17.	to	N.24.b.15.28.
B/177 from	N.24.b.15.28.	to	N.18.d.22.47.
C/177 from	N.18.d.22.47.	to	N.18.b.20.55.
D/177 from	N.24.d.27.20.	--	N.24.d.68.62.
	O.19.a.04.92.	--	N.18.d.86.22.
	O.13.c.13.48.	--	N.18.b.80.22.

14.
Returns. A detailed list of returns required will be issued to all batteries concerned by the Adjutant, 180th. Brigade RFA.

ACKNOWLEDGE.

Lt-Col., R.F.A.

27.5.17. Comdg., 180th. Brigade R.F.A.

Copies to ;-

A/113.	C/177	O.C. 113th. Bde.
B/113.	D/177.	O.C. 177th. Bde.
C/113	A/180	O.C. 49th. Inf. Bde.
D/113	B/180	16th . Div. Art y.
A/177	C/180	O.C. DIEPENDAAL Gp.
B/177	D/180	O.C. SPANBROEK Gp.

War Diary, File.

SECRET. Copy No. 14

ROSS GROUP OPERATION ORDER No.2.

by

Lieut-Colonel L. E. S. WARD, D.S.O., R.F.A., Commdg.

---

1. The Right Group (vide Appendix 1 of 16th. Divisional Artillery Instructions for the Offensive, Part 1, Operations) assumes it's duties from today (31st May) inclusive.

2. The following number of guns and howitzers will take part in bombardments and barraging communications.

No.1. Right Group ... 36 18-pdrs.
No.3. Right Sub-Gp. .. 12 4.5" Hows.

Daily ammunition expenditure will be ;-

18-pdrs. - 600 rounds per battery, of which 180 rounds per battery will be expended on night firing. This allowance for night firing does not include what Battery Commanders fire for keeping open wire.

For night firing 75% "AX" will be used. In day firing the proportion of "AX" to "A" will be so adjusted as to make the proportions for the total daily expenditure not less than 50% "AX".

4.5" Hows.- 600 rounds per battery of which 100 rounds per battery will be expended on night firing.

3. Lieut-Col. C.de L.WINTER,D.S.O., Commanding No.3. Right Sub-Group will allot all targets to the two 4.5" How. Batteries of his Group now in action (D/113 and D/180).

In this connection the attention of O.C. No.3. Right Sub-Group is invited to 16th. Divisional Artillery "Instructions for the Offensive" Part 1 Operations, para 53.

4. All orders dealing with defensive measures which have been issued by the ROSS Group remain in force.

5. ACKNOWLEDGE

D Mackay Lieut., R.F.A.

31.5.17. Adjt., ROSS GROUP.

No.1.	O.C. A/113	R.F.A.
2.	" B/113	"
3.	" C/113	"
4.	" D/113	"
5.	" A/180	"
6.	" B/180	"
7.	" C/180	"
8.	" D/180	"
No.9.	O.C. 58th. Bde.	R.F.A.
10.	" C/58th.Bde.	"
11.	" 113th.Bde.	"
12.	" 48th. Inf. Bde.	
13.	" 16th. Div. Arty.	
✓ 14.	War Diary.	
✓ 15.	File.	

10. Batteries of 180th. Brigade will take over all ammunition at present in positions of batteries they relieve. Receipts in triplicate will be forwarded to this office by 10.0. p.m. 19th. June.
A guard will be left on ammunition in present positions.

11. Batteries will report by wire to Brigade H.Q. (using the code word "SATISFACTORY") as soon as possible after 8.0. p.m. that the relief has been completed.

12. 180th. Brigade HQ. will remain at BYRON HOUSE.

13. ACKNOWLEDGE.

D Maclloy Major R.F.A.

19.6.17. for O.C., 180th. Brigade R.F.A.

Copies to ;-
A/88th. Battery
B/180 "
C/180 "
D/180 "
16th. D.A.
19th. D.A.
88th. Bde. R.F.A.
177th. Bde. R.F.A.
57th. Inf. Bde.
War Diary. ✓
File.

76

WAR DIARY.

FOR MONTH OF JUNE, 1917.

VOLUME:- 14

UNIT:- 180th Brigade R.F.A.

Vol 17

Page 1.

Instructions regarding War Diaries and Intelligence Summaries are contained in F. S. Regs., Part II. and the Staff Manual respectively. Title pages will be prepared in manuscript.

WAR DIARY No 17
or
~~INTELLIGENCE SUMMARY.~~
(Erase heading not required.)

180th Bde R.F.A

Army Form C. 2118.

Place	Date	Hour	Summary of Events and Information	Remarks and references to Appendices
ROSSIGNOL WOOD	1/6/17		Practice Barrage No 1 carried out	RIGHT GROUP O.O. No 3
			No 36054 Bdr DALLMAN B/180 slightly wounded, remaining at duty.	
			No 41100 Gnr DAVIS. A. B/180 " " " " "	
"	2/6/17		No 37929 Sgt MARSHALL W.J. C/180 Wounded. (to hospital)	
			No 39295 Gnr PARKER A.G. C/180 " " "	
			2/Lt T.C. HIPWELL D/180 slightly wounded, remaining at duty.	
"	night 2-3 June		D/180 fired gas shell	16th DA OO 79
"	3/6/17		Bombardment and Practice Barrage No 2 at 11 am and 11.30 am.	RIGHT GROUP O.O. No 5
			Army bombardment and barrage for 15 minutes	RIGHT GROUP O O No 6
"			No 39295 Gnr PARKER C/180 died of wounds	
"			No 106350 Gnr ATKINS W A/180 wounded (to hospital)	
"			No 38842 Gnr STRANG F A/180. " " "	
"			No 156164 Gnr WEBSTER W " " "	
	4/6/17		No 36072 Gnr STIMSON G.E. A/180 wounded (remaining at duty)	
			No 109721 Gnr SWAINE C. A/180 Wounded (to hospital.	
"	5/6/17		No 170890. Gnr STOKES D/180 Killed in action	
			No 122593 Gnr WILSON J.H.T D/180 wounded in thigh (slight)	

2353 Wt. W2544/1454 700,000 5/15 D. D. & L. A.D.S.S./Forms/C. 2118.

Page 2

Army Form C. 2118.

WAR DIARY or ~~INTELLIGENCE SUMMARY.~~ No 17

180th Bde RFA

(*Erase heading not required.*)

Instructions regarding War Diaries and Intelligence Summaries are contained in F. S. Regs., Part II. and the Staff Manual respectively. Title pages will be prepared in manuscript.

Place	Date	Hour	Summary of Events and Information	Remarks and references to Appendices
ROSSIGNOL WOOD	5/6/17	3pm	ARMY PRACTICE BARRAGE	RT GP OO No 9
ROSSIGNOL WOOD	5/6/17		2/LT HINDS G.H. Wounded (to hospital) a/Capt LYNCH G.T. B/180 posted to 5th (ARMY) RHA Brigade, to command a battery.	
			No 36141 a/Bdr WHITAKER J C/180 Wounded.	
			No 21027 FTR. CRAGG J. C/180 wounded.	
			No 74394 a/Bdr MORGANS J.W. C/180. Wounded (remaining at duty)	
			No 152153 a/Bdr MORRIS H H C/180 " " "	
			No 34946 Gnr BASS J.H. C/180 " " "	
"	5th-6th/6/17	10.30pm	Raid by 6th CONNAUGHT RANGERS Successful. 7 prisoners taken	OO. No 7
	6/6/17		No 114193 Gnr BRACKEN H. (C/180) Wounded (remaining at duty)	
			No 43065 Gnr BARRETT L.J. C/180 Wounded (to hospital)	
"	7/6/17		Attack on WYTSCHAETE began at 3.10 am and all objectives taken up to BLACK LINE 500 yds East of WYTSCHAETE taken by 8.30 am.	
			180th Bde RFA got the order to advance to positions near MAEDELSTEDE FARM in "NO Man's Land" N24c. Headquarters at IRISH HOUSE N23c95. Advance on OOSTTAVERNE LINE commenced at 3.10pm Successful. O.P.s established on WYTSCHAETE RIDGE. ROCKET GUARD near WYTSCHAETE CHURCH. Visual signalling stations at church, and lip of MAEDELSTEDE CRATER. Location of Infantry Front Line reported at 12 midnight by 2/Lt F.E. DAVY, (Advanced Intellig. Off.)	
IRISH HOUSE N23c95				

2353 Wt. W2544/1454 700,000 5/15 D. D. & L. A.D.S.S./Forms/C. 2118.

Page 3.

Army Form C. 2118.

Instructions regarding War Diaries and Intelligence Summaries are contained in F. S. Regs., Part II. and the Staff Manual respectively. Title pages will be prepared in manuscript.

WAR DIARY

or

~~INTELLIGENCE SUMMARY.~~

(Erase heading not required.)

No 17 . 180th Bde RFA

Place	Date	Hour	Summary of Events and Information	Remarks and references to Appendices
IRISH HOUSE	7/6/17		2/Lt ~~G.B.~~ B.G. LEE D/180 Wounded (GSW) (to hospital)	
" "	8/6/17		H.Q. remaines at IRISH HOUSE Batteries fired on SOS call at 9 pm. Enemy counter attack on a 7 mile front. No enemy infantry entered our trenches. Many enemy dead in front of our lines.	
" "	9/6/17		Reconnaissance made for battery positions in (Sheet 28) N12d and O7c	
S.P. 13	10/6/17		H.Q. moves to S.P. 13 to occupy late H.Q. of 59th Bde RFA. Batteries remained at MAEDELSTEDE Quiet day. No 36320 Gnr. HAZEL A.G. C/180. wounded (to hospital)	
BYRON ~~HOUSE~~ FARM	11/6/17		Batteries moved to positions just W and N of the NAG'S NOSE in N12d H.Q. at dugouts near BYRON FARM. (N18a 25). 180th Bde forms part of Left Group 19th Div. Arty. (with 88th Bde RFA) under Col. Tovey 88th Bde RFA. Maj. N.A. STEBBING, DSO, RFA assumed command of 180th Bde RFA. Col L.E.S. WARD DSO RFA proceeded to England on leave. 2/Lt H.M. CHARTER ~~RFA~~ joined the Brigade and was posted to B/180.	
" "	12/6/17		Left Group 19th DA OO NO A1, Firing at O16d 75 55 with 4.5 How + 18 pdrs.	L.G. 19th DA OO No A1.
" "	16/6/17		A/180 withdrew from action on the night 16th-17th June to join the Second Army Artillery School	
" "	14/6/17		Batteries of 180th Bde assisted 41st DA in 19th Div. Art. OO No 125	SF 186.

2353 ~~Wt.~~ W2544/1454 700,000 5/15 D. D. & L. A.D.S.S. Forms/C. 2118.

Page 4

Army Form C. 2118.

Instructions regarding War Diaries and Intelligence Summaries are contained in F. S. Regs., Part II. and the Staff Manual respectively. Title pages will be prepared in manuscript.

WAR DIARY or ~~INTELLIGENCE SUMMARY.~~ No 17

(*Erase heading not required.*)

180th Bde RFA.

Place	Date	Hour	Summary of Events and Information	Remarks and references to Appendices
BYRON FARM	17/6/17	3.30am	A/180 left wagon line to proceed to TILQUES	16th DA OO No 88
" "	19/6/17		180th Bde RFA relieves opposite numbers of 88th Bde RFA in their position in action and took over the defence of the line at 8pm. Zone - O7c 50 30 to O11c 38 10. A/88 remained in action in place of A/180 under 180th Bde RFA.	~~[illegible]~~ 180th Bde OO A1.
" "	20/6/17		No 39600 SGT KING P. C/180 + No 35962 Cpl McCOLL C/180 Killed in action No 64937 SGT STENNING W, No 31084 FTR MARTIN W.H. No 36160 Gnr HYMNS E, No 110605 Gnr. WOOD, T No 39381 A/BDR WATSON E.C., all of C/180, and No 13520 Gnr SPEAKMAN A., D/180 — Wounded.	
" "	21/6/17		Wagon Lines of Brigade heavily shelled at 8.15pm + 1.15am. About 20 horses hit and a few men. No 22211 SGT STRANG J C/180 wounded.	
" "	22/6/17		No 34598 SGT JEFFREY SMITH, L.C. B/180 Killed in action No 135542 Gnr STEVENS E.C., C/180 and No 92763 Br. REDDIE T, C/180 Wounded. Wagon lines shifted to rear area. B/180, C/180 at M21c. D/180 M26d 38 HQ wagon line at LOCRESTRAAT FARM No 43106 Dr. PRINCE G B/180 Wounded	

2353 Wt. W2544/1454 700,000 5/15 D. D. & L. A.D.S.S. Forms/C 2118.

Army Form C. 2118.

WAR DIARY No 17
or
~~INTELLIGENCE SUMMARY~~.
(Erase heading not required.)

180th Bde. RFA

Instructions regarding War Diaries and Intelligence Summaries are contained in F. S. Regs., Part II. and the Staff Manual respectively. Title pages will be prepared in manuscript.

Place	Date	Hour	Summary of Events and Information	Remarks and references to Appendices
BYRON FARM	23/6/17		2/Lt W.H. HURSTBOURNE D/180 Killed in action while on Liaison Duty with Infantry Battalion (109th Bde).	180th Bde
"	27.6.17		Relief of 180th Bde began. See OO No A2	OO No A2.
	26.6.17		2/Lt B.H. LANE C/180 posted to trench mortars	
	28.6.17		Relief of 180th Bde completed. Batteries withdrew to wagon lines	
"	~~30.6.17~~		Bde H.Q. at M8c04 near WESTOUTRE.	
M8c04.	30.6.17		Batteries still remaining at wagon lines in M8c + M14a.	

[signature] 2/Lt for.
O.C. 180th Bde RFA

SECRET. Practice 1. O.O. Cpy.No. 10

RIGHT GROUP OPERATION ORDER No. 4. 3

by

Lieut-Colonel L. E. S. WARD, D.S.O., R.F.A., Comdg.

Ref . Map WYTSCHAETE 28 S.W.2. Edn. 5.a. 1/10,000.

1. A practice barrage will be carried out at 6. p.m. June 1st. on IXth. Corps Front.

2. A table of tasks for the creeping barrage is issued herewith to all batteries concerned.

3. O.C. No.3. Right Sub-Group will issue tasks for the standing barrage. This will include K.49.

4. Watches will be synchronized under arrangements by the Adjutant, 180th. Brigade R.F.A., for No.1. Right Group.
O.C. No.3. Right Sub-Group will arrange for synchronization of his Group and include K.49.

5. Zero hour will be <u>6. p.m.</u> 1st. June.

6. The rate of fire will be three rounds per gun per minute for 18-pdrs.
The creeping barrage will be 100 % "A". One section per battery will ~~ex~~ fire smoke shell if available.

7. All guns will cease firing at Zero plus 10 minutes.

8. Batteries will each detail one Officer specially selected to watch the barrage and report on ;-

(a) The efficacy of our own barrage, special note beinga made of any gaps, high fuzes, or irregularities.

(b) The time of starting, nature, intensity, duration, locality etc., of the enemy reply.

Written reports will be rendered to this office by 7.30. p.m.

9. ACKNOWLEDGE.

[signature] Lieut., R.F.A.

1.6.17. Adjt., ROSS GROUP.

Copies to ;-		
	K.67.	K.49. (for information)
	K.73.	O.C. No.1 Right Sub-Group
	K.69.	16th. D.A.
	K.42.	War Diary
	K.4[illegible].	File
	K.48.	Spare.

Battery.	Hour	Task	Remarks.
K.42.	Zero to zero plus two.	N.24.c.96.93. to N.24.c.81.61.	
	Zero plus two to zero plus 4.	N.24.d.18.90. to N.24.d.03.60.	
	Zero,plus 4 to zero plus 6.	N.24.d.37.98. to N.24.d.29.70.	
	Zero plus 6 to zero plus 8.	N.24.b.58.02. to N.24.d.50.72.	
	Zero plus 8 to zero plus 10.	N.24.d.18.90. to N.24.d.03.60.	
K.41.	Zero to zero plus two.	N.24.c.81,61. to N.24.c.80.24.	160 yds. front.
	Zero plus 2 to zero plus 4.	N.24.d.03.60. to N.24.c.97.29.	--do--
	Zero plus 4 to zero plus 6.	N.24.d.29.70. to N.24.d.21.39.	150 --do--
	Zero plus 6 to zero plus 8.	N.24.d.50.72. to N.24.d.44.42.	140 --do--
	Zero plus 8 to zero plus 10.	N.24.d.03.60. to N.24.c.97.29.	160 --do--
K.48.	Zero to zero plus two.	N.24.a.95.52. to N.24.c.96.93.	320 --do--
	Zero plus 2 to zero plus 4.	N.24.b.16.54. to N.24.d.12.90.	320 --do--
	Zero plus 4 to zero plus 6.	N.24.b.38.56. to N.24.d.37.98.	300 --do--
	Zero plus 6 to zero plus 8.	N.24.b.58.56. to N.24.b.58.02.	280 --do--
	Zero plus 8 to zero plus 10.	N.24.b.16.54. to N.24.d.12.90.	320 --do--

CREEPING : PRACTICE BARRAGE TABLE.

Battery.	Hour	Task	Remarks.
K.67.	Zero to zero plus two.	N.24.b.00.56. to N.24.a.95.52.	160 yds. front.
	Zero plus two to zero plus	N.24.b.13.86. to N.24.b.16.54.	--do--
	Zero plus to zero plus	N.24.b.37.85. to N.24.b.38.56.	150 yds. front.
	Zero plus 6. to zero plus 8.	N.24.b.57.85. to N.24.b.58.56.	140 yds. front.
	Zero plus 8 to zero plus 10.	N.24.b.13.86. to N.24.b.16.54.	160 --do--
K.73.	Zero to zero plus two.	N.24.a.95.52. to N.24.a.98.24.	160 --do--
	Zero plus 2 to zero plus 4.	N.24.b.16.54. to N.24.b.18.22.	160 --do--
	Zero plus 4 to zero plus 6.	N.24.b.38.56. to N.24.b.38.28.	150 --do--
	Zero plus 6 to zero plus 8.	N.24.b.58.56. to N.24.b.58.29.	140 --do--
	Zero plus 8 to zero plus 10.	N.24.b.16.54. to N.24.b.18.22.	160 --do--
K.69.	Zero to zero plus two.	N.24.a.98.24. to N.24.c.96.93.	
	Zero plus 2 to zero plus 4.	N.24.b.18.22. to N.24.d.18.90.	
	Zero plus 4 to zero plus 6.	N.24.b.38.28. to N.24.d.37.98.	
	Zero plus 6 to zero plus 8.	N.24.b.58.29. to N.24.b.58.02.	
	Zero plus 8 to zero plus 10.	N.24.b.18.22. to N.24.d.18.90.	

SECRET
****

Copy No....2.....

16th DIVISIONAL ARTILLERY
OPERATION ORDER No. 79.

Ref. 1/10,000 WYTSCHAETE
Trench Map.

Carried out

2nd June, 1917.

1. Bombardments with Gas Shell will be carried out by all 4.5" Hows (less D/58 Brigade, R.F.A.) on the nights of 2nd/3rd June; 3rd/4th June.

2. The localities to be bombarded and the number of shell to be employed are shown in the attached tables.

3. If weather conditions are unfavourable and gas shell bombardments are not to take place, or are postponed, a message will be sent to all concerned "Ref para. 56, conditions do not permit."

4. Figures against objectives refer to the map issued to Groups under this Office No. R.17/37 dated 1st June, 1917.

5. Rate of fire in firing Lethal shell will be two rounds per gun per minute.

6. All Gas shell other than S K may be taken to be Lethal.

7. (a) At 2.0 a.m. on night 2nd/3rd June, 50 rounds of B S K will be fired by each Sub-Group on each of the objectives allotted to it in attached table. Rate of fire not faster than 2 rounds per gun per minute.

(b) Similarly at 3.15 a.m. on 4th June, 30 rounds of B S K will be fired by each Sub-Group on each of the objectives allotted to it for the night 3rd/4th June.

8. ACKNOWLEDGE.

[signature] Major, R.A.,
Brigade Major, 16th Divl.Arty.

Issued at 12.30 pm

Copies to:-

1. 177th Bde, R.F.A.
2. 180th Bde, R.F.A.
3. 113th Army F.A.Bde.
4. 58th Bde, R.F.A.
5. 59th Bde, R.F.A.
6. 5th Army Bde, R.H.A.
7. 19th Div. Arty.
8. 36th Div. Arty.
9. 11th Div. Arty.
10. 47th Inf. Bde.
11. 48th Inf. Bde.
12. 49th Inf. Bde.
13. 16th Div. "G".
14. R.A., IX Corps.
15. H.A., IX Corps.
16. 16th Div. Signals.
17. 53rd Sqdn, R.F.C.
18. No. 5 Balloon Coy.
19. D.T.M.O., 16th Div.
20. Chemical Advisor, IX Corps.
21. Bde Maj., 16th D.A.
22. Staff Capt., 16th D.A.
23. War Diary.
24.) File.
25.)
26.)

S E C R E T
****

(0.0.79)

GAS SHELL BOMBARDMENT TABLE 2nd/3rd JUNE.

HOWITZERS

Batteries	Time	Objective *	Ammunition	Remarks
Right Sub-Group 12 Howitzers.	10.0 p.m.	(A) Houses on WYTSCHAETE-OOSTAVERNE ROAD between 0.19.d.85.90 and 0.20.c.15.80 paying particular attention to 14 and 15.	Lethal 200 rds	
Left Sub-Group 12 Howitzers	- do -	Houses on above road between 0.19.b.60.00 and 0.19.d.85.90.	Lethal 200 rds.	
Right Sub-Group 12 Howitzers	10.40 p.m.	(B) Houses between 0.19.d.43.76. and 0.19.d.27.90. paying special attention to 10.	Lethal 200 rds.	
Left Sub-Group 12 Howitzers	- do -	Houses between 0.19.d.27.95. and 0.19.b.23.28. paying special attention to 11.	Lethal 200 rds.	
Right Sub-Group 12 Howitzers	11.50 p.m.	(C) Between 0.19.a.99.65. and 0.19.b.15.42. paying special attention to 12.	Lethal 200 rds.	
Left Sub-Group 12 Howitzers.	- do -	Between 0.19.b.02.60 and 0.19.b.32.67. paying special attention to 13.	Lethal 200 rds.	
Right Sub-Group 12 Howitzers	1.25 a.m.	(D) House at 0.20.a.17.00 (16) and dump 0.20.a.37.05.	Lethal 200 rds.	
Left Sub-Group 12 Howitzers	- do -	Dugouts at 0.20.a.20.35 (17)	Lethal 200 rds.	

* Numbers refer to Hdqrs., etc., marked on Map issued under this Office No. R.17/36 dated 1/6/17.

S E C R E T
****

(O.O.79)

GAS SHELL BOMBARDMENT TABLE FOR 3rd/4th JUNE.

HOWITZERS.

Battery	Time	Objective	Ammunition	Remarks
Right Sub-Group 12 Howitzers	1.0 a.m.	(A) Dugouts and trenches along the line O.19.b.47.58. to O.19.b.85.68.	Lethal 200 rds.	
Left Sub-Group 12 Howitzers	- do -	Dugouts and trenches and junction within a 50 yards radius of O.19.b.90.43.	Lethal 200rds.	
Right Sub-Group 13 Howitzers	1.25 a.m.	(B) Task "C" as shown in Table for 2nd/3rd June.	Lethal 200 rds.	
Left Sub-Group 12 Howitzers	- do -	- ditto -	Lethal 200 rds.	
Right Sub-Group 12 Howitzers	1.50 a.m.	(C) OCCASION ALLEY O.19.d.20.95 to O.19.c.94.87.	Lethal 200 rds.	
Left Sub-Group 12 Howitzers	- do -	OCCASION ALLEY O.19.d.20.95 to O.19.b.49.02.	Lethal 200 rds.	
Right Sub-Group 12 Howitzers	2.45 a.m.	(D) Task "A" as shown in Table for 2nd/3rd June.	Lethal 182 rds.	
Left Sub-Group 12 Howitzers	- do -	- ditto -	Lethal 180 rds.	

S E C R E T.
-:-:-:-:-:-

Copy No. 11

RIGHT GROUP OPERATION ORDER No.5.

by

Lieut-Colonel L. E. S. WARD, D.S.O., R.F.A., Comdg.

Ref. Map WYTSCHAETE, 1/10,000. Trench Map.

1. Commencing at 11.0. a.m. (ZERO hour) on June 3rd, a concentrated bombardment will be carried out on WYTSCHAETE by Heavy Artillery.

2. The bombardment will last 30 minutes.

3. From Zero plus one to Zero plus thirty :

(a) A/113 will fire on the Western exits of WYTSCHAETE from O.19.b.00.57. (communication trench inclusive) to O.19.b.00.23.
(b) B/113 will fire on Western exits of WYTSCHAETE from O.19.b.00.23. to O.19.b.00.00.
(c) B/180 will fire on Western exits of WYTSCHAETE from O.19.b.00.00. to the KEMMEL - WYTSCHAETE Road inclusive.

Rate of fire one round per gun per minute.
75 % "AX" will be used.

4. ZERO hour will be 11.0. a.m.

5. Practice Barrage No.2.

Immediately following the combined bombardment of WYTSCHAETE, a practice barrage will be carried out on the IXth. Corps front.

6. A Table of Battery Tasks is attached.

7. ZERO hour will be 11.30. a.m. At Zero plus ten m minutes all batteries will cease fire.

8. Rates of fire. 18-pdrs. 3 rounds per gun per minute.

9. Nature of shells. 18-pdrs. ... 100 % "A".
One Section per 18-pdr. Battery will fire smoke shell.

10. Adjutant, 180th. Brigade R.F.A. will syncronize watches at 9.30. a.m., 3rd. June.

11. Right Group O.O. No.3. para. 8. will again hold good. Reports to be in this office by 12 noon.

12. ACKNOWLEDGE.

D Mackay Lieut., R.F.A.
Adjt., RIGHT GROUP.

2.6.17.

Copies to :-

A/113.
B/113.
C/113.
A/180
B/180
C/180
C/58th. Bde.
O.C. No.3.Rt.Sub-Group.
47th. Inf. Bde.
16th. D.A.
War Diary.
File.

TABLE OF TASKS.

-:-:-:-:-:-:-:-:-:-:-:-:-:-

attery	Hour	Task.		
K.42.	Zero to zero plus 2.	N.24.a.98.03.	to	N.24.c.83.66.
	Zero plus 2 to zero plus 4.	N.24.b.18.02.	to	N.24.d.04.62.
	Zero plus 4 to zero plus 6.	N.24.b.38.12.	to	N.24.d.29.72.
	Zero plus 6 to zero plus 8	N.24.b.57.13.	to	N.24.d.49.78.
	Zero plus 8 to zero plus 10.	N.24.b.18.02.	to,	N.24.d.04.62.
K.41.	Zero to zero plus 2	N.24.c.83.66.	to	N.24.c.79.29.
	Zero plus 2 to zero plus 4	N.24.d.04.62.	to	N.24.c.97.33.
	Zero plus 4 to zero plus 6	N.24.d.29.72.	to	N.24.d.20.40.
	Zero plus 6 to zero plus 8	N.24.d.49.78.	to	N.24.d.43.42.
	Zero plus 8 to zero plus 10.	N.24.d.04.62.	to	N.24.c.97.33.
K.48.	Zero to zero plus 2	N.24.a.98.03.	to	N.24.c.79.29.
	Zero plus 2 to zero plus 4	N.24.b.18.02.	to	N.24.c.97.33.
	Zero plus 4 to zero plus 6	N.24.b.38.12.	to	N.24.d.20.40.
	Zero plus 6 to zero plus 8	N.24.b.57.13.	to	N.24.d.43.42.
	Zero plus 8 to zero plus 10.	N.24.b.18.02.	to	N.24.c.97.33.

TABLE OF TASKS.

Battery	Hour	Task		
K.67.	Zero to zero plus 2.	N.24.b.00.86.	to	N.24.a.95.44.
	Zero plus 2 to zero plus 4	N.24.b.14.83.	to	N.24.b.17.43.
	Zero plus 4 to zero plus 6	N.24.b.37.83.	to	N.24.b.38.49.
	Zero plus 6 to zero plus 8.	N.24.b.53.82.	to	N.24.b.56.49.
	Zero plus 8 to zero plus 10.	N.24.b.14.83.	to	N.24.b.17.43.
K.73.	Zero to zero plus 2.	N.24.a.95.44.	to	N.24.a.98.03.
	Zero plus 2 to zero plus 4	N.24.b.17.43.	to	N.24.b.18.02.
	Zero plus 4 to zero plus 6.	N.24.b.38.49.	to	N.24.b.38.12.
	Zero plus 6 to zero plus 8.	N.24.b.56.49.	to	N.24.b.57.13.
	Zero plus 8 to zero plus 10.	N.24.b.17.43.	to	N.24.b.18.02.
K.69.	Zero to zero plus 2	N.24.b.00.86.	to	N.24.a.98.03.
	Zero plus 2 to zero plus 4.	N.24.b.14.83.	to	N.24.b.18.02.
	Zero plus 4 to zero plus 6	N.24.b.37.83.	to	N.24.b.38.12.
	Zero plus 6 to zero plus 8.	N.24.b.53.82.	to	N.24.b.57.13.
	Zero plus 8 to zero plus 10.	N.24.b.14.83.	to	N.24.b.18.02.

8 pages.

S E C R E T.
-:-:-:-:-:-

Copy No. 11

RIGHT GROUP OPERATION ORDER No.6.

by

Lieut-Colonel L. E. S. WARD, D.S.O., R.F.A., Comdg.

Ref. Map WYTSCHAETE 1/10,000.
Trench Map.

June 3rd,1917.

1. A demonstration will be made on the whole front of the Second Army today, June 3rd. and will commence at 3. p.m.
If weather conditions are unfavourable the demonstration will be postponed to 4.p.m. June 3rd. or till 3.p.m.June 4th.

2. ZERO hour will be 3.15. p.m. (unless otherwise postponed vide para.1) at which time the barrage opens.

3. <u>ZERO minus 15 to zero.</u>
Groups will vigorously carry out the normal bombardment with those batteries not employed on special tasks.
The majority of the fire should be directed on the enemy's front and support line.

4. <u>At ZERO (315. p.m.)</u>
(a) The first 15 minutes of the barrage programme as shewn On the Second Army Barrage Map will be carried out, this will include the barrage on the PETIT BOIS Salient.

(b) Table of Tasks attached.

(c) 16th. Division "G" are arranging for our trenches to be cleared in front of the PETIT BOIS Salient.

(d) <u>Rates of fire.</u>

<u>18-pdrs.</u> 4 rounds per gun per minute for two minutes.
then 3 rounds per gun per minute.
18-pdr. batteries of the Standing Barrage will fire Smoke Shell for the first two minutes at a rate of 8 rounds per gun per minute.

<u>4.5" Hows.</u> 2 rounds per gun per minute for 2 minutes.
then one round per gun per minute.

5. ACKNOWLEDGE.

Lieut., R.F.A.

Adjt., RIGHT GROUP.

Copies to :-

K.67.	K.49. (for information)
K.73.	O.C. No.3. Right Sub-Group.
K.69.	16th. Div. Arty.
K.42.	47th. Inf. Bde.
K.41.	War Diary.
K.48.	File.

Contd.

T A B L E O F T A S K S

Battery	Hour	Task		
K.42.	Zero to zero plus 4	N.24.a.98.03.	to	N.24.c.83.66
	Zero plus 4 to zero plus 6	N.24.b.18.02	to	N.24.d.04.62
	Zero plus 6 to zero plus 8	N.24.b.38.12	to	N.24.d.29.72
	Zero plus 8 to zero plus 12	N.24.b.57.13	to	N.24.d.49.78
	Zero plus 12 to zero plus 15	N.24.b.78.18	to	N.24.d.75.80
K.41	Zero to zero plus 4	N.24.c.83.66	to	N.24.c.79.29
	Zero plus 4 to zero plus 6	N.24.d.04.62	to	N.24.c.97.33
	Zero plus 6 to zero plus 8	N.24.d.29.72	to	N.24.d.20.40
	Zero plus 8 to zero plus 12	N.24.d.49.78	to	N.24.d.43.42
	Zero plus 12 to zero plus 15	N.24.d.75.80	to	N.24.d.63.48
K.48	Zero to zero plus 4	N.24.a.98.03	to	N.24.c.79.29
	Zero plus 4 to zero plus 6	N.24.b.18.02	to	N.24.d.97.33
	Zero plus 6 to zero plus 8	N.24.b.38.12	to	N.24.d.20.40
	Zero plus 8 to zero plus 12	N.24.b.57.13	to	N.24.d.43.42
	Zero plus 12 to zero plus 15	N.24.b.78.18	to	N.24.d.63.48

TABLE OF TASKS

Battery	Hour	Task		
K.67.	Zero to zero plus one	N.24.a.60.86.	to	N.24.a.60.68.
	Zero plus one to zero plus 2	N.24.a.76.86.	to	N.24.a.76.62.
	Zero plus 2 to zero plus 4	N.24.b.00.86.	to	N.24.a.95.44.
	Zero plus 4 to zero plus 6	N.24.b.14.83	to	N.24.b.17.43
	Zero plus 6 to zero plus 8	N.24.b.37.83	to	N.24.b.38.49.
	Zero plus 8 to zero plus 12	N.24.b.53.82	to	N.24.b.56.49
	Zero plus 12 to zero plus 15	N.24.b.75.85.	to	N.24.b.74.52
K.73.	Zero to zero plus 4.	N.24.a.95.44.	to	N.24.a.98.03
	Zero plus 4 to zero plus 6	N.24.b.17.43.	to	N.24.b.18.02
	Zero plus 6 to zero plus 8	N.24.b.38.49.	to	N.24.b.38.12
	Zero plus 8 to zero plus 12	N.24.b.56.49.	to	N.24.b.57.13
	Zero plus 12 to zero plus 15	N.24.b.74.52	to	N.24.b.78.18
K.63	Zero to zero plus 4	N.24.b.00.86.	to	N.24.a.98.03.
	Zero plus 4 to zero plus 6	N.24.b.14.83.	to	N.24.b.18.02.
	Zero plus 6 to zero plus 8	N.24.b.37.83.	to	N.24.b.38.12
	Zero plus 8 to zero plus 12	N.24.b.53.82.	to	N.24.b.57.13
	Zero plus 12 to zero plus 15	N.24.b.75.85.	to	N.24.b.78.18

SECRET
-:-:-:-:-:-

Copy No. 19

RIGHT GROUP OPERATION ORDER No.7

by

Lieut-Colonel L. E. S. WARD, D.S.O., R.F.A., Comdg.

Ref. Map 1/10,000 WYTSCHAETE Trench Map.

1. An enterprise will be carried out by the 6th. Battalion Connaught Rangers on the night 4th/5th June.
Objectives :

NANCY SWITCH from N.24.b.30.75 to N.24.b.30.30.
NANCY SUPPORT from N.24.b.60.78 to N.24.b.62.48.

2. A Table of Tasks for the supporting Artillery is attached.
18-pdr. Batteries will fire 50% "A" and 50% "AX".

3. ZERO hour will be 10.30. p.m.

4. Lieutenant G.H. HINDS will act as Liaison Officer with O.C. Enterprise, with whom he will remain throughout the operation.
Further instructions will be issued to this Officer.

5. Batteries will continue to fire on the last task shown until "Stop Firing" is issued from Group H.Q., when normal night tasks will be resumed.

6. Watches will be synchronised by telephone under arrangements by Adjutant, 180th. Brigade R.F.A.

7. ACKNOWLEDGE.

D Mackenzie
for Lt-Col., R.F.A.

3.6.17. Comdg., RIGHT GROUP.

Copies to ;-

A/58 F9 87	B/177 FO40	58th. Bde. R.F.A.
B/58 FO57	A/180 FO56	113th. Bde. R.F.A.
C/58 FO7	B/180 FO53	177th. Bde. R.F.A.
A/113 FO55	C/180 FO54	War Diary
B/113 FC45	D/180 FO27	File.
C/113 FO9	16th. D.A.	Spare.
D/113 FO58	47th. Inf. Bde.	Liaison Officer.

"7 prisoners.

CREEPING BARRAGE

-:-:-:-:-:-:-:-:-:-:-:-:-:-

Battery	Hour	Task	Remarks.
K.67	Zero to zero plus 2	N.18.c.94.00 to N.24.a.94.75	3 rounds per gun per min.
	Zero plus 2 to zero plus 4	N.18.d.18.00 to N.24.b.17.75	
	Zero plus 4 to zero plus 6	N.18.d.39.00 to N.24.b.37.75	
	Zero plus 6 to zero plus 8	N.18.d.60.00. to N.24.b.58.75	
	Zero plus 8 to zero plus 10	N.18.d.83.00 to N.24.b.82.75	
	Zero plus 10 to zero plus 12	O.13.c.00.00 to O.19.a.00.75	
	From zero plus 12 to stop firing	O.13.c.00.00 to O.19.a.00.75	1½ rounds per gun per min.
K.73	Zero to zero plus 2	N.24.a.94.75 to N.24.a.94.50	3 rounds per gun per min.
	Zero plus 2 to zero plus 4	N.24.b.17.75 to N.24.b.17.50	
	Zero plus 4 to zero plus 6	N.24.b.37.75 to N.24.b.36.51	
	Zero plus 6 to zero plus 8	N.24.b.58.75 to N.24.b.59.50	
	Zero plus 8 to zero plus 10	N.24.b.82.75 to N.24.b.82.50	
	Zero plus 10 to zero plus 12	O.19.a.00.75 to O.19.a.00.50	
	From zero plus 12 to stop firing	O.19.a.00.75 to O.19.a.00.50	1½ rounds per per gun per min
K.42	Zero to zero plus 2	N.24.a.94.50 to N.24.b.00.25	3 rounds per gun per min.
	Zero plus 2 to zero plus 4	N.24.b.17.50 to N.24.b.22.25	
	Zero plus 4 to zero plus 6	N.24.b.36.51 to N.24.b.38.25	
	Zero plus 6 to zero plus 8	N.24.b.59.50 to N.24.b.59.25	
	Zero plus 8 to zero plus 10	N.24.b.82.50 to N.24.b.85.26	
	Zero plus 10 to zero plus 12	O.191a.00.50 to N.24.b.00.27 O19a	
	From zero pls 12 to stop firing	O.19.a.00.50 to N.24.b.00.27 O19a.	1½ rounds per per gun per min

Contd.

CREEPING BARRAGE

Battery	Hour	Task	Remarks.
K.41	Zero to zero plus 2	N.24.b.00.25. to N.24.b.06.00	
	Zero plus 2 to zero plus 4	N.24.b.22.25 to N.24.b.27.00	
	Zero plus 4 to zero plus 6	N.24.b.38.25 to N.24.d.48.98	3 rounds per gun per min.
	Zero plus 6 to zero plus 8	N.24.b.59.25 to N.24.b.60.00	
	Zero plus 8 to zero plus 10	N.24.b.85.26. to N.24.b.84.03	
	Zero plus 10 to zero plus 12	N.24.b.00.27 (O 19 a) to O.19.a.00.08	
	Zero plus 12 to stop firing	N.24.b.00.27 (O 19 a) to O.19.a.00.08	1½ rounds per gun per min.
K.69	Zero to zero plus 2	N.18.c.94.00 to N.24.a.94.50	
	Zeroplus 2 to zero plus 4	N.18.d.18.00 to N.24.b.17.50	
	Zero plus 4 to zero plus 6	N.18.d.39.00 to N.24.b.36.51	3 rounds per gun per min.
	Zero plus 6 to zero plus 8	N.18.d.60.00 to N.24.b.59.50	
	Zero plus 8 to zero plus 10	N.18.d.83.00 to N.24.b.82.50	
	Zero plus 10 to zero plus 12	O.13.c.00.00 to O.19.a.00.50.	
	From zero plus 12 to stop firing	Enfilade NAME DRIVE from front line to O.19.a.10.92.	1½ rounds per gun per min.
K.48	Zero to zero plus 2	N.24.a.94.50 to N.24.b.06.00	
	Zero plus 2 to zero plus 4	N.24.b.17.50 to N.24.b.27.00	
	Zero plus 4 to zero plus 6	N.24.b.36.51 to N.24.d.48.98	3 rounds per gun per min.
	Zero plus 6 to zero plus 8	N.24.b.59.50 to N.24.b.60.00	
	Zero plus 8 to zero plus 10	N.24.b.82.50 to N.24.b.84.03	
	Zero plus 10 to zero plus 12	O.19.a.00.50 to O.19.a.00.08	

STANDING BARRAGE

Battery	Hour	Task	Remarks.
K.44	Zero to zero plus 4	N.18.d.39.00 to N.24.b.36.50	1½ rounds per gun per minute
	Zero plus 4 to zero plus 8	NANCY SUPPORT from N.18.d.59.00 to N.24.b.62.50	
	Zero plus 8 to stop firing	The following points and Trench Junctions : N.18.d.20.31 N.18.d.37.30 N.18.d.88.23 O.19.a.12.91 N.24.d.49.79 N.24.d.30.66	1 round per gun per minute
K.59	Zero to zero plus 4	N.24.b.36.50 to N.24.d.47.98	1½ rounds per gun per minute
	Zero plus 4 to zero plus 8	NANCY SUPPORT from N.24.b.62.50 to N.24.b.58.00	
	Zero plus 8 to stop firing	The following points and Trench Junctions : O.19.a.18.48 O.19.a.28.22 O.19.c.06.79 N.24.d.80.73 N.24.c.89.53 N.24.c.83.43	1 round per gun per minute
K.66.	Zero to zero plus 4	Sweep from N.18.d.39.00 to N.24.b.58.00	1½ rounds per gun per minute
	Zero plus 4 to zero plus 8	Sweep from N.18.d.39.00 to O.19.a.00.05	
	Zero plus 8 to stop firing	Barrage NANCY AVENUE from N.24.b.70.00 to O.19.a.15.06	
A Batty. 177.Bde.	Zero to stop firing.	Barrage hostile front line from N.18.d.18.20 to N.18.d.20.60 ~~sweeping~~ Search. back to NAIL SWITCH	1½ rounds per gun per minute
K.49.	Zero to stop firing	Barrage hostile front line from N.24.d.32.90 to N.24.d.10.57	1½ rounds per gun pr minute
K.47.	Zero to stop firing	Sweep NAP RESERVE.	
	One Section from	O.19.a.18.82 to O.19.a.35.63	1½ rounds per gun pr minute
	One Section from	O.19.a.47.52 to O.19.a.42.30	
	One Section from	O.19.a.52.06. to O.19.c.42.87	

Assistance from Heavy Artillery : Zero to zero plus 60. — 1 round per gun pr minute
One 6" How. on each of the following points ;-

N.18.d.50.69	O.13.c.15.49.
O.13.c.60.30	O.19.a.60.89
O.19.a.42.70	O.19.a.43.58
O.19.a.41.27	O.19.a.47.13
O.19.c.30.74	N.24.d.55.67.

Contd.

CREEPING BARRAGE

Battery	Hour	Task	Remarks.
K.48. (Contd)	Zero plus 12 to stop firing	Barrage NANCY AVENUE from it's junction with front line to N.24.d.68.98.	1½ rounds per gun per min.

S E C R E T.

O.O. No.7/1.

O.C. K.41.
" K.42.
" 47th. Inf. Bde.
" 16th. Div. Arty.
" 6th. Btn.Connaught Rngrs.

Reference Right Group Operation Order No.7

Please notethe following corrections in the "CREEPING BARRAGE" Table.

<u>K.42. Zero Plus 10 to zero plus 12</u>

For 0.19.a.00.50. to N.24.b.00.27.

Substitute 0.19.a.00.50. to 0.19.a.00.27.

<u>K.42. From zero plus 12 to Stop Firing.</u>

For 0.19.a.00.50. to N.24.b.00.27.

Substitute 0.19.a.00.50. to 0.19.a.00.27.

<u>K.41. Zero plus 10 to zero plus 12</u>

For N.24.b.00.27. to 0.19.a.00.08

Substitute 0.19.a.00.27 to 0.19.a.00.08.

<u>K.41. From zero plus 12 to stop firing.</u>

For N.24.b.00.27. to 0.19.a.00.08.

Substitute 0.19.a.00.27. to 0.19.a.00.08.

Lieut., R.F.A.

4.6.17. Adjt., RIGHT GROUP.

SECRET.
SECOND ARMY BARRAGE MAP.
June, 1917.
CORPS BOUNDARY
DIVISIONAL BOUNDARY
(SPECIAL) 1:10,000 MAP 8150/2.
19th DIV.
16th DIV.
36th DIV.
OOSTTAVERNE LINE
DOTTED BLACK LINE
BLACK LINE
IX CORPS GREEN LINE
BLUE LINE
RED LINE
Oosttaverne
Wambeke
Vierstraat
CONVERSION TABLE
MINUTES — HOURS.
61 mins. = 1 hour 1 min.
62 2
64 4
65 5
67 7
69 9
70 10
71 11
72 12
73 13
77 17
82 22
85 25
90 30
91 31
100 40
104 44
105 45
108 48
110 50
113 53
115 55
116 56
118 58
119 59
120 2 hours 0 mins.
122 2
125 5
127 7
129 9
130 10
131 11
132 12
220 mins. = 3 hours 40 mins.
224 44
228 48
229 49
230 50
232 52
234 54
236 56
240 4 hours 0 mins.
244 4
245 5
246 6
248 8
249 9
250 10
255 15
264 24
272 32
275 35
280 40
284 44
286 46
288 48
300 5 hours 0 mins.
304 4
318 18
322 22
326 26

S E C R E T

Copy No. 12

RIGHT GROUP OPERATION ORDER No.9.

by

Lieut-Colonel, L. E. G. WARD, D.S.O., R.F.A., Comdg.

Ref. Map. 1/10,000. WYTSCHAETE Trench Map.

1. Today, 5th. June, there will be a practice barrage on the whole Army Front lasting ten minutes.

2. ZERO hour will be 3.0. p.m.

3. From ZERO to zero plus 10 minutes the Right Group will carry out the first 10 minutes of the attack programme for "Z" day, except that K.67. (B/113) and K.69 (A/180) detailed to fire on the PETIT BOIS Salient , will conform to the remainder of the barrage line at ZERO.

4. No smoke shell will be fired during ZERO to zero plus 10 minutes.

5. Watches will be synchronised under arrangements by the Adjutant, 180th. Brigade R.F.A.

6. ACKNOWLEDGE.

D Macday Lieut., R.F.A.

5.6.17. Adjt., RIGHT GROUP.

Copies to ;-

1. A/113
2. B/113
3. C/113
4. A/180
5. B/180
6. C/180
7. C/ 58 (for information)
8. No.3. Right Sub.Group.
9. 47th. Inf. Bde.
10. 113th. Brigade R.F.A.
11. War Diary.
✓12. File

AFTER ORDER.

7. During the practice barrage this afternoon a patrol will leave our trenches about N.24.a.58.52 and enter the hostile front line about N.24.a.70.62.

Inf. Offensive

S E C R E T   47th Inf. Bde. No. G. 3221.

6th Connaught Rangers.	47th T.M.Battery.
1st Royal Munster Fusrs.	49th Inf. Bde.
6th Royal Irish Regt.	108th Inf. Bde.
7th Leinster Regt.	Right Group R.F.A.
47th M.Gun Company.	16th Division.

1. 6th Connaught Rangers will carry out a raid on the night of June 4th/5th.

2. Objectives will be:-

First Objective about N.24.b.3.4. to N.24.b.32.73.

Second Objective about N.24.b.6.4. to N.24.b.60.74.

3. Strength of the attacking party will be 3 Coys less 2 platoons or about 11 Officers and 280 O.R. with 6 Lewis Guns under command of Lieut. TUITE.

4. Zero hour will be 10.30 p.m. at which hour the troops will leave our trenches.

5. The attack will be made under a creeping artillery barrage supported by a bombardment of heavy howitzers on selected points.
The liftsof the creeping barrage will be in accordance with the attached table and map

6. 2 Coys will attack in two waves, the 1st wave seizing the 2nd objective and the 2nd wave the 1st objective. Flank protection will be afforded by a platoon on either flank moving in artillery formation.
The first wave will pass through the second wave on withdrawal and return in artillery formation.

7. The O.C. raid will establish his H.Q. in the neighbourhood of the junction of NANCY SWITCH and NANCY SUPPORT.

8. To guide the parties on their return, some or all of the following methods will be employed:-
(a) Bonfire East of ROSSIGNOL WOOD.
(b) Gold and silver rain rockets fired from vicinity of LUNETTE DUGOUTS.
(c) Oil barrel to be fired at each extremity of the 2nd objective.

9. 1st Royal Munster Fusrs. will detail 4 Lewis guns with teams to be at H.Q. 6th Connaught Rangers at 8 p.m. on June 4th as reinforcements for holding the line.

10. O.C. Enterprise and the Artillery Liaison Officer will be at LUNETTE DUGOUTS.

Captain,
3-6-17.   Brigade Major, 47th Infantry Brigade.

Barrage Table to accompany 47th Infantry Brigade No. G. 3221.

	Infantry.	Artillery.	Stokes Mortars.
Zero	Leave trenches.	Barrage opens.	Intense fire N.24.c.90.55 - 24.d.30.70 - 24.d.30.80.
Zero plus 8.	Reach 1st Objective.	Barrage lifts from 1st objective to NANCY SUPPORT.	Slackens to slow fire.
Zero plus 12.	Reach 2nd Objective.	Lifts to furthest point and forms a box barrage until stop firing is ordered	
Zero plus 32.	Commence withdrawal.		Intense fire on above targets.
Zero plus 45	To be back in our lines.		

SECRET. Copy No: 5 .

LEFT ARTILLERY GROUP 19th DIVISION
--OPERATION ORDER NO: A.1--------

12th JUNE 1917.

1. In accordance with instructions received for Headquarters 19th D.A. 180th and 88th Brigades R.F.A. will now comprise "The Left Artillery Group 19th Division."

2. In addition to the continuation of registration, firing on points that contain enemy, and tracks used by him, F.A.Brigades will to-day, 12th instant, engage objectives as follows:-

<u>180th Brigade R.F.A.</u> Between 2.0 pm - 3.0 pm.

Building at O 16 D 75 55 with 4.5" Hows: and 18-prs. The 4.5" Hows: will fire about 100 rounds for effect, the 18-prs registering, watching for, and engaging movement.

<u>88th Brigade R.F.A.</u> Between 30 pm - 4.0 pm.

"D"/88 and "A"/88 will in conjunction with each other, register SUNKEN ROAD O 17 A 20 25 - suspected 15 cm position. Batteries will not fire for effect on this objective until reports have been received from infantry patrols going out tonight.

<u>180th Brigade R.F.A.</u> Between 5.0 pm - 6.0 pm.

Will register suspected 15 cm position at SUNKEN ROAD O 16 D 95 85 with 4.5" Hows: and 18-pdrs, but will not fire for effect until reports have been received from the infantry.

3. "A"/88 Battery will move forward to a position about O 7 B 6 1 moving by the most Northerly track through BOIS QUARANTE.
This battery will commence improving the route and preparing the position to-day, and will commence moving up ammunition at dusk this evening 12th inst.
Guns will be moved forward between 3.0 am and 6.0 am
"B"/88 and "C"/88 will each be responsible for half of "A"/88 Zone from 2.0 am until "A"/88 has reported registrations carried out from new position.

4. The normal hours for bringing up ammunition, supplies etc. to gun positions will be from dusk to daylight, but advantage will be taken of dull and misty weather for bringing up ammunition etc.

5. At 10.0 am 12th inst., the front line is approximatly:-

O 10 D 0 0 - O 16 D 15 55 - East edge of HOVE FARM.

Issued at 11.30....a.m.
12/6/17

Lieut: R.F.A.
Adjutant, 88th Brigade, R.F.A.

Copy No: 1 to "A"/88.
" " 2 to "B"/88.
" " 3 to "C"/88.
" " 4 to "D"/88.
" " 5 to 180th F.A.Bde
" " 6 to Senior Liaison Offr.
" " 7 to 58th Infy. Bde.
" " 8 to 19th D.A.
" " 9 & 10 to File.

ADDENDUM TO LEFT ARTY: GROUP OPERATION ORDER NO: A.1.

From 2.0 pm onwards, Brigades will engage objectives as follows, firing about 100 rounds 4.5" Hows: and 100 18-pdr shrapnel and H.E. as required, at each objective.

180th Brigade R.F.A.

Buildings O 16 D 7 5
Buildings O 17 C 3 4
Buildings O 17 C O 3

"A"/88 and "D"/88.

Buildings O 17 C 6 6
Buildings O 17 C 8 8
Buildings O 17 D O 8

Lieut: R.F.A.
12/6/17. Adjutant LEFT ART: GROUP 19th DIVN:

Copies to:-
All recipients of Left Arty: Group Operation Order No: A.1.

SECRET
-:-:-:-:-:-

180. Bde.RFA. No.SF. 186.

O.C. A/180 O.C. C/180
B/180 D/180

Ref. 19th. Div. Arty. O.O. 125 attached.

1. A/180 and C/180 will undertake the Creeping Barrage and B/180 and D/180 will be on the Standing Barrage.

2. A/180 is allotted an opening line from O.16.d.7.8. to O.16.d.7.4.
B/180 is allotted an opening line from O.16.b.7.2. to O.16.d.7.8.

3. One Section each of A/180 and C/180 will remain on the protective barrage line at ZERO plus 37 and sweep to cover the battery zone allotted above.

4. B/180 will search and sweep within the limits of the Sub-Group zone, (i.e. between a line running East and West through O.16.b.7.2. and a line running East and West through O.16.d.7.4.) from a line N. and S. through O.17.a.8.0. up a limit of range of 5800 yards.

5. D/180 : objectives as laid down in para 3 (b).

6. Watches will be synchronised by Adjutant, 180th. Brigade R.F.A.

7. ACKNOWLEDGE.

D Mackay
Lieut., R.F.A.

14.6.17. Adjt., 180th. Brigade R.F.A,

M28a 55 38

60 Bty No 27

S E C R E T.

19th Divisional Artillery Operation Order No 125.

Reference Maps:-
Sheet 28 S W 1/20,000
1/10,000 Trench Maps.

14th June 1917.

1. The IInd Anzac and X Corps are carrying out operations today, 14th instant, with the object of gaining more ground.

The 41st Division and 24th Division on our Left are to capture and consolidate the following objectives :-

(a) That point of OLIVE TRENCH which is not yet held by us from about O 10 d 70 85., OBTIC TRENCH to its junction with OBLIQUE ROW, and thence northwards along OBLIQUE ROW to the CANAL.
This will be carried out by the 41st Division.

(b) SPOIL BANK in O 5 b up to LOCK 6 bis, thence to the railway at I 36 c 3 0, thence North along the railway to IMPARTIAL TRENCH
This will be carried out by the 24th Division.

2. Zero hour will be 7.30p.m.

3. The Left Group will co-operate with the 41st Division by extending the lines of the 41st Divisional Artillery Creeping Barrage within the limits of the Group Zone (i.e. a zone between an E and W line through O 10 d 0 0 and an E. and W. line through O 16 d 0 4).

A Standing Barrage will search approaches from Zero onwards.

Details as follows :-

(a) Creeping Barrage.

26 18-pdr. guns.	Zero to Zero plus 10.	Open on a line O 10 d 7 0 - O 16 d 7 4.
	Zero plus 10 to Zero plus 25	Lift 150 yards.
	Zero plus 25 to Zero plus 29	Lift 100 yards
	Zero plus 29 to Zero plus 33	Lift 100 yards.
	Zero plus 33 to Zero plus 37	Lift 100 yards.

At Zero plus 37 18 guns of the Creeping Barrage will search . . ex and sweep forward by lifts of 100 yards up to a limit of 600 yards beyond protective barrage line.

The remaining 8 guns will form a protective barrage line sweeping so as to cover the zone.

(b) Standing Barrage.

10 18-pdr. guns. 12 4.5-inch howitzers.

18-pounders. Search and ~~sweep~~ within the limits of Group Zone from a line North and South through O 17 a 8 0 up to a limit of range of 5,800 yards.

4.5-inch Howitzers.

D/88. Bridges over YPRES COMINES CANAL (P 13 a 60 55. P 13 d 4 4).

D/180. WARNETON LINE TRENCH within limits of Group zone.

/Rates of Fire

Rates of Fire. (rounds per gun per minute).

	Creeping Barrage. 18-pdr.	Standing Barrage. 18-pdr.	4.5"how.
Zero to Zero plus 7	3	2	2
Zero plus 7 to Zero plus 37	2	2	1
Zero plus 37 to Zero plus 50	1	1	1
Zero plus 50 to Zero plus 60	½	½	½

Nature of Shell for Creeping and Standing Barrages -
75% Shrapnel 25% H.E.

4. In conjunction with the operation indicated in para. 1 a raid covered by an Artillery Barrage will be carried out by the 56th Infantry Brigade against the group of houses at O 22 b 9 7 and VERHAEGE FARM.

5. The G.O.C. 56th Infantry Brigade will arrange with the Right Artillery Group Commander as to his requirements for the Artillery Barrage to cover the raid.

When these requirements are known the arrangements will be co-ordinated by C.R.A. 19th Division so as to synchronize, as far as possible, with the co-operation of the Left Group as indicated above and with the action of the 11th Divisional Artillery.

6. ACKNOWLEDGE by WIRE.

[signature]

Major R.A.,
Brigade Major, 19th Divisional Artillery.

Issued at 10.30a.m. to :-

Copy	To.
1/2	19th Division "G"
3	R.A. IX Corps.
4	H.A. IX Corps.
5	56th Infantry Brigade.
6	58th Infantry Brigade.
7	11th Divisional Artillery.
8	41st Divisional Artillery.
9/13	87th F.A.Brigade.
14/18	88th F.A.Brigade.
19/23	177th F.A.Brigade.
24/28	180th F.A.Brigade.
29	19th D.T.M.O.
30	19th D.A.C.
31/32	War Diary.
33	File.

S E C R E T   Copy No.......

LEFT ARTILLERY GROUP 19th DIVISION

OPERATION ORDER No.A.2.

Reference 1/10,000 Trench Map, 28 S.W. 2.

Reference 19th D.A. O.O. No.125 dated 14/6/17, sufficient copies of which have been issued for 1 for each Brigade H.Q. and Battery

1. Reference para 3 (a)

13 guns of Creeping barrage will be 120th Brigade R.F.A.
12 guns of Creeping barrage will be 88th Brigade R.F.A.

For 88th Brigade R.F.A. A/88 will provide 4 guns
B/88 " " 4 "
C/88 " " 4 "

Each Battery firing within its battery zone.

At Zero plus 37 minutes 9 guns of each Sub-Group will search and sweep forward by lifts of 100 yards up to a limit of 600 yards beyond Protective Barrage.
For 88th Brigade R.F.A. each Battery will sweep forward with 3 guns

2. Reference para 3 (b)

Each Sub-Group will provide 5 18-pdrs for Standing barrage within the limit of the Sub-Group zone.
For 88th Brigade R.F.A.:-
A/88 will provide 2 for Standing barrage.
B/88 " " 2 " " "
C/88 " " 1 " " "

Lieut: R.F.A.

Issued at 5.10 pm
14/6/17.

Adjutant Left Arty: Group 19th Divn:.

O.O. A.2.

RELIEF TABLE 27th/28th. June.

Relieving Unit.	Unit Relieved.		Location of Guns.
B/88	B/180	2 guns	O. 7.b.30.60.
		1 gun.	N.12.d.35.30.
Battery of 318th. Army Brigade R.F.A.	C/180	2 guns	O. 7.b.60.70.
		1.gun.	O. 7.c.00.40.
D/88	D/180	2 guns.	O. 7.a.60.00.
		1 gun.	N.12.d.05.55.

28th/29th. June.

Relief will be completed (vide O.O. No. A.2) and Units of the 180th. Brigade R F.A. will withdraw to Wagon Lines as under.

H.Q/180 R.F.A. to N.8.c.0.4.

B/180 R.F.A. to N.5.c.3.3.

C/180 R.F.A. to Present Wagon Lines at N.21.c.6.8.

D/180 R F.A. to N.14.a.4.8.

SECRET
-:-:-:-:-:-

180. Bde.RFA. No.SF.18.

O.C. A/180 O.C. C/180
B/180 D/180

Ref. 19th. Div. Arty. O.O. 125 attached.

1. A/180 and C/180 will undertake the Creeping Barrage and B/180 and D/180 will be on the Standing Barrage.

2. A/180 is allotted an opening line from O.16.d.7.8. to O.16.d.7.4.
C B/180 is allotted an opening line from O.16.b.7.2. to O.16.d.7.8.

3. One Section each of A/180 and C/180 will remain on the protective barrage line at ZERO plus 37 and sweep to cover the battery zone allotted above.

4. B/180 will search and sweep within the limits of the Sub-Group zone (i.e. between a line running East and West through O.16.b.7.2. and a line running East and West through O.16.d.7.4.) from a line N. and S. through O.17.a.8.0. up to a limit of range of 5,800 yards.

5. D/180 : objectives as laid down in para 3 (b).

6. Watches will be synchronised by Adjutant, 180th. Bde. R.F.A.

7. ACKNOWLEDGE.

Lieut., R.F.A.

14.6.17. Adjt., 180th. Brigade R.F.A.

S E C R E T.
-:-:-:-:-:-

16th. DIVISIONAL ARTILLERY
OPERATION ORDER No. 88.

Ref. Map BELGIUM
HAZEBROUCK 5 a.
1/100,000.

16th. June, 1917.

1. A/180 Brigade R.F.A. will march on 17th. instant at 3.30. a.m. from present Wagon Lines to Second Army Artillery School.

They will halt for the night 17th/18th June at HARDIFORT and will reach Second Army Artillery School, TILQUES, on 18th. June.

2. Billeting Parties will be sent on in advance under Battery arrangements.

3. Orders regarding rations for consumption on 18th. inst. will be issued later.

4. Arrival at Second Army Artillery School will be reported by wire to this office.

5. ACKNOWLEDGE.

(sd) R.A. SPENCER, Major, R.A
a/Brigade Major, 16th. Div. Artilley

O.C. A/180

180th. Bde. R.F.A. No. S.6/18/ 16.6.17.

For information and necessary action, please.

Lieut., R.F.A.

Adjt., 180th. Brigade R.F.A.

S E C R E T
-:-:-:-:-:-

Copy No. 5

180th. BRIGADE OPERATION ORDER No.A.2.

by

Major N. A. STEBBING, D.S.O., R.F.A., Commanding.

Ref. 1/20,000 Trench Map.
Sheet 28 S.W.

26th. June, 1917

1. B/180 and D/180 will be relieved by B/88 and D/88 respectively on the 27th. and 28th. June, in accordnace with attached relief table.

2. C/180 will be relieved by a Battery of the 315th Army Bde R.F.A

3. Guns of B/180 and D/180 will be left in situ; the personnel will be relieved by day, the relief to be complete by 12 noon on each day.

4. C/180 will withdraw guns from its position and exchange with C/88 in Wagon Lines.

5. No movement of vehicles will take place East of YORK ROAD before 9.0. p.m.

6. All local maps, panoramas, air photos, battery boards, Defence Schemes and all orders and information concerning the front will be handed over to incoming units.

7. On relief, H.Q/180, B/180 and D/180 will exchange billets and Wagon lines with corresponding Units of 88th. Brigade R.F.A.
   Wagon Lines will be exchanged on 28th. June, the exchange to be completed by 6.0. p.m.
   C/180 will remain in their present Wagon Lines.

8. No less than 500 rounds per 18-pdr. gun and 400 rounds per 4.5" howitzer will be handed over at gun positions.
   Receipts will be taken in triplicate for all amounts of ammunition according to natures handed over, and two copies sent to this office by 2.0. p.m. 28th, June.

9. Command of batteries will pass on completion of relief.
   Completion of relief will be reported to this office by wire using the code word "PERTH".

10. Certificates of cleanliness for billets, wagon lines and gun-lines will be taken.

11. ACKNOWLEDGE.

N. Stebbing Major R.F.A.

Comdg., 180th. Brigade R.F.A.

Copies to ;-
1. B/180 Bde. R.F.A.
2. C/180 " "
3. D/180 " "
4. 16th. D.A.
5. 109th. Inf. Bde.
6. 88th. Brigade R.F.A.
7. A/88th. Bde. R.F.A.
8. War Diary.
9. File.

W A R D I A R Y

FOR MONTH OF OCTOBER, 1917.

UNIT 180 Brigade R.F.A.

VOLUME NUMBER 21

Vol 21

Instructions regarding War Diaries and Intelligence Summaries are contained in F. S. Regs., Part II. and the Staff Manual respectively. Title pages will be prepared in manuscript.

WAR DIARY

or

~~INTELLIGENCE SUMMARY.~~

(Erase heading not required.)

No 20.

180th Bde RFA.

Army Form C. 2118.

Place	Date	Hour	Summary of Events and Information	Remarks and references to Appendices
near ST LEGER. (G22a 28)	5.10.17		Lt A.B. WEEKES rejoined the Brigade from 16th D.A.C and was posted to B/180. 2/Lt V G WILLIAMS evacuated to England and struck off the strength.	
"	6.10.17		A/180 returned to action from Wagon line. Lt-Col L.E.S. Ward DSO. went to Command 16th Div. Arty. during absence on leave of Brig. Gen Charlton D.S.O. Major N.A. Stebbing D.S.O. in command of 180th Bde RFA.	
"	12.10.17		2/Lt L BARNES reposted to D.A.C 2/Lt T. HORSFIELD joined the Brigade from 16th D.A.C and was posted to D/180.	
"	13.10.17		2/Lt R. E. FREEMAN posted to 16th D.A.C. 2/Lt H.E. FAWKES posted to 16th D.A.C.	
	14.10.17		B/180 tactically under 51st D.A.	
	night 15/16.10.17		Raid carried out on TUNNEL TRENCH by 7th Leinster Regt. 180th Bde cooperated. Raid successful.	
	18.10.17		2/Lt B D M BREWER posted to Y/16 T M Battery.	
	19.10.17		2/Lt R.H.A LUCAS joined the Brigade and was posted to C/180.	
	20.10.17.		2/Lt E.D. STURROCK joined the Brigade and was posted to A/180 2/Lt W. I. LINKLATER joined the Brigade and was posted to D/180.	

2353 Wt. W2544/1454 700,000 5/15 D. D. & L. A.D.S.S. Forms/C 2118.

Instructions regarding War Diaries and Intelligence Summaries are contained in F. S. Regs., Part II. and the Staff Manual respectively. Title pages will be prepared in manuscript.

WAR DIARY
or
INTELLIGENCE SUMMARY.
(Erase heading not required.)

Army Form C. 2118.

Place	Date	Hour	Summary of Events and Information	Remarks and references to Appendices
near ST LEGER.	27.10.17		Successful daylight raid carried out by 2nd Royal Dublin Fusiliers 180th Bde cooperated.	
	27.10.17.		A/77 Bde RFA came into action, and came under tactical command of O.C. 180th Bde.	
	29.10.17.		Successful raid by 7/8th Royal Inniskilling Fusiliers. 180th Bde cooperated.	
	30.10.17		B/180 reverted under tactical command of O.C. 180th Bde.	
			~~Dur~~ During the month weekly bombardments in cooperation with trench mortars, gas shell bombardments, and nightly harassing fire, have been carried out.	
			Batteries have been engaged in improving battery positions, preparing re-inforcing positions, and constructing horse standings.	
			[signature] Capt RFA for Major RFA Comd. 180th Bde RFA	

2353 Wt. W2544/1454 700,000 5/15 D. D. & L. A.D.S.S. Forms/C 2118.

W A R   D I A R Y

FOR MONTH OF NOVEMBER, 1917.

VOLUME :- 22

U N I T :- 180th Bde R.F.A.

Vol 22

Instructions regarding War Diaries and Intelligence Summaries are contained in F. S. Regs., Part II. and the Staff Manual respectively. Title pages will be prepared in manuscript.

WAR DIARY No 22

or

~~INTELLIGENCE SUMMARY.~~

(Erase heading not required.)

180th BRIGADE, R.F.A. No. 2/203 DATE 1/12/17

Army Form C. 2118.

180th Bde RFA.

Place	Date	Hour	Summary of Events and Information	Remarks and references to Appendices
T 28 a 2 8 near ST LEGER	1.11.17.		No 33537 Gr. R Rutherford B/180. wounded (slightly). Major N.A. STEBBING D.S.O B/180 posted to command 95th Bde RFA. Major H K DANIEL posted to command B/180. 2/Lt P.J.W STRAUS A/180 posted to H.Q. as Orderly Officer. 2/Lt J. S DUNCAN, B/180 posted to H.Q as Signals Officer.	
	5th		2/Lt R.E. FREEMAN rejoined from 16th DAC & was posted to C/180. 2/Lt H.E. FAWKES rejoined from 16th DAC and was posted to D/180.	
	7th		2/Lt W. J. LINKLATER D/180 posted to 77th (Army) Bde RFA. A/77 and B/77 left the tactical command of O.C. 180th Bde, and went out of action.	
	16th		A/180 and C/180 moved their detached sections to their main positions in preparation for the offensive operation.	
	20th	6.20 am	Attack by 16th Division on TUNNEL TRENCH and TUNNEL	

Page 2

Army Form C. 2118.

Instructions regarding War Diaries and Intelligence Summaries are contained in F. S. Regs., Part II. and the Staff Manual respectively. Title pages will be prepared in manuscript.

WAR DIARY
or
INTELLIGENCE ~~SUMMARY~~.

(*Erase heading not required.*)

No 22

180th Bde RFA

Place	Date	Hour	Summary of Events and Information	Remarks and references to Appendices
T28 a 28 near ST LEGER			SUPPORT. 48th Inf. Bde. supported by 180th Bde RFA.	
			Attack successful. Over 500 unwounded prisoners.	
	22.11.17		2/Lt R.H.A. Lucas. C/180 admitted to hospital (sick)	
	21.11.17		152nd Bde RFA. came under tactical command of OC. 180th Bde RFA, forming, with 180th Bde, the Left Artillery Group.	
	23.11.17		2/Lt P. Oakley, C/180 to hospital, sick.	
	25.11.17		2/Lt J. Horsfield posted from D/180 to 16th D.A.C.	
	26.11.17		Lt W.A. Simmons, joined the command and was posted to D/180.	
	28.11.17		18pdr batteries of 152nd Bde RFA left the tactical command	
	29.11.17		4.5 How battery " " " " " " "	
			Heavy bombardment of our trenches about 5.30 am. Enemy infantry left their trenches on Right Battalion Front, but did not reach our trenches.	
	30.11.17		Heavy bombardment of our trenches about 6 am and at	

2353 Wt. W2544/1454 700,000 5/15 D. D. & L. A.D.S.S. Forms/C. 2118.

WM 23

WAR DIARY

FOR MONTH OF DECEMBER, 1917.

VOLUME : - 23.

UNIT:- 180th Brigade R.F.A.

Original.

Instructions regarding War Diaries and Intelligence Summaries are contained in F. S. Regs., Part II. and the Staff Manual respectively. Title pages will be prepared in manuscript.

WAR DIARY
or
~~INTELLIGENCE SUMMARY.~~
(Erase heading not required.)

No 22

180th Bde R.F.A.

Army Form C. 2118.

Page 3.

Place	Date	Hour	Summary of Events and Information	Remarks and references to Appendices
			intervals during the morning. 4 heavy bombardments in all. No infantry action.	
	29th 30th		A/180 and C/180 moved a section each to Detached Section Position, A on 29th Nov C on 30th Nov.	
			1.12.17.	
			[illegible] Lt Col. RFA Comdg 180th Bde R.F.A.	

Page 1.

Army Form C. 2118.

WAR DIARY
or
~~INTELLIGENCE SUMMARY.~~

(*Erase heading not required.*)

No 23.

180th Bde RFA

Instructions regarding War Diaries and Intelligence Summaries are contained in F. S. Regs., Part II. and the Staff Manual respectively. Title pages will be prepared in manuscript.

Place	Date	Hour	Summary of Events and Information	Remarks and references to Appendices
ST LEGER	1.12.17		Batteries still in action near CROISILLES.	
"	3.12.17		2/Lt W G GLENISTER and 2/Lt J.E.S. SPINNER joined the Brigade and were posted to B/180 and A/180 respectively.	
"			180th Bde came under tactical command of 40th D.A.	
"	5.12.17	9.43 pm	Raid carried out by 103rd Inf. Bde (on left). 180th Bde assisted in artillery support.	
"	9.12.17		Batteries commenced filling 3 reinforcing positions up to 100 rds per gun.	
	11.12.17		Two batteries of 14th Army Bde RFA came into action in reinforcing positions, under command of O.C. 180th Bde.	
	12.12.17		One battery 14th Army Bde, and four batteries of 178th Bde RFA went into action in reinforcing positions, under command of O.C. 180 Bde.	
			Left Group 40th D.A. composed as follows:- 14th Army Bde, 178th Bde, and 180th Bde., under tactical command of O.C. 180th Bde.	
	13.12.17		2/Lt W. WIMBURY joined Brigade and posted to B/180.	
	14.12.17		Wagon lines of 180th Bde moved to tented Camp North of ERVILLERS.	
	15.12.17	3 pm	Left Gp. cooperated in artillery support of Raid carried out by 119th Inf. Bde. 6 pm Firing carried out in connection with gas projection near FONTAINE LES CROISILLES. 2/Lt E. D STURROCK rejoined from hospital.	

Page 2.

Army Form C. 2118.

Instructions regarding War Diaries and Intelligence Summaries are contained in F. S. Regs., Part II. and the Staff Manual respectively. Title pages will be prepared in manuscript.

WAR DIARY
or
~~INTELLIGENCE SUMMARY.~~
(Erase heading not required.)

No 23

180th Bde RFA

Place	Date	Hour	Summary of Events and Information	Remarks and references to Appendices
ST LEGER	16.12.17		1 section of D/178 transferred to Right Group.	
	17.12.17		1 battery of 14th Army Bde transferred to Right Group.	
	19.12.17		One half of each battery of 180th Bde withdrew to wagon lines. A, B, & D batteries relieved by corresponding batteries of 178th Bde.	
"	20.12.17		Lt T. C. HIPWELL joined the Brigade and was posted to D/180.	
near ERVILLERS	20.12.17		Remainder of each battery, and Bde H.Q. moved to wagon lines.	
	21.12.17		Batteries & Bde H.Q. remained in wagon lines. Major J. W. HUGHES, Comdg C/180 admitted to hospital (sick).	
near BEAULENCOURT	22.12.17		Brigade marched to camp near BEAULENCOURT.	
HAUT ALLAINES	23.12.17		" " " " " HAUT ALLAINES	
near ROISEL	24.12.17		" " " " " ROISEL	
	25.12.17		Batteries relieved corresponding batteries of 276th Bde RFA at RONSSOY.	
STE EMILIE	26.12.17		Guns of 276th Bde taken over. Bde H.Q. removed to STE EMILIE.	
" "	28.12.17		Major P. J. B. HEELAS, Comdg A/180, admitted to hospital. (sick).	
" "	28.12.17		No 93436, Gunner D. WATSON, C/180. awarded military medal. (authority dated 23.12.17.).	
	31.12.17		2/Lt R RUDDLE joined the Brigade & was posted to C/180 with effect from 23.12.17	

[illegible] Lt Col RFA
Comdg 180th Bde RFA

2353 Wt. W2544/1454 700,000 5/15 D. D. & L. A.D.S.S. Forms/C. 2118.

Vol 24

W A R   D I A R Y,

FOR MONTH OF JANUARY, 1918.

VOLUME :- 24

U N I T :- 180th Brigade R.G.A.

Instructions regarding War Diaries and Intelligence Summaries are contained in F. S. Regs., Part II. and the Staff Manual respectively. Title Pages will be prepared in manuscript.

WAR DIARY or ~~INTELLIGENCE SUMMARY~~

(Erase heading not required.)

No 24. (Jan 1918)

180th Bde RFA

Army Form C. 2118.

Place	Date	Hour	Summary of Events and Information	Remarks and references to Appendices
	Jan			
STE EMILIE	1st.		Batteries still in action at RONSSOY. New battery positions being constructed East of STE EMILIE	
	2nd		Maj. P.J. BHEELAS D.S.O. rejoined from hospital.	
	3rd		Maj J. W. HUGHES M.C. rejoined from hospital.	
	6th.		189th Bde withdrawn from Rt Group. 180th Bde now forms Rt Gp.	
	13th		2/Lt R RUDDLE C/180 thrown from horse, & admitted to hospital.	
	17th		72003 Sgt ~~H~~ HIBBS A/180 wounded.	
	18th		109332 Bdr McKINNON M. B/180 Killed in action.	
			112895 Gr ROTHERHAM W. & 36197 Gr BOND W. (B/180) wounded.	
	20th	6.45 am	A/180 & B/180 Co-operated in artillery support for raid carried out by 17th Inf. Bde on our right. Raid successful.	
			Lt-Col L.E.S. WARD D.S.O. commanding 16th Div. Artª.	
			Lt Col W.R. WARREN, 177th Bde commds Right Gp.	
			Major H.K. DANIEL B/180 commds 180th Bde.	
	21st.		Visual signalling only. (24 hours test)	
	25th.		do do do.	
	28th		2/Lt R RUDDLE C/180 Struck off the strength, with effect from	

2449 Wt. W14957/M90 750,000 1/16 J.B.C. & A. Forms/C.2118/12.

Army Form C. 2118.

Instructions regarding War Diaries and Intelligence Summaries are contained in F. S. Regs., Part II. and the Staff Manual respectively. Title Pages will be prepared in manuscript.

WAR DIARY or INTELLIGENCE SUMMARY

(Erase heading not required.)

No 24 page 2

180th Bde RFA

Place	Date	Hour	Summary of Events and Information	Remarks and references to Appendices
STE EMILIE			21/1/18 on evacuation to England.	
	31st		Lt A.E.N. CLARK joined the Brigade & was posted to C/180	
			Relief of 180th Bde by 177th Bde postponed.	
			During the month, hostile artillery activity on our front system has been slight. There has been the usual desultory shelling of RONSSOY & back areas. There have been several aerial bombing raids on back areas & in the wagon line area, but 180th Bde has not been affected. Our Batteries have been engaged in the construction of new positions and improvement of wagon lines.	
			J Miller Capt for OC 180th Bde RFA	
			31/1/18	

2449 Wt. W14957/M90 750,000 1/16 J.B.C. & A. Forms/C.2118/12.

Vol 25

WAR DIARY.

FOR MONTH OF FEBRUARY, 1918.

VOLUME:- 25

UNIT:- 180th Brigade R.F.A.

Army Form C. 2118.

Instructions regarding War Diaries and Intelligence Summaries are contained in F. S. Regs., Part II. and the Staff Manual respectively. Title Pages will be prepared in manuscript.

WAR DIARY
or
~~INTELLIGENCE SUMMARY~~
(Erase heading not required.)

NO 25

180th Bde RFA.

Place	Date	Hour	Summary of Events and Information	Remarks and references to Appendices
MARQUAIX	1st.		HQ. at MARQUAIX. Batteries still in action at RONSSOY.	
"	2nd.		On redistribution of artillery, 177th + 180th Bde form Right Group 16th DA. under command of Lt Col W R Warren, DSO.	
			Lt. C.W. COCKRILL C/180 killed in action.	
"	6th		2/Lt RW ATKINSON joined the Brigade. Posted to C/180.	
"	9th		Major R.A. SPENCER DSO. took over command of 180th Bde. RFA.	
	14th		a/Major O STEVEN M.C. posted to command C/180. a/Major J.W. HUGHES posted to D/180 as Captain. Lt (a/Capt) B.G. LEE relinquishes rank of a/Capt on ceasing to be second in command of D/180	
			2/Lt. E.N. TAYLOR joined the Brigade + was posted to C/180.	
	17th		227668 Dr. LIDDLE R wounded.	
	18th		Wagon Lines moved to North west of TINCOURT. HQ at TINCOURT	
TINCOURT	19th		Lt J.M.S. LIVESAY + 2/Lt A ELLIOTT joined the Brigade + were posted to C/180 + A/180 respectively	
			1 section per battery of 180th Bde relieved by 282nd Bde.	
	20th		Remaining sections relieved. Batteries withdrew to wagon lines for training.	
			Major P.J.B HEELAS DSO took over command of the Brigade.	
	26th		2/Lt O.M. BROWN joined the Brigade + was posted to B/180	

2449 Wt. W14957/M90 750,000 1/16 J.B.C. & A. Forms/C.2118/12.

Army Form C. 2118.

Instructions regarding War Diaries and Intelligence Summaries are contained in F. S. Regs., Part II. and the Staff Manual respectively. Title Pages will be prepared in manuscript.

WAR DIARY
or
INTELLIGENCE SUMMARY
(Erase heading not required.)

Place	Date	Hour	Summary of Events and Information	Remarks and references to Appendices
TINCOURT	26th		Lt W.A.B. EDE posted to take charge of Signal Subsection attached to Bde.	
"	27th		Brigade went into action into positions near STE EMILIE as a practice test, & withdrew the same night	
QUARRY near STE EMILIE	28th		Brigade went into action, to reinforce the front. Batteries in action East of STE EMILIE. H.Q. at the QUARRY. 180th Brigade forms the Left Sub Group, 16th D.A.	
			1/3/18	
			[signature] Capt for Major ~~LIEUT COL.~~ R.F.A. COMDG. 180th BRIGADE, R.F.A.	

2449 Wt. W14957/M90 750,000 1/16 J.B.C. & A. Forms/C.2118/12.

16th Divisional Artillery.

180th BRIGADE R. F. A.

MARCH 1918

Appendix attached:-

Battle Casualties.

180th Bde RFA. 14 **WAR DIARY.** **No 26.** March 1918 AF C2118.

Place	Date	Hour	Summary of Events & Information	Remarks &c.
QUARRY near STE EMILIE	1st	–	Batteries still in action between STE EMILIE and RONSSOY.	26
"	7th		Enemy made an unsuccessful raid on MULE TRENCH. 2 prisoners taken by us.	
"	13th	12 midnight	Raid carried out on KILDARE POST by 2nd Royal Munster Fusiliers. 3 prisoners captured.	
			Capt D. Mackay, B/180. posted to command B/177 Bde RFA.	
			Lt J. S. Evans, D/180. appointed a/Capt. in D/180.	
	14th		2/Lt J B. Wilson + 2/Lt W.A.R Rees joined the brigade and were posted to A/180 + D/180 respectively.	
	15th	3am	1st Royal Dublin Fusiliers raided KILDARE POST, but found the post empty.	
	16th	6.30 am	Batteries fired on S.O.S. in response to S.O.S. rocket signals. No enemy infantry action.	
	20th		2nd Lt. L. J. Woodland and 2nd Lt J. L. Smith joined the Brigade, and were posted to A/180 and C/180 respectively.	
	21st	4.30am	Enemy Attack, Commencing at 4.30am with a heavy bombardment of Gas and H. E. Shell.	
		12.15pm	Reported "Enemy holding part of RED LINE."	
		12.30pm	C & D/180 ordered to withdraw by Sections to Rear positions.	

180th BRIGADE R.F.A. — WAR DIARY No. 26. — MARCH 1918. — A.F. C2118.

PLACE	DATE	TIME	SUMMARY OF EVENTS AND INFORMATION	REMARKS.
	Mch 21st	2.16pm	Orders to retire to positions covering RED LINE [illegible] to A & B.	
			Bde. Headquarters moved to SPUR QUARRY.	
		5.30pm	Batteries to withdraw to positions covering BROWN LINE.	
		7.0pm	MAJOR O. STEVEN M.C. given command of C/180.	
		7.30pm	Bde. Hdqrs were moved to Hdqrs 16th Div. Arty. MARQUAIX. During night Batteries kept up a slow rate of fire on barrages protecting BROWN LINE.	
	Mch 22nd	4.15am	Batteries opened out on S.O.S. lines which were constantly varied to meet the situation.	
		7.10am	Orders sent to Batteries to move into positions covering G.H.Q. line. Headquarters moved to BUIRE.	
		10.30am	Verbal orders received from 16 D.A. to move Bde Hdqrs to BUSSU.	
	23/3/18	8.15am	Orders received to withdraw all Batteries by sections. These to proceed at once via PERONNE to positions in I.20.a. Hdqrs 180 Bde to be in HALLE.	
		8.55	Last Battery reported all clear.	
		9.0am	H.Q. Staff left BUSSU for HALLE.	

180th BRIGADE R.F.A. WAR DIARY No. 26. MARCH 1918 A.F. C 2118

PLACE	DATE	TIME	SUMMARY OF EVENTS AND INFORMATION.	REMARKS
	Mch 23rd	12 NOON	All Batteries reported in action in new positions	
		2 P.M.	Orders received to withdraw by BAZENCOURT (I 19 c 0.0) to positions in H 28 a & b, to cover the line from ST. RADEGONDE to right of Div. front at LA MASONETTE. Fire will not be opened except by direct observation.	
		2.30 PM	Batteries had considerable difficulty in crossing bridge at BAZENCOURT on account of extraordinary congestion of traffic. C/80 which was at the end of the column crossed the Bridge at 4.15 P.M.	
		7 PM.	H.Q. Staff proceeded west of HERBECOURT where they reported to temporary D.A.H.Q.	
		7.35 PM.	Following orders received and issued to Batteries; "All Batteries will withdraw at once and take up positions in valley H 26 a. O.P. to be established in HERBECOURT, and visual arranged for between STN. and Hdqrs. Refilling point "CAPPY." Bde Hdqrs at H 25 c 40.15." 2nd Lt. C.L. [illegible] and 2nd Lt. S.R. Thomas joined the Bde and posted to A/80.	

180th BRIGADE R.F.A. — WAR DIARY No. 26 — March 1918 — A.F.C.2118.

PLACE	DATE	TIME	SUMMARY OF EVENTS AND INFORMATION	REMARKS
	March 24th	12.45am	All Batteries reported in action.	
		3.0am	Command of 16th Div Group passed to 39th Div Group.	
		6.10pm	Owing to situation of 9th Div it is necessary for the 39th Div to take up line :- B 15 CENTRAL - B21 CENTRAL - B27 CENTRAL - H3 CENTRAL with right on River Somme.	
		6.45pm	Zones altered are now as follows:- H11c 8.0 to H9d0.1. S.O.S. Lines to the HEM-CLERY Road.	
		6.30pm	O.C. 177 Bde. R.F.A. reported that he had heard rumours that the enemy was in DEMPIERE. Upon communication of the situation to D.A. we received permission to withdraw to CAPPY. Having received no orders at CAPPY the Bde proceeded to BRAY and arrived at 11 p.m.	
		11.0pm	Orders were received by special D.R. from Brigade Major 39th D.A., to the effect that as there appeared to be no truth in the rumours stated the Bde would return at once to positions in HERBECOURT and be in action before dawn. The Bde was in action by 5.15am morning of 25th. C/180 Wagon Lines remained at BRAY.	

180th BRIGADE R.F.A. — WAR DIARY No 26 — MARCH 1918 — A.F. C2118

PLACE	DATE	TIME	SUMMARY OF EVENTS AND INFORMATION	REMARKS
	Mch 25th	12.30pm	Enemy reported to have broken through at CLERY.	
			Situation now as follows:- 21st Div on our left are withdrawing tonight to the line CURLU-MAUREPAS 39th Div will extend its left to FRISE inclusive. Zones allotted to 180th Bde R.F.A. for observation as follows:- from FEUILLERES to HEM.	
		4.20pm	Orders to C/180 to march via CAPPY to BOIS D'OLYMPE.	
		6.30pm	Following orders were received from 39th D.A. and passed to all Batteries. 39th Div. retiring to take up general line ASSEVILLERS, HERBECOURT, FEUILLERES - HEM. If further withdrawal is necessary the general line will be DEMPIERE - FRISE. If it is decided to hold the first of these two lines the 180th Bde will take up positions in G33 and G34. To cover the second line the Bde will hold positions CHUIGNES - BOIS OLYMPE (Ref Map FRANCE 62c.)	
		7.30pm	180th Bde moved to positions in G 33 a & b.	
			All Batteries reported in action at 9.45pm.	
	March 26th	9.40am	Orders received to proceed to MORCOURT via CHUIGNES, FOUCAUCOURT and PROYART.	
		9.45am	Headqrs left for MORCOURT, leaving B/180 in action.	

180th BRIGADE R.F.A.

WAR DIARY No. 26

MARCH 1918.

A.F. C.2118.

PLACE	DATE	TIME	SUMMARY OF EVENTS AND INFORMATION.	REMARKS.
	March 26th	10.5am	B/180 [illegible] all clear and proceeded to MORCOURT.	
		11.40am	The Bde came under the orders of 16th D.A.	
		12 NOON	Batteries took up positions in MORCOURT Q.20 & C. Message to Batteries. The 16th Div. is to hold the line from PROYART - R.21.c to FROISSY.	
			The 177th & 180th Bdes R.F.A. will be known as Right group & cover the 47th Inf. Bde.	
			Zone covered by 180th Bde R.21.c.0.0. to R.15.b.50.00.	
			Headquarters 180th Bde at Q.18.d.80.60.	
		4 P.M.	Warning Order to Batteries "In event of a retirement Batteries will proceed to HAMEL."	
		10.0 P.M.	Orders for Night Firing (AREA SEARCHES) 100 Rounds per gun sent out.	
	March 27th	8.30am	Enemy attacked in large numbers on our front, and batteries commenced firing on their S.O.S. lines.	
		9.30am	Enemy reported to be gaining ground on left bank of River.	
		10.0am	Provisional orders of retirement sent out indicating rendezvous to be between CACHY and BOIS L'ABBE.	

80th BRIGADE R.F.A. — MARCH 1918

WAR DIARY No. 26

PLACE.	DATE.	TIME.	SUMMARY OF EVENTS AND INFORMATION.	REMARKS.
	27th	10.30am	Enemy reported to have crossed River and taking CERISY.	
		11.0am	Owing to hostile shelling we were obliged to move Hdqrs to a steep bank on the opposite side of the Road.	
		11.30am	Received a message from Liaison Officer with 4th Inf Bde. "Infantry are retiring and communication is bad." In agreement with [illegible] Inf Bde we decided to retire.	
		1.0pm	Established provisional Hdqrs at LAMOTTE and batteries were brought into action in P20 a. Batteries did not fire in this position but retired to positions in P23 b with the exception of D/80 which was taken out of action and sent to CACHY.	
		5.15pm	After having fired a few rounds on the infantry seen advancing in direction of MORCOURT the Bde was retired along the LAMOTTE - VILLERS BRETONNEUX ROAD to about P26c where it remained out of action.	
		7.0pm	The actual position of our front was obscure, and after having reconnoitred the front A & B Batteries went forward to positions in R27 b at 8.30pm. D/80 came up from CACHY and remained out of action in P26d throughout the night, but went forward into action at dawn.	

180th BRIGADE R.F.A. 1918 A.F. C2118

WAR DIARY

PLACE	DATE	TIME	SUMMARY OF EVENTS AND INFORMATION	REMARKS
	Mch 28th	3.30am	Received orders from D.A. to move forward bty. into action at once in P16a.	
		6.30am	The Bde started in action.	
		10.15am	Order sent to all Batteries "The General Commanding wishes it to be made known to all ranks that he [illegible] to [illegible] guns at all costs and under all circumstances."	
		12.15pm	Owing to heavy hostile fire the Batteries were moved under cover of the BOIS DE VAIRE to positions in P15c.	
		4pm	Infantry in the line are made up of Cavalry, remnants of 16th Div, and Carey's Force.	
		8.30pm	Large numbers of our Infantry were seen to be retiring, and as no information could be obtained from them, we opened fire on our S.O.S. line. This however proved a false alarm, as no attack had taken place on our front.	
			Quiet night.	
	March 29th		Throughout the day we engaged the enemy with observed fire.	
		1.0pm	Batteries moved to positions in P14c.	
			A night firing programme of 150 Rounds per battery was carried out.	

180th BRIGADE R.F.A. — MARCH 1918

WAR DIARY No 26

PLACE	DATE	TIME	SUMMARY OF EVENTS AND INFORMATION	REMARKS
	Mar 30th	11.25am	S.O.S. lines are now laid at 500 yards in front of following guns:- P17 central - P11 b 0.6.	
		11.30am	Enemy attacked on our [illegible] after putting down an extremely heavy barrage on our front line. Our O.P. Officer, who was wounded, reports that our barrage was holding the enemy.	
		2.20pm	Attack still in progress. Received following message from Liaison Officer: "[illegible] appears to be held. There is no sign of the enemy anywhere."	
		4pm	Enemy again launched an attack, but was brought to our barrage and did not reach our front line. Light firing 150 rds per Battery carried out.	
	Mar 31st		Quiet day. Quite an enemy [illegible] harassed fire. Harassing fire was carried out throughout night. A list of casualties for the month is attached.	

J Miller Capt
for LIEUT.-COL, R.F.A.
COMDG. 180th BRIGADE, R.F.A.

BATTLE CASUALTIES.

Regtl. No	Rank.	Name.	Bty	Casualty & Date.
	2/Lt.	A.P. WOODLAND	A Bty	Killed in action 21/3/18
	LIEUT.	W.A. SIMMONS	A/180	
	LIEUT.	B.G. LEE	D/180	Gsw. 21·3·18.
	LIEUT.	E.D. STURROCK	D/180	
40948	Gnr	L. Whale		
211978	GNR.	H. WESTBURY		
144292	"	MOULTRIE	A/180	KILLED IN ACTION 21·3·18
241503	"	MAXIM E.F.		
64893	"	PINCHES E.		
656278	FTR. SGT	BLAKELEY		
1771	SGT.	T. DEALEY		
36081	BDR.	F. BIGGS		
117258	4/BDR.	G. STEPHENSON		
36280	GNR.	A.H. HOLLOWAY	A/180	G.S.W. 21/3/18.
212745	GNR.	A.Y. WEST		
203472	GNR.	W. METCALF		
37272	GNR.	W.E. JERMEY		
32069	B.S.M	W. FITZPATRICK		
205575	A/L/BDR	T. TARRANT		
208885	DR.	D.J. KENT	A/180	ACCIDENTALLY WOUNDED 21/3/18
118636	GNR	B. ARMITAGE	B/180	KILLED IN ACTION 21·3·18.
34732	DR.	J.R. CREATES.	"	
36103	CPL.	W.G. NORRIS	"	
114366	BDR.	G. BOWLES	"	
24410	GNR.	S. MORGAN	"	G.S.W. 21·3·18
40065	GNR.	CF. CANDY	"	
38793	CPL.	C.G. JAMES	"	
34925	GNR.	J. GANGE	"	
956180	SGT.	G.A. BENNETT	"	GASSED 21·3·18
170291	GNR.	A.P. SMITH	"	
93242	GNR.	J. MORRICE	"	
~~71221~~	~~GNR.~~	~~G. BEWLEY~~	~~"~~	
34810	GNR	T.E. WATTS	"	
36075	DR.	M. LONG	"	MISSING SINCE 21·3·18.
31093	L/BDR.	C.W. PEARCE	"	
14325	L/BDR	S. SLATER	C/180	
36106	FTR.	G. HAYWOOD	"	
34703	TRUMPTR.	J.B. RANK	"	G.S.W. 21·3·18
12169	GNR.	A. KITCHEN	"	
114385	GNR.	J.C. JACKSON	"	KILLED IN ACTION 21·3·18.

Regt'l No	Rank	Name	Bty	Casualty Date
19532	CPL	J. GIBBONS		
124194	BDR.	A. ROBERTS		
85225	GNR.	W. LIGERTWOOD		
245495	GNR.	C.E. PERKINS		
~~[illegible]~~ 129059	GNR	S. RILEY	D/180	G.S.W. 21·3·18.
968252	GNR.	A.E. STEVENS		
41576	GNR.	R.C. CLAXTON		
84642	BDR.	W. ROWLEY	→	GASSED 21·3·18.
40822	DR.	COOKSLEY	D/180	
50941	DR.	LOXTON		G.S.W
47698	DR.	P. ROCK	A/180	G.S.W. 22·3·18
71224	GNR.	G. BEWLEY	B/180	ACC. INJURED 22·3·18.
36121	DR.	W. GARDNER	"	
28847	~~GNR.~~ DR	A. FORD	C/180	G.S.W (AT DUTY) 22·3·18.
21158	DR.	W. CLAYTON	"	
170906	DR.	A. SMITH	D/180	GASSED 22·3·18.
224575	CPL.	J. KEYWORTH	"	
128322	GNR.	J.R. BARTLETT	"	KILLED IN ACTION 22·3·18.
204390	GNR.	J.W. STELL	"	
~~190906~~ 173139	DR.	J. CONNOR.	"	G.S.W. 22·3·18.
13823	GNR.	T. MASON	"	ACC. INJURED 22·3·18.
230017	GNR.	Mc GAWLEY T	B/180	ACC. INJURED 23·3·18.
34810	GNR.	E. TITHERLY	"	MISSING 23·3·18
36084	CPL.	C. WESTROP	"	G.S.W. 29·3·18.
945761	GNR.	C. ORCHARD		
217833	GNR.	ASHLEY C	A/180	MISSING 23·3·18.
43066	GNR.	RATCLIFF	A/180	
222300	DR.	LAMB	"	
71856	DR.	W. PEARCE	"	
39401	GNR.	H.W. Mc CARTHY	"	G.S.W. 28·3·18.
244401	GNR.	T. MASON	"	
19103	GNR.	G. HOLYOAK	"	
36306	GNR	G. FULLER	"	
13477	DR.	W. METCALF	C/180	KILLED IN ACTION 29·3·18.
9384	GNR.	L. HILL	A/180	G.S.W. 29·3·18.
97055	GNR.	L. KAY	"	
87694	GNR.	E. LAKEY	"	G.S.W. 29·3·18
20098	GNR.	H. EDWARDS	"	
219601	GNR.	R. SMITH	"	
~~15960~~	~~GNR.~~	~~A. BUTT~~		
46774	BDR.	F.G. HUNT	B/180	G.S.W. 30·3·18
23392	DR	MIZON J.	"	

Regt. No	Rank	Name	Bty	Casualty & Date
51738	BDR.	E. EDWARDS		
95634	BDR.	E.C. HART		
843	GNR.	C. MILNE	D/180	G.S.W 30/3/18
248712	GNR.	J.H. LAWTON		
895247	GNR	W.E. SMITH		
202796	GNR.	S. DYER	D/180	KILLED IN ACTION 30/3/18.

180th BRIGADE R.F.A. — APRIL 1918

1/16 | 4

WAR DIARY No 27

PLACE	DATE	TIME	SUMMARY OF EVENTS AND INFORMATION	REMARKS
WEST OF BOIS DE VAIRE Nr. HAMEL.	APRIL 1st	4.0PM.	Battery moved to position in O.18 central (Ref. map 62D)	
			Subsequently moved to FOUILLOY.	
FOUILLOY	" 3rd		[illegible] of the [illegible] rejoined [illegible] from leave.	
			[illegible] day [illegible] engaged [illegible] with [illegible] effect [illegible]	
	" 4th	5.30AM	Enemy attacked [illegible] barrage of [illegible] shells.	
		10.0AM	Enemy occupied our original front line.	
		12 NOON	C/180 moved in [illegible] to engage enemy massing in BOIS DE VAIRE	
		3.30PM	A & B/180 came into action near [illegible]	
		4.0PM	C/180's position becoming untenable, the Battery was withdrawn to position just West of FOUILLOY	
		5.30PM	Enemy attack repulsed [illegible] the order STOP FIRE was communicated to all Batteries. These had been firing intensely since 5.30AM.	

180th BRIGADE R.F.A. WAR DIARY No. 27 APRIL 1918 A.F.C. 2118

PLACE	DATE	TIME	SUMMARY OF EVENTS AND INFORMATION	REMARKS
FOUILLOY	Apl 4th	7.30PM	Remaining Btys withdrawn to positions west of FOUILLOY.	
		10.0PM	Wagon lines moved to western outskirts of FOUILLOY.	
	" 5th		Moved one section of "A" & "B" Batteries to forward position in O 18 central.	
		11.0PM & 6AM	Fired in response to S.O.S. signals	
	" 6th		C/180 moved detached section forward.	
			The Batteries fired a heavy concentration on the BOIS DE VAIRE	
		DUSK	[illegible] on the S.O.S. line. Infantry action took place.	
	" 7th		Came out of action at dusk, and marched via AUBIGNY, BLANGY-TRONVILLE, GLISY, LONGUEAU, CAGNY, BOUTILLERIE, DURY, SALEUX, VERS to BACOUEL arriving 4AM morning of 8th.	
	" 8th		The Bde marched off at 7am for PONT DE METZ via VERS, SALEUX and BACOUEL, arriving at destination at 1.30PM.	

180th BRIGADE R.F.A.

A.F. C.2118.

APRIL 1918

WAR DIARY No. 17.

PLACE	DATE	TIME	SUMMARY OF EVENTS AND INFORMATION	REMARKS
	April 9th		The Bde left at 4.30 AM proceeding via RENANCOURT, DREUIL, AILLY-SUR-SOMME, PICQUIGNY, LE CHAUSSE, BELLOY, FLEXICOURT, BETENCOURT, ST. OUEN, DOMART EN PONTHIEU, to RIBEAUCOURT.	
			"C" & "B" Bty were billeted in DOMESMONT.	
			Bde reached RIBEAUCOURT at 8 P.M.	
	Apl. 10th		Left at 5am for BOUBERS-SUR-CANCHE proceeding via BEAUMETZ, MAIZICOURT, AUXI-LE-CHATEAU, LA VACQUERIE.	
	Apl 11th		The Bde started at 7am via HAUTECOTE, HUNCQ, ST. POL, and arrived at HERNICOURT at 12NOON.	
	Apl 12th		The Bde left at 8.0am for WITTERNESSE via TANGRY, PERNES, AMES, ST. HILAIRE. On arriving at ST HILAIRE orders were received to go into action in the MERVILLE front.	
			Batteries proceeded to HAM EN ARTOIS.	
		5.0 PM	The Bde came under the orders of the 51st Div and orders were received from them for the Bde to come into action at HAMET BILLET.	

180th BRIGADE R.F.A. APRIL 1918 A.F. C.2118.

WAR DIARY No 27.

PLACE	DATE	TIME	SUMMARY OF EVENTS AND INFORMATION.	REMARKS.
	Apl 12th		Proceeded to HAMET BILLET via BERGUETTE and GUARBECQUE	
			Bde reported in action at 2.30am 13.4.18.	
	Apl 13th		Headquarters at HAMET BILLET	
			Btys in position in P 3 a & b	
			[illegible] to Eastern edge of HAMET BILLET.	
	Apl 14th		[illegible] attacked on 3 different occasions during the day	
	Apl 15th		Enemy harassing fire on all roads and approaches [illegible] by Batteries during the day	
	Apl 16th		Normal harassing fire carried out.	
	Apl 17th		Capt J. MILLER and Lt J. BARNET HUNT wounded.	
			Lt R. ROBINSON joined the Bde and posted to "C" Battery	
	Apl 18th		GUARBECQUE shelled by heavy guns. D/180 had 3 men killed and 10 wounded. Battery began being moved out of GUARBECQUE [illegible]	

180th Brigade R.F.A. — WAR DIARY No 27 — APRIL 1918 — A.F. C.2118.

PLACE	DATE	TIME	SUMMARY OF EVENTS AND INFORMATION	REMARKS
HAMET BILLET	Apl 20th		"A" & "C" Batteries moved to positions further forward. D/180 to a position South of South of ST. VENANT.	
			A/Major C.B. Locke, and 2nd Lieut G.J. Ellis joined the Bde and posted to command "A" & "C" Batteries respectively.	
			2Lt. [illegible] Linfield joined the Bde and posted to A/180.	
	Apl 21st		B/180 moved about 1000 yards N.E.	
		3.0pm	D/180 co-operated in concentration carried out by H.5" & 6" hows. [illegible] on houses in CORNET MALO (Q2)	
	Apl 22nd	3.0am	D/180 bombarded L'ECANG FARM and road East of farm with gas shells.	
			D/180 co-operated in 2 concentrations carried out on CORNET MALO (Q2)	
	Apl 23rd	3.0am	D/180 co-operated in concentration on houses in CORNET MALO (Q2)	
			Capt. P. Reid A.V.C. attached as Veterinary Officer to Bde.	
	Apl 24th	12.0am	D/180 again carried out a gas shell bombardment of L'ECANG FARM and Road East of Farm.	
	Apl 30th		Since coming into action in this sector, Batteries have carried out vigorous harassing fire on enemy approaches by night and by day. cont.	

180th Bde R.F.A. — April 1918 — A.F. C2118

WAR DIARY No 41

PLACE	DATE	TIME	SUMMARY OF EVENTS AND INFORMATION	REMARKS
	Apl 30th		About 100 Rounds per gun per 24 hours being fired. Enemy harassing fire has on several occasions been fairly heavy.	
			Lt Col [illegible] D.S.O. left Bde for temporary attachment to 16th Div	
			Lt Col J.H. [illegible] assumed temporary command of the Bde	
			A List of casualties for the month is attached	

[signature] LIEUT.-COL, R.F.A.
COMDG. 180th BRIGADE, R.F.A.

BATTLE CASUALTIES

DATE.	RANK.	NAME.	UNIT.	CASUALTY.	
88933	DR.	LANE A.R.	A/180	G.S.W.	
198438	DR.	ROBERTS W.			
39256	DR.	MATHURIN E			1·4·18.
124049	L/BDR.	WOODGATE W.J.	B/180	G.S.W.	
212515	GNR.	KIRK. J.			
32899	GNR.	BATTIN A.	B/180	KILLED IN ACTION. 2·4·18.	
701106	GNR.	EDMUNSON	B/180	MISSING SINCE 2·4·18. (WAS WITH GNR. BATTIN)	
	2/LIEUT.	BYRNE R.E	C/180	KILLED IN ACTION	
	A/MAJOR	O. STEVEN M.C.	C/180	G.S.W.	
14507	GNR.	J. BAKER	A/180	KILLED IN ACTION	
117637	GNR.	R. KIDD	"	G.S.W.	
36277	CPL.	H. QUINCE	"	"	
241877	DR	E. TENNANT.	"	"	
687498	GNR.	J. COLE	B/180	KILLED IN ACTION	
100982	DR.	D. QUIRKE	B/180	" " "	
58475	SGT.	E. HALLIDAY	"	G.S.W.	
36146	GNR.	C. BROWN	"	"	
129970	GNR.	WHITEHEAD	"	"	
	~~GNR.~~	~~WELLS~~	~~"~~	~~(AT DUTY)~~	
160865	GNR.	H. HUTTER	C/180	KILLED IN ACTION	
36214	CPL.	F. BENDER	"	G.S.W.	4/4/18
170892	BDR.	S. KEMPSTER	"	"	
39335	BDR.	J. DUNN	"	"	
169601	L/BDR.	J. LAMB	"	"	
68216	GNR.	H. COSHAM.	"	"	
741134	GNR.	H. STOKES	"	"	
211156	GNR.	COOPER	"	"	
28797	GNR.	A.E. WRIGHT	"	"	
90647	GNR.	J. BROWERS	"	"	
39760	GNR.	W. HARDING	"	"	
36230	GNR.	W.F. LEWIS	"	"	
37718	SGT.	F. WILTSHIRE	"	"	
92643	DR.	G. CROCKETT	"	"	
114096	BDR.	F. SKELTON	"	"	
400556	BDR.	G. BAKER	"	"	
36161	GNR.	E. COWLEY.	"	"	
23606	GNR.	D. CURRY	"	G.S.W. AT DUTY	
38815	GNR.	W. RILEY	D/180	G.S.W	
70704	DR.	W.F. SUMNER	"	"	

REGT'L NO	RANK	NAME.	BTY.	CASUALTY.
38815	GNR.	W.P. WYLIE	D/180	G.S.W 5/4/18.
70286	GNR.	R.E. RUSSELL	"	G.S.W 6/4/18
113521	GNR.	A. TIBBETTS	"	G.S.W. 6/4/18
40039	SGT.	A.F. BECKER	C/180	G.S.W. 13/4/18.
40008	DR.	A. MANNAKEE	"	
40068	L/BDR.	E. BARRETT	B/180	G.S.W. 14/4/18.
242842	GNR.	W. DUNCAN	"	KILLED IN ACTION 14/4/18.
120496	GNR	A.E. GAMBLE	C/180	KILLED IN ACTION 18/4/18
242946	GNR	GREIG W	"	
30198	GNR	BRIDGER F.	"	G.S.W. 18/4/18.
56197	GNR.	THREFALL J	"	
191103	GNR.	ARYTON	"	G.S.W.
725448	GNR.	R.W. ROPER	D/180	
681463	GNR.	P.F. OWEN	"	KILLED IN ACTION
101273	GNR.	A. BULLOCK	"	
48720	SGT.	C.H. HARRIS	"	
69898	DR.	T. DONNELLY	"	
68333	DR.	J. GILL	"	
89207	DR.	S. MADELL	"	19/4/18
147464	DR.	P.J. NEVE	"	
229590	DR.	H. PRIORY	"	G.S.W.
71154	DR.	J. RIDING	"	
31089	DR.	C.W. SMITH	"	
114972	GNR.	G. SOUTH	"	
249322	GNR.	J. PRICE	"	
234134	DR.	H.G. GODFREY	"	G.S.W. 21.4.18.
24189	CPL.	J. SHARKEY	D/180	
114819	GNR.	S.E. FREED	"	G.S.W. 25/4/18.
57033	GNR.	W. TROUGHT	"	
	A/CAPT.	J.S. EVANS	"	
	2/LIEUT.	T. HORSFIELD	"	G.S.W 29/4/18.
	2/LIEUT. (16DAC)	R.E. HENDERSON	ATTACHED D/180	
38760	GNR.	A. BUTT	A/180	G.S.W. 29/4/18.
38793	CPL.	G. JAMES	B/180	ACCIDENTALLY
115634	GNR.	A. FAIRHURST	"	WOUNDED 29/4/18.
155485	GNR.	C.F. KNIGHT.	"	(BACK BURST)

Army Form C. 2118.

Instructions regarding War Diaries and Intelligence Summaries are contained in F. S. Regs., Part II. and the Staff Manual respectively. Title pages will be prepared in manuscript.

WAR DIARY or ~~INTELLIGENCE SUMMARY.~~ No 28. MAY 1918.

(Erase heading not required.)

180th Bde R.F.A. Pg 1

Vol 28

Place	Date	Hour	Summary of Events and Information	Remarks and references to Appendices
HAMET BILLET	1st.		Batteries still in action west and South west of ST VENANT.	
(near ST. VENANT)			Following men of B/180 wounded: 42161 Dr C. Sharpe, 137074 Dr C Lee	
			96806 Gr M Wynne. Following of B/180 died of wounds 127478	
			Dr W.H. Sykes, 651943 Gr W. Maltby. LT. W.H.F. OLLIS joined Bde & is posted to D/180.	
	2nd	10pm	Successful minor operation carried out by Left Battalion.	
			3 prisoners taken.	
	3rd		A/180's forward Section moved to ASILE D'ALIENES.	
		4am	Corps H.A. bombarded CALONNE with Gas shell. 180th Bde	
			cooperated with bursts of fire	
	4th		Following casualties in A/180: 39341 Gr H Gill killed; 70870	
			Gr W.J. Knowles and 23284 Gr H. Mossdale died of wounds;	
			204559 Gr G. Eastwood, wounded. (died of wounds on 5th)	
	6th	4am	D/180 carried out Gas shell bombardment of L'ECLANG FME.	
			LT-COL L.E.S. WARD DSO resumed command of the Brigade	
	7th		7556 Gr D. Steven MM. D/180 wounded.	
			42963 Dr F.C. Lucas & 36080 Dr E. Sale of A/180 wounded.	

A6945 Wt. W11422/M1160 350,000 12/16 D. D. & L. Forms/C./2118/14.

Instructions regarding War Diaries and Intelligence Summaries are contained in F. S. Regs., Part II. and the Staff Manual respectively. Title pages will be prepared in manuscript.

WAR DIARY
or
INTELLIGENCE SUMMARY.
(*Erase heading not required.*)

Army Form C. 2118.

Place	Date	Hour	Summary of Events and Information	Remarks and references to Appendices
HAMET BILLET	8th	4.15am	D/180 bombarded L'ECANG FME with Gas Shell.	
		Evening	C & D batteries moved to alternative positions, in anticipation of expected attack.	
	9th		A & B Batteries moved to alternative positions.	
	10th		A B & C Batteries moved back to old positions.	
	11th	2am.	Minor Enterprise carried out by 183rd Inf. Bde (on our left) 180th Bde co operated in artillery support.	
	14th	11.30pm	Minor operation carried out by 182 Inf Bde, supported by 180 Bde and other artillery of 16th DA group. 1 prisoner.	
			795535 Sgt A McGuinness C/180 wounded.	
			2/Lt J. B. WILSON A/180 to hospital accidentally injured.	
	17th		2/Lt P. Oakley rejoined from hospital	
	18th		2/Lt S. R. THOMAS posted from C/180 to A/180.	
	16th		D/180 established a detached section about 1000 yds forward of battery.	
	20th		Lt. J. M. S Livesay to hospital. Accidentally injured.	

A6945 Wt. W11422/M1160 350,000 12/16 D. D. & L. Forms/C./2118/14.

Instructions regarding War Diaries and Intelligence Summaries are contained in F. S. Regs., Part II, and the Staff Manual respectively. Title pages will be prepared in manuscript.

WAR DIARY
or
INTELLIGENCE SUMMARY.
(*Erase heading not required.*)

Army Form C. 2118.

Place	Date	Hour	Summary of Events and Information	Remarks and references to Appendices
HAMET BILLET.	22nd		180th Bde (less A/180) forms Centre Group, covering 182nd Infantry Bde. A/180 in Left Group.	
	28th.	2am	182nd Inf. Bde, covered by 180 Bde. & other artillery of 16th D.A. group, raided an enemy post, but found it unoccupied.	
			Lt J. M. S. Livesay rejoined from hospital	
			84109 L/Bdr J. J. Moffatt, 755607 Gr A. Thomson, and 209361 Ftr Winter T.H. of A/180 wounded.	
			Left Group became a Subgroup under O.C. 180th Bde. B/180 & C/180 established detached sections. South of ST VENANT.	
	29th.		22545 Sgt S.H. Alderton MM, 94126 Gr W Delve, and 19612 Gr W. E. King of D/180 wounded.	
			2/Lt J. B. WILSON rejoined from hospital.	

J. P. L. Ward LIEUT.-COL. R.F.A.
COMDG. 180th BRIGADE, R.F.A.

A6945 Wt. W11422/M1160 350,000 12/16 D. D. & L. Forms/C./2118/14.

9 16

WAR DIARY
or
~~INTELLIGENCE~~ SUMMARY. No 29 JUNE 1918
180 Bde RFA

(*Erase heading not required.*)

Army Form C. 2118.

Instructions regarding War Diaries and Intelligence Summaries are contained in F. S. Regs., Part II, and the Staff Manual respectively. Title pages will be prepared in manuscript.

Vol 29

Place	Date	Hour	Summary of Events and Information	Remarks and references to Appendices
Hamet	1st		Batteries still in action west and south west of St Venant.	Pages
Billet			Lieut (a/Capt) J. Miller adjt 180 Bde RFA posted to D/180 with effect from	
near			30/5/18) as Second in Command of 6 gun battery vice Lieut a/c Capt	
St VENANT			J.S. Short Evans MC. wounded	
			2/Lt J.S. Duncan HQ 180 appointed acting adjt with effect from this	
			date vice Lieut a/c Capt J Miller posted to D/180 Bde RFA	
	3rd		The left group is formed as follows 177 with A/180 attached	
			and 180 with C 282 attached under the Command of OC 180 Bde	
	5.		Brigade carried out a special shoot against hostile M.G.s	
			which have been very active of late.	
	10.		Hostile activity slight during past few days	
	14		C/180 moved their Wagon Lines to Guarbecq	
	16		D/180 shot their guns with aeroplane observation	
			on targets in Calonne	
	15	5pm	C/282 was withdrawn at 5 pm all ammunition	
			and documents were handed over to A/180	

A6945 Wt. W11422/M1160 350,000 12/16 D. D. & L. Forms/C./2118/14.

Instructions regarding War Diaries and Intelligence Summaries are contained in F. S. Regs., Part II, and the Staff Manual respectively. Title pages will be prepared in manuscript.

WAR DIARY
or
INTELLIGENCE SUMMARY.
(Erase heading not required.)

Army Form C. 2118.

Page 2.

Place	Date	Hour	Summary of Events and Information	Remarks and references to Appendices
Hamet	15	5pm	A/180 returned to the 180 Bde. The Left Group is now	
Billet.			composed of the 177 Bde and 180 Bde under O.C. 180 Bde	
	18		Gnr Kershaw B/180 Killed in action	
	21.		One section per battery relieved by one section per battery	
			of the 330 Bde RFA	
	22		A/c Capt. J.S. Duncan and Capt E.E. Lightwood went to	
			hospital with P.U.O.	
	22	9.30p	Batteries relieved remaining sections and withdrew to	
			Enquin les Mines	
		11.pm	Brigade handed over to the 330 Bde RFA at 11 pm	
ENQUIN-les-Mines.	23		Brigade in bivouac at Enquin les Mines	
			2/Lt J.E.S. Spooner to hospital P.U.O.	
Bois du Hazois	24		Brigade moved off to Bois du Hazois	
	25		A/c Capt. J.S. Duncan, Capt E.E. Lightwood returned from Hospital	
	26		Brigade commenced training programme.	

A6945 Wt. W11422/M1160 350,000 12/16 D. D. & L. Forms/C./2118/14.

Army Form C. 2118.

Instructions regarding War Diaries and Intelligence Summaries are contained in F. S. Regs., Part II. and the Staff Manual respectively. Title pages will be prepared in manuscript.

WAR DIARY
or
INTELLIGENCE SUMMARY.
(*Erase heading not required.*)

Place	Date	Hour	Summary of Events and Information	Remarks and references to Appendices
Bois du	27		Brigade continued its training programme.	
Hazois.	28			
	29			
	30			
			L. E. S. Ward Lieut.-Col.	
			Cmdg 184th Bde R.F.A.	

A6945 Wt. W11422/M1160 350,000 12/16 D. D. & L. Forms/C./2118/14.

Instructions regarding War Diaries and Intelligence Summaries are contained in F. S. Regs., Part II. and the Staff Manual respectively. Title pages will be prepared in manuscript.

WAR DIARY
or
INTELLIGENCE SUMMARY.
(Erase heading not required.)

No 30 July 1918
180 Bde RFA

Army Form C. 2118.

Vol 30

Place	Date	Hour	Summary of Events and Information	Remarks and references to Appendices
Bois du Hazois.	1.7.18.		Brigade is still out at rest in the Bois du Hazois. All batteries are carrying out an active training programme.	
ACQ	17.7.18		Brigade marched from Bois du Hazois to ACQ where H.Q. and batteries were established for the night. A ~~detached~~ section of each battery went into action at 9 pm. in positions on the eastern outskirts of Arras relieving a section of the 277 A.F.A. Bde.	
Arras.	18.7.18		H.Q. and remaining sections relieved the 277 A.F.A in their positions East of Arras (south of the Arras Cambrai Road) The Right Group 1st Can. D.A. is now commanded by O.C. 180 Bde and is composed of the 180 and 177 Bde	
	19.7.18.		Right Group 1st Can. D.A. becomes Centre Group and is composed of 180 Bde and 177 Bde under Command of O.C. 180 Bde.	

Page 2.

Instructions regarding War Diaries and Intelligence Summaries are contained in F. S. Regs., Part II. and the Staff Manual respectively. Title pages will be prepared in manuscript.

WAR DIARY
or
INTELLIGENCE SUMMARY.
(Erase heading not required.)

Army Form C. 2118.

Place	Date	Hour	Summary of Events and Information	Remarks and references to Appendices
Arras.	20.7.18		Centre Group 1st Can. D.A. becomes Left Group 1st Can. D.A. Its composition and command remains unchanged.	
"	26.7.18		A raid on Enemy Out posts in which all the Left Group Artillery took part was carried out by the 2nd Can. Inf. Bde. Zero hour was 9. p.m.	
"	27.7.18.		Lieut A. M. Champion is posted to A/180. Capt. (A/Major) R.A. Spencer DSO RFA is posted to 16th Div. Artillery H.Q.	
"	28.7.18		A raid is carried out on our right by the 16th Can. Inf. Bde. B/180 co.operated. Zero hour 12.50 a.m.	
"	31.7.18		Nil.	
			L. E. S. Ward O.C. 180 Bde R.F.A.	

A6945 Wt. W11422/M1160 350,000 12/16 D. D. & L. Forms/C./2118/14.

180th Brigade R.F.A.
8th Divisional Artillery

Instructions regarding War Diaries and Intelligence Summaries are contained in F. S. Regs., Part II, and the Staff Manual respectively. Title pages will be prepared in manuscript.

WAR DIARY
or
INTELLIGENCE SUMMARY.
(Erase heading not required.)

August.
No. 40.

Army Form C. 2118.

Place	Date	Hour	Summary of Events and Information	Remarks and references to Appendices
ARRAS.	1.8.18	–	Major H J Glendinning posted to D/180 authority RARO No AD.430	
"	2-8/18		The 180 Bde becomes the left group 56 Div Arty. covering the left Sector of	
			the 56 Inf. Division	
			D/180 Carried out a Gas bombardment (50 BNC) on Enemy dug-outs	
	7.8.18		Major W.H.P Johnston DSO posted to A/180 – Lt (a/Major) A.B. Weekes	
			relinquishes a/rank of Major. Lt A.B.Weekes to be a/Capt.	
			A/Capt R.C Archbutt posted to A/180 from B/180	
			A/Capt F.J Newman M.C Relinquishes a/rank of Capt.	
			A/Capt A.B.Weekes posted from A/180 to B/180	
	9.8.18		113413 Dr White J. (C/180) G.S. W slight L arm (at duty	
	13.8.18		Capt E.E Lightwood RAMC returned from leave to UK.	
	14.8.18		Enemy raided our posts but failed to get in. we sustained no casualties.	
	16.8.18		180 Bde becomes Independent Group 56 Div Arty	
East of	16.8.18		Moved the Brigade to positions East of Arras (H.Q G17 a 1.0) relieved the	
Arras.			286 Bde.	
	17.8.18		At 9 pm we came under the 51 Division Arty. and we cover the 152	Inf Bde

A6945 Wt. W11422/M1160 350,000 12/16 D. D. & L. Forms/C./2118/14.

Instructions regarding War Diaries and Intelligence Summaries are contained in F. S. Regs., Part II. and the Staff Manual respectively. Title pages will be prepared in manuscript.

WAR DIARY
or
INTELLIGENCE SUMMARY.
(*Erase heading not required.*)

Army Form C. 2118.

page 2

Place	Date	Hour	Summary of Events and Information	Remarks and references to Appendices
	17.8.18		in the Feuchy South sector	
	18.8.18		Assisted in an operation of the 170 Inf Bde to capture the IONIAN and Iceland Trench. Zero hour was 1am barrage lasted until 0+50. All objectives were gained	
	20.8.18		Covered the 152 Inf Bde in an operation to capture trench along Sunken Road in H17b (ref. map 51B NW) Zero hour 3.35 am. All objectives gained. MORAY and IONIAN TR previously captured by us (18.8.18) retaken by enemy during a counter attack at 4.50 am	
	21.8.18		Assisted by our Bde the 152 Inf Bde carried out an operation to capture CAMEL Ave. Zero hour at 1.30 am. Ceased fire 0+30 All objectives gained	
			From 4.45 am to 6.45 am we carried out a bombardment of Enemy front line as a demonstration in support of operations South of us	
	22.8.18		Moved our HQ from G17a 1.0 to H18a 90 20	
	23.8.18		The 51 DA came under Canadian Corps ~~[illegible]~~ at 12 noon	
	24.		Carried out an operation to capture Zion Alley - TROY Alley - PIPPIN TR	

A6945 Wt. W11422/M1160 350,000 12/16 D. D. & L. Forms/C./2118/14.

Instructions regarding War Diaries and Intelligence Summaries are contained in F. S. Regs., Part II, and the Staff Manual respectively. Title pages will be prepared in manuscript.

WAR DIARY
or
INTELLIGENCE SUMMARY.
(Erase heading not required.)

Army Form C. 2118.

page 3.

Place	Date	Hour	Summary of Events and Information	Remarks and references to Appendices
	24.8.18		Zero hour 4.30 am. All objectives taken. Casualties slight.	
	25.8.18		Supported an operation to capture HOLLY - HOARY and HAGGARD TR. Zero hour 5 am all objectives taken. casualties slight	
			Enemy raided Brigade on our left at 4.09 am we fired on SOS until 4.34 am	
	26.8.18		Supported an attack by the 3rd & 1st Canadians on the enemy lines South of the Scarpe Zero hour 3 am - all objectives gained.	
			Covered the 51st Div in an attack on enemy front system North of Scarpe. All objectives were taken.	
			At 7.30 pm we supported the 152 Inf/Bde in an operation to exploit their morning success - all objectives were taken	
			Casualties 36132 Driver E Hurradine Killed	
			29093 Cpl FW Motby Wounded	
			5212 Bdr BJ Luckie "	
			123486 Gnr HJ Reeves "	
			Moved our HQ to H13 b 8.5	

A6945 Wt. W11422/M1160 350,000 12/16 D. D. & L. Forms/C./2118/14.

Instructions regarding War Diaries and Intelligence Summaries are contained in F. S. Regs., Part II, and the Staff Manual respectively. Title pages will be prepared in manuscript.

WAR DIARY
or
INTELLIGENCE SUMMARY.
(Erase heading not required.)

page 4

Army Form C. 2118.

Place	Date	Hour	Summary of Events and Information	Remarks and references to Appendices
	27.8.18		Covered an attack by the 153 Inf Bde to capture Greenland Hill. Zero hour 10 am. Owing to heavy hostile MG fire our objectives were not completely held.	
			At 2.30 am we covered the 152 Inf Bde in an operation to capture Cabin, Carpet and Cat TR. We were unable to maintain our line in these positions owing to enfilade MG fire and opposition from Hausa Wood	
	28.8.18.		Moved our Bde HQ to H 15 c 80.20.	
	29.8.18		Covered the 154 Inf Bde in an operation to capture Clod TR, [illegible] and Whisper TR Zero hour was at 6 30 am. All objectives were taken.	
			C/180 pushed forward their battery to a position in rear of Fampoux and D/180 occupied a position in Fampoux	
	30.8.18		A and B/180 moved to positions N.E of Fampoux (H18a and b) HQ moved forward to H10 d.	
			Casualties No 154504 Dr Miller F W wounded. The Brigade becomes Left Group 56 DA. with the 256 Bde as a Sub-Group.	

A6945 Wt. W11422/M1160 350,000 12/16 D. D. & L. Forms/C./2118/14.

Instructions regarding War Diaries and Intelligence Summaries are contained in F. S. Regs., Part II. and the Staff Manual respectively. Title pages will be prepared in manuscript.

WAR DIARY
or
INTELLIGENCE SUMMARY.
(Erase heading not required.)

Army Form C. 2118.

Place	Date	Hour	Summary of Events and Information	Remarks and references to Appendices
	31.8.18.		Crenalter Gnr. 21602 Causby J.C. Killed	
			Cpl. James N. 94399 Wounded.	
			Gnr 244527 Horne E.J. wounded.	
			" 219206. Gnr. Shaffery B. wounded.	
			B/180 and C/180 moved forward to positions N.E. of Sainghin	
			L. E. S. Ward Lieut. Col Cmdg 180th Bde R.F.A.	

A6945 Wt. W11422/M1160 350,000 12/16 D. D. & L. Forms/C./2118/14.

SEPTEMBER 1918

Instructions regarding War Diaries and Intelligence Summaries are contained in F. S. Regs., Part II. and the Staff Manual respectively. Title pages will be prepared in manuscript.

WAR DIARY
or
INTELLIGENCE SUMMARY.
(Erase heading not required.)

No 32

180 Bde RFA

Army Form C. 2118.

Place	Date	Hour	Summary of Events and Information	Remarks and references to Appendices
				pages 32
EAST of FAMPOUX	1 Sept.		HQ Bde H10 d 8000 – Batteries NE of FAMPOUX – The 180 Bde with the 256 Bde as Sub Group forms the Left Group 51st DA. Our front line now runs GAVRELLE SUPPT – WIBBLE TR – WAVY Supt – WASTE TR – CRIB TR	
			Casualties. B/180 56286 Cpl Barker Wounded	
			" 87753 Bdr H Gibbs "	
			" 233402 Gnr S Reeve "	
			C/180 244527 Gnr E J. Home "	
			219206 Gnr B. Shaffrey "	
			A/180 37766 Cpl B France "	
	2/9/18		Casualties C/180 A/Capt J.R. Kent "	
	3/9/18		Each battery moved 4 guns back to positions West of Fampoux	
	4.9.18		Detached Sections relieved at 10 p.m. by sections of 175 A.F Bde	

A6945 Wt. W11422/M1160 350,000 12/16 D. D. & L. Forms/C./2118/14.

* Instructions regarding War Diaries and Intelligence Summaries are contained in F. S. Regs., Part II, and the Staff Manual respectively. Title pages will be prepared in manuscript.

WAR DIARY
or
INTELLIGENCE SUMMARY.
(Erase heading not required.)

Army Form C. 2118.

page 2.

Place	Date	Hour	Summary of Events and Information	Remarks and references to Appendices
Famfoux	5.9.18		Remaining Guns relieved by 175 Army Bde RFA and marched	
ANZIN			to ANZIN	
			Casualties: 57180 Lt R Robinson M.C. Gassed 2/Lt H E Fawkes	Gassed
			65101 Sgt H Taylor. Gassed. 134124 Gnr J Michael	"
			13441 BSM J H White M.M. Gassed. 1257 Gnr J Martindale	"
			931505 Sgt Darling " 12821 Gnr J Owen	"
			13993 Cpl Tennant " 247726 " J Pearce	"
			30972 Cpl J Ellis " 610 " J Renton	"
			31096 Cpl G. Wells " 201033 " Seeker	"
			39776 Gnr Miller " 177458 " H N Steer	"
			930766 Gnr AH Holliday " 37967 " R E Segnet	"
VIELFORT	6.9.18.		Bde marched to VIELFORT today.	
	7.9.18		Detached Sections went into action today relieving detached	
			Sections of 84th Army Bde RFA in positions East of Annequin.	

A6945 Wt. W11422/M1160 350,000 12/16 D. D. & L. Forms/C./2118/14.

Instructions regarding War Diaries and Intelligence Summaries are contained in F. S. Regs., Part II. and the Staff Manual respectively. Title pages will be prepared in manuscript.

WAR DIARY
or
INTELLIGENCE SUMMARY.
(*Erase heading not required.*)

Army Form C. 2118.

page 3.

Place	Date	Hour	Summary of Events and Information	Remarks and references to Appendices
ANNEQUIN	8.9.18		Remaining Guns went into action today – Relief complete 10.30 pm The 180 Bde is known as the CAMBRIN GROUP – and occupies positions East of Annequin.	
	11.9.18		Took part in an operation to capture Railway Triangle, Railway Cottage and TR Junct. A22c 95 15. Zero hour was at 5.15 am. A Counter attack drove us out of these positions at 9 am – At Zero hour 5.45 pm we assisted the 49th Inf Bde in an operation to recapture positions lost at 9 am. Operation was successful 26 prisoners being taken.	
	12.9.18		Assisted 49th Inf Bde in exploiting yesterdays success Infantry have now established themselves in Cemetery TR west of Auchy	
	13.9.18		Front line post advanced beyond Auchy.	

A6945 Wt. W11422/M1160 350,000 12/16 D. D. & L. Forms/C./2118/14.

Instructions regarding War Diaries and Intelligence Summaries are contained in F. S. Regs., Part II. and the Staff Manual respectively. Title pages will be prepared in manuscript.

WAR DIARY
or
INTELLIGENCE SUMMARY.
(*Erase heading not required.*)

Page 4

Army Form C. 2118.

Place	Date	Hour	Summary of Events and Information	Remarks and references to Appendices
H.Q. ANNEQUIN	14.9.18.		The 49th Bde continued its forward movement today and assisted by our Artillery established posts on the general line Canal Bank A17 d 6.3 - Railway and TR junct A17d 60.10. A17d 75.00 thence due south to A29 b 45.45	
	15.9.18		Assisted the 49 Inf Bde in a small operation to establish posts East of Auchy - These posts were subsequently retaken by the Enemy	
	16.9.18		Capt Weeks posted from B/180 to C/180. Capt Archbutt posted from A/180 to B/180. Capt Morice from C/77 to A/180. A gas bombardment was carried out on Cité de Douvrin tonight	
	17.9.18		Capt Hoodjemukle attached to A/180. The 180 Bde supported the 165 Inf Bde in an operation to capture the line APSE House - A11 c 95.50 to the La Bassée Canal A17 d 70 50. Zero hour 5.20 am. Simultaneously the Brigade assisted in an operation carried out by the 49th Bde to establish post on the line Canal Bank A17d 6.3 Railway and Trench Junct. A17 d 60.10. Road & Railway Junct A17d 75.00	

A6945 Wt. W11422/M1160 350,000 12/16 D. D. & L. Forms/C./2118/14.

Instructions regarding War Diaries and Intelligence Summaries are contained in F. S. Regs., Part II, and the Staff Manual respectively. Title pages will be prepared in manuscript.

WAR DIARY
or
INTELLIGENCE SUMMARY.
(Erase heading not required.)

page 5

Army Form C. 2118.

Place	Date	Hour	Summary of Events and Information	Remarks and references to Appendices
AQ Annequin.		18.9.18.	Advanced post taken during the morning operations having been evacuated we assisted in an operation to recapture same and established our line in A17 d 7040 – A17 d 8000	
		18.9.18	Batteries ~~—~~ moved to positions East of Cambrai	
		20/9/18.	Gas bombardment (23 Rds BNC) on HAINES –	
		22.9.18		
			2 Hows of D/177 have now been included in the Cambrai Group	
		23.9.18	Casualties 22360 Gnr E. S. Rumbles, A/180 Killed	
			850795 Sgt RL Day " Wounded	
			223034 Bdr J. J. Newton " "	
			104680 Gnr J. Yeardley.	
		25/9/18	Gas bombardment by D/180 on Brickstacks A25a (120 BNC)	
			2/Lt HS Ramsay posted to B/180	
		26/9/18	Gas bombardment by D/180 on Haisnes – (100 BNC)	

A6945 Wt. W11422/M1160 350,000 12/16 D. D. & L. Forms/C./2118/14.

Instructions regarding War Diaries and Intelligence Summaries are contained in F. S. Regs., Part II. and the Staff Manual respectively. Title pages will be prepared in manuscript.

WAR DIARY
or
INTELLIGENCE SUMMARY.
(Erase heading not required.)

page 6

Army Form C. 2118.

Place	Date	Hour	Summary of Events and Information	Remarks and references to Appendices
HQ Annequin	28.9.18		D/180 and D/177 (2 Hows) carried out gas bombardments on points East of the Hulluch Labassée line throughout the night (800 BWC)	
			Commenced a programme of increased Artillery activity	
	29.9.18		Continued increased activity programme including wire cutting operations.	
	30.9.18		Co-operated in an operation conducted by the 55th Division to advance and establish posts on the line A18c 3.9 – 150 yds E of distillery A18c 7.1. – A24a 87 and Canal alley A24a 7.4.	
			Operation was successful although later in the day we were obliged to evacuate these posts.	
			Gas bombardment was carried out by D/180 and D/177 on B19c and B25a (ref Map. La Bassée Canal 10a)	
			L E S Ward Lieut Col O.C. 180 Bde RFA	

A6945 Wt. W11422/M1160 350,000 12/16 D. D. & L. Forms/C./2118/14.

180 Bde RFA

Instructions regarding War Diaries and Intelligence Summaries are contained in F. S. Regs., Part II. and the Staff Manual respectively. Title pages will be prepared in manuscript.

WAR DIARY
or
~~INTELLIGENCE SUMMARY.~~
(Erase heading not required.)

Army Form C. 2118.

No 33

Vol 33

Place	Date	Hour	Summary of Events and Information	Remarks and references to Appendices
ANNEQUIN	1/10/18		55 Div carried out an operation establishing posts on a line A 18 c – E of Distillery – A 24 a 7.4. Zero hour 06 15 – Operation successful. Batteries of the 180 Bde are situated E of CAMBRIN.	
	2-10/18		Capt J R KENT rejoined the Unit today.	
			Casualties B/180. 154189 Gr J. Porter wounded	
			C/180 313 Dr J. Campbell "	
			In the early morning patrols of the 48th Inf Bde lost touch with the enemy who had retired all along the divisional front. Batteries were pushed forward to positions E of CAMBRIN and S of AUCHY and later in the day detached sections came into action E of AUCHY. The Infantry established themselves on the VENDIN – DOUVRIN – LABASSE LINE	
	3.10.18		Line advanced to approximately BILLY – BERCLAND	

Army Form C. 2118.

Instructions regarding War Diaries and Intelligence Summaries are contained in F. S. Regs., Part II. and the Staff Manual respectively. Title pages will be prepared in manuscript.

Page 2.

WAR DIARY
or
INTELLIGENCE SUMMARY.
(Erase heading not required.)

Place	Date	Hour	Summary of Events and Information	Remarks and references to Appendices
	3.10.18		BERCLAND. Batteries moved ~~up~~ a section at a time to positions E of HAINES and W. of DOUVRIN. HQ moved to ROBERTSON'S TUNNEL. The 177 Bde comes under the Command of O.C. 180 Bde as a Sub Group.	
AUCHY.	4.10.18.		Our line is now established as follows BERCLAND – B24 Central – DYNAMITE FACTORY W. outskirts of WINGLES – HQ moved to AUCHY – Batteries in action with main position W. of DOUVRIN and detached sections W of BILLY	
"	5.10.18		Gas bombardment (100 Rds) on ~~AN~~ PROVIN – One section was move into action W. of BERCLAND	
			Casualties L/Bdr J. Johnston. 39852	
			Gnr. J. Farr 35519 — A/180. Gassed	
			" Murrican 205729	
			" Gubby 54203	

A6945 Wt. W11422/M1160 350,000 12/16 D. D. & L. Forms/C./2118/14.

Instructions regarding War Diaries and Intelligence Summaries are contained in F. S. Regs., Part II. and the Staff Manual respectively. Title pages will be prepared in manuscript.

Page 3.

WAR DIARY
or
INTELLIGENCE SUMMARY.
(Erase heading not required.)

Army Form C. 2118.

Place	Date	Hour	Summary of Events and Information	Remarks and references to Appendices
Auchy	6/10/18		Gas bombardment was carried out by D/180 on BAUVIN (100 Rds)	
"	7 "		" " " " " " PROVIN (80 Rds)	
"	8 "		Casualties A/180 Gassed 2Lt J Hawks – Lt SJ Weaver	
"	9/10/18		Gas bombardment was carried out by D/180 on PROVIN (70 Rds)	
"	10.10.18.		" " " " " " " " BAUVIN (100 Rds)	
BILLY	15.10.18.		Enemy retired on our Divisional front. Infantry moved forward to a line running W of ANNOELIN and E of PROVIN. Batteries came into action E. of Billy with detached sections E of Canal. HQ moved to BILLY	
			2/Lt W ELLIOT posted to 19th DIV	
			2/Lt EN TAYLOR " " " "	
ANNOELIN	16.10.18		Infantry established a line EW of CAMPHIN and CHEMY. An advance artillery guard composed of one battery of 18 Pdrs and one section of Hows co-operated with Infantry. Remaining batteries occupied positions SE of CANAL & E of BAUVIN SE of ANNOELIN = HQ ANNOELIN	

A6945 Wt. W11422/M1160 350,000 12/16 D. D. & L. Forms/C./2118/14.

Instructions regarding War Diaries and Intelligence Summaries are contained in F. S. Regs., Part II. and the Staff Manual respectively. Title pages will be prepared in manuscript.

page 4.

WAR DIARY
or
INTELLIGENCE SUMMARY.
(Erase heading not required.)

Army Form C. 2118.

Place	Date	Hour	Summary of Events and Information	Remarks and references to Appendices
CAMPHIN.	17.10.18		Infantry established a line through MARTINSART and WAHAGNIES batteries came into action E of PHALEMPIN. One battery cooperated with Infty as Advance artillery Guard. HQ CAMPHIN	
PONT A MARQ	18.10.18		Infantry advanced to a line E of TEMPLEUVE. Two 18 Pdr Batteries were detached as Advance artillery Guard. Batteries came into action E of LATOURBE and W. of PONT.A.MARQ. HQ PONT A MARQ.	
TEMPLEUVE	19.10.18		Infantry established a line of outposts E of COBRIEUX batteries cover this line from positions E of TEMPLEUVE — HQ TEMPLEUVE	
SENTIER	20.10.18		Infantry established a line through WILLEMEAU – TAINTIGNIES batteries were moved up to positions E of LES PATURES and subsequently E of RUMES one battery acting in cooperation with Infty as Adv. Arty Guard	
TAINTIGNIES.	21.10.18		Batteries moved to positions west of TAINTIGNIES and came into action to cover the line St MAUR – MERLIN. HQ TAINTIGNIES Major H K Daniels proceeded to England on a tour of duty and …	

A6945 Wt. W11422/M1160 350,000 12/16 D. D. & L. Forms/C./2118/14.

Instructions regarding War Diaries and Intelligence Summaries are contained in F. S. Regs., Part II, and the Staff Manual respectively. Title pages will be prepared in manuscript.

Papers

WAR DIARY
or
INTELLIGENCE SUMMARY.
(*Erase heading not required.*)

Army Form C. 2118.

Place	Date	Hour	Summary of Events and Information	Remarks and references to Appendices
TAINTIGNIES	21.10.18		off the Strength of the Unit.	
			Casualties. 25046. Gnr McDonald M. } wounded.	
			" 711469 Sig. Lawton A.E. }	
"	22.10.18		Batteries moved to positions in GUIGNIES and VEZ VELVAIN	
			Line now runs from St MAUR to W. outskirts of BRUYELLE - Casualties	
	24.10.18	C/180	217170 Dr Marks Killed. 42351 Dr W. Moore - Gnr 715203	
"			J NIXON wounded. D/180. 153836 Gnr A E RALPH wounded	
"				
	27.10.18		B/180 Gassed 16953 Sgt W. Henson — 39698 Gnr W. Thorne	
"			33537 Gnr R. Rutherford 675860 Gnr J. Woods 210821 Gnr J. W King	
"			152895 Gnr J. Hudson 117818 Gnr S. Chester 901639 Gnr J. Hughes	
"			245595 " E M Hiles 33009 Gnr W H Morgan 36102 Bdr J. Church	
"	29.10.18		900744 Gnr W. Balstone A/180 Gassed.	
	31.10.18		One section of each battery was relieved by a section of the 177 Bde	
			at 0630 and one section at 1800. - HQ remained at	
			TAINTIGNIES.	
			L. E. S. Ward Lieut Col	
			OC 180 Bde RFA	

A6945 Wt. W11422/M1160 350,000 12/16 D. D. & L. Forms/C./2118/14.

Instructions regarding War Diaries and Intelligence Summaries are contained in F. S. Regs., Part II. and the Staff Manual respectively. Title pages will be prepared in manuscript.

WAR DIARY
or
INTELLIGENCE SUMMARY.
(Erase heading not required.)

180 Bde RFA
NO 34
VR 34

Army Form C. 2118.

Place	Date	Hour	Summary of Events and Information	Remarks and references to Appendices
TAINTIGNIES	1/11/18		Remaining two sections of each battery and HQ came out of action and went into Divisional Reserve at RUMES.	
RUMES			Lt J M S Livesay struck off the strength (authy WO AG 4a)	
	5/11/18		Lt F F Newman M.C. appt. A/Capt vice Capt. J A Morrice posted to 5 Army re-inforcement Camp	
	7/11/18		Lieut R. Robinson M.C. rejoined A/180	
	11/11/18		Hostilities ceased at 11. am	
	13/11/18		Brigade Educational scheme started	
ENEVELIN	15/11/18		Brigade marched to ENNEVELIN	
WAHAGNIES	16/11/18		Brigade marched to WAHAGNIES	
	18/11/18		Lt O. M. Brown struck off strength of unit	
MONS EN PEVELE	20/11/18		Brigade " " MONS-EN-PEVELE and took up quarters as follows. HQ MONS-EN-PEVELE two batteries	

(A9175) Wt W2358/P.60 600,000 12/17 D. D. & L. Sch 52a. Forms/C2118/15.

Instructions regarding War Diaries and Intelligence Summaries are contained in F. S. Regs., Part II, and the Staff Manual respectively. Title pages will be prepared in manuscript.

2

WAR DIARY
or
INTELLIGENCE SUMMARY.
(Erase heading not required.)

Army Form C. 2118.

Place	Date	Hour	Summary of Events and Information	Remarks and references to Appendices
			in BELLINGAMP and two batteries in LA PETRIE	
	26/11/18		A/Capt R.C. Archbutt. ~~[illegible]~~ posted from B/180 to A/180	
			A/Capt F.J. Newman M.C. posted from A/180 to B/180	
			[signature] Major RFA	
			Commanding ~~[illegible]~~ 180 Brigade RFA	

Instructions regarding War Diaries and Intelligence Summaries are contained in F. S. Regs., Part II. and the Staff Manual respectively. Title pages will be prepared in manuscript.

WAR DIARY

or

~~INTELLIGENCE SUMMARY.~~

(Erase heading not required.)

Army Form C. 2118.

180 Bde RFA

No 46

Vol 35

Place	Date	Hour	Summary of Events and Information	Remarks and references to Appendices
	1.12.18.		Bde HQ are still in MONS-EN-PEVELE with batteries in MONCHAUX and LAPETRIE.	
	5.12.18.		Major HS Ellis took over command of the Bde from Brevet-Major HJ Glendinning	
	13.12.18.		Lt. Col LES Ward DSO again assumed command of the Brigade	
	15.12.18		8882 T/RSM A Grant DCM admitted to Hospital. sick.	
	28.12.18		2Lt W. Wembury B/180 temporarily attached to ROD Audricq	

Jas. J Duncan Capt

(A9475) Wt W2358/P560 600,000 12/17 D. D. & L. Sch 52a. Forms/C2118/15.

Instructions regarding War Diaries and Intelligence Summaries are contained in F. S. Regs., Part II. and the Staff Manual respectively. Title pages will be prepared in manuscript.

January 1919

WAR DIARY
or
~~INTELLIGENCE SUMMARY.~~
(*Erase heading not required.*)

No 36

Army Form C. 2118.

180 Bde RFA 16/

98 36

Place	Date	Hour	Summary of Events and Information	Remarks and references to Appendices
MONS-EN-PEVELE	1/1/19		Bde HQ still at MONS-EN-PEVELE. Batteries billeted in LA PETRIE and MONCHEAUX.	
			LT-COL L.E.S. WARD, DSO, Commanding, awarded the C.M.G. Lt (a/Major) A.B. WECKES, B/180 awarded the MC	
"	14/1/19		Lt W.H.E. OLLIS D/180, and Lt R.E. FREEMAN C/180, struck off the strength (demobilised).	
"	21/1/19		Lt A.M. CHAMPION, A/180 and 2/Lt J.E.S. SPINNER A/180 struck off the strength. (demobilised)	
"	28/1/19		Lt (a/Capt) F.F. NEWMAN MC. B/180 struck off the strength (demobilised)	
			During the month 148 NCOs and men were demobilised.	
			Muller Capt. for O.C. 180th Bde RFA	

(A9175) Wt W2358/P.60 600,000 12/17 D. D. & L. Sch 52a. Forms/C2118/15.

Instructions regarding War Diaries and Intelligence Summaries are contained in F. S. Regs., Part II. and the Staff Manual respectively. Title pages will be prepared in manuscript.

WAR DIARY or ~~INTELLIGENCE SUMMARY.~~

(*Erase heading not required.*)

Army Form C. 2118.

Feb 1919 No ~~36~~ 37 180 Bde RFA

98 37

Place	Date	Hour	Summary of Events and Information	Remarks and references to Appendices
MONS-EN PEVELE	1/2/19		Bde HQ still at MONS-EN-PEVELE. Batteries in LA PETRIE and MONCHEAUX.	
			Lt (a/Capt) J. R. KENT MC C/180 and 2/Lt R.V.I. ATKINSON D/180 struck off the strength (demobilised).	
"	2/2/19		H.R.H. The Prince of Wales visited the Brigade.	
"	7/2/19		Lt W.A.S. PENLEY MC HQ, 180 Bde ~~and~~ struck off the strength. (demobilised).	
			~~Lt (a/Capt) F. E. NEWMAN MC B/180 struck off the strength (demobilised).~~ JM	
"	15/2/19		Maj. W.M.P. JOHNSTONE D.S.O. A/180 struck off the strength (demobilised).	
"	26/2/19		All ammunition on charge of batteries handed in to Ammunition Dump at TEMPLEUVE.	
			During the month 47 NCO's + men were demobilised, thus reducing the Brigade to Cadre "B".	

Miller Capt
for OC 180th Bde RFA

(A9175) Wt W2358/P.60 600,000 12/17 D. D. & L. Sch 52a. Forms/C2118/15.

Army Form C. 2118.

Instructions regarding War Diaries and Intelligence Summaries are contained in F. S. Regs., Part II. and the Staff Manual respectively. Title pages will be prepared in manuscript.

MAY 1919.

WAR DIARY

~~or~~

~~INTELLIGENCE SUMMARY.~~

(Erase heading not required.)

No. 39.

180th Brigade R.F.A.

Place	Date	Hour	Summary of Events and Information	Remarks and references to Appendices
CAPPELLE. (Chateau du Bron.)	1st.		Brigade Headquarters still at CAPPELLE with Batteries at CAPPELLE and WATTINES.	
"	23.4.19.		2/Lieut. R.E.HENDERSON. taken on strength of Repatriation Camp WINCHESTER on 23.4.19. and struck off strength of this Bde. from that date (Authy. Document Office Repatriation Camp WINCHESTER.)	
"	5th	May.	Lieut. H.E.FAWKES to WINCHESTER for Repatriation (Group 45 b U.K.6.)	
"	6th	"	Lt. (A/Major. A.B.WEEKES M.C. taken on strength of Repatriation Camp PIRBRIGHT from 6.5.19. (Authy. Officers Wing Repatriation Camp No. 1/2107/19 d/20.5.19.)	
"	10th	"	Lieut. J.B.WILSON posting to Light Div'l Arty. is cancelled, this officer is therefore taken on the strength from 10.5.19. (Auhy. DOUAI CADRES :- Wire No. 442 A dated 10.5.19.)	
WATTINES.	12th	"	Headquarters moved to "C" and "D" Batteries at WATTINES.	
"	26th	"	Imprest Account with the Chief Paymaster i/c Clearing House BASE. closed.	
			During the month 83 O.Ranks were demobilized.	

A H [signature] Major R.F.A. ~~Captain, R.F.A.~~

~~for~~

O.C. 180th Brigade R.F.A.

(A9475) Wt W2358/P360 600,000 12/17 D. D. & L. Sch. 52a. Forms/C2118/15

Instructions regarding War Diaries and Intelligence Summaries are contained in F. S. Regs., Part II. and the Staff Manual respectively. Title pages will be prepared in manuscript.

WAR DIARY or ~~INTELLIGENCE SUMMARY~~.

(Erase heading not required.)

June 1919 — No 40 — 180th Bde RFA

Army Form C. 2118.

Place	Date	Hour	Summary of Events and Information	Remarks and references to Appendices
WATTINES	1		Bde HQ, C, & D/180 at WATTINES (S. of CAPPELLE), A & B/180 at CAPPELLE.	Ceased
"	7		"Cadre" proceeded to UK as a dispersal draft, leaving an "Equipment Guard" of 1 officer & 15 O.R. per battery 1 officer & 4 O.R. on H.Q. Capt a/Maj. H.S. ELLIS, C/180 Lt a/Maj. H.E. SEALY D/180 & Lt a/Capt R.C. ARCHBUTT A/180 proceeded with this draft.	
	3		Lt. a/Capt J. MILLER awarded Military Cross. Cutting King's Birthday Honours Gazette of 3rd June.	
CAPPELLE	8.		HQ, C, & D/180 moved to CAPPELLE.	
	21		Brigade proceeded with vehicles & equipment by train to DUNKERQUE	
DUNKERQUE	28		Brigade commenced loading vehicles & Equipment on barges	

J. Miller Capt. RFA
O.C. 180 Bde RFA
Equipment Guard

(A9475) Wt W2358/P360 600,000 12/17 D. D. & L. Sch. 52a. Forms/C2118/15.

www.ingramcontent.com/pod-product-compliance
Lightning Source LLC
Chambersburg PA
CBHW080920230426
43668CB00014B/2163

* 9 7 8 1 4 7 4 5 2 3 2 7 1 *